Youth and Society: Patterns of Alcohol and Drug Use

Youth and Society: Patterns of Alcohol and Drug Use

Natalia Clibburn

CLANRYE
INTERNATIONAL
www.clanryeinternational.com

Clanrye International,
750 Third Avenue, 9th Floor,
New York, NY 10017, USA

ISBN: 978-1-64726-627-1

Cataloging-in-Publication Data

Youth and society : patterns of alcohol and drug use / Natalia Clibburn.
p. cm.
Includes bibliographical references and index.
ISBN 978-1-64726-627-1
1. Youth--Alcohol use. 2. Youth--Drug use. 3. Youth--Social conditions.
I. Clibburn, Natalia.

HV5135 .Y68 2023
362.292 083 5--dc23

For information on all Clanrye International publications
visit our website at www.clanryeinternational.com

CLANRYE INTERNATIONAL

Contents

Preface

This book aims to highlight the current researches and provides a platform to further the scope of innovations in this area. This book is a product of the combined efforts of many researchers and scientists, after going through thorough studies and analysis from different parts of the world. The objective of this book is to provide the readers with the latest information of the field.

Alcohol and drug use is a leading public health problem in most societies. There are several consequences of alcohol and drug use in adolescents that encompass a range of physical, academic, and social problems. Apart from these problems, excessive alcohol and drug use among adolescents is also associated with certain negative consequences and harmful behaviors such as high-risk sexual behaviors (unplanned and unprotected intercourse), sexual misconduct, accidents, fights, and assaults. Among the youth, alcohol use has become a principal factor responsible for high rate of morbidity and mortality. Alcohol and drug use has become the primary cause of death due to injuries in individuals younger than twenty-one years of age. This book explores the patterns of alcohol and drug use among adolescents as well as its impacts on their lives. It will prove to be immensely beneficial to students and researchers in this area of study.

I would like to express my sincere thanks to the authors for their dedicated efforts in the completion of this book. I acknowledge the efforts of the publisher for providing constant support. Lastly, I would like to thank my family for their support in all academic endeavors.

Natalia Clibburn

1

Youth and Chemicals: An Overview

My friend Hannah is worried. Her 18-year-old son Fedde is traveling through Australia, as some young people do after completing high school, and he is broke. He intends to sign up as a paid volunteer for a clinical trial in Sydney to finance the rest of his travels. Hannah wonders if she should advise against doing this. Having worked for years on issues of pharmaceutical safety, I ask for details during our dinner-table conversation. What kind of drug is involved? Is it an early trial? My daughter, who grew up with Fedde, joins the discussion, asking: "Why are you so concerned about him participating in a hospital experiment? Surely if something goes wrong he is in good hands. Do you know what he experiments with when he is in Amsterdam?"

I came of age in the 1970 and 1980s, and was engaged in activism against pharmaceutical company misinformation and greed. I scrutinize the safety profiles of pharmaceuticals; I buy organic food, checking its origins; and I take detours when cycling to work to avoid streets that have bad air quality. How do youth today experience the chemical environments in which they grow up? What do chemicals do for them? After more dinner-table discussions with my daughter and her friends, and exploratory talks with other young people, I became intrigued by how many young people are embracing all kinds of substances, whether to feel good, be creative, have more focus, or stamina, or meet some other purpose. How do young people "do" chemicals? And why do they do what they do?

Social and behavioral scientists have tended to focus on young people's use of (both legal and illegal) psychoactive and addictive substances, largely ignoring their use of other kinds of chemicals. There are four broad trends in this body of research: one set of studies defines substance use as risky behavior, something that needs to be prevented by understanding the determinants of use. These studies usually have a narrow focus on particular drugs, such as alcohol, cigarettes, cannabis, heroin, and ecstasy; they present statistics on the use of these "problem drugs" and seek to identify associated risk factors. These surveys show that factors such as education, poverty, violence, and peer pressure are associated with drug use (for example, Assanangkornchai et al. 2007; Kokkevi et al. 2007; Hibell et al. 2009; Legleye et al. 2011). For example, a study of cannabis experimentation among French teenagers found that one out of five 8th to 10th graders had tried cannabis (Jovic et al. 2014). The researchers report that teenagers of low socioeconomic status who were living with both parents, feeling well monitored, and had good communication with their mothers were less likely to experiment with cannabis than those who did not like school and felt undervalued by teachers. In the Netherlands, a study found that parents had little influence on young adults' cannabis use, which was instead associated with the actions of their peers and partners (Liebregts et al. 2013).

A second group of studies maintains that drug use is often a survival strategy for young people growing up in risky environments and under conditions of structural violence (Bourgois 1998; Rhodes 2002; Pilkington 2007; Singer 2008). For example, in urban poor communities in Makassar, Indonesia, young men consume locally brewed spirits, along with psychoactive prescription drugs, cannabis, and heroin to project "rewa"—masculine bravery. As one informant put it: "To survive and to be respected, you need to be rewa. Indeed, you're not a real lorong guy if you don't put on a brave face against dangers" (Nasir and Rosenthal 2009, p. 240). Lasco examines how a group of young men, working stand-by as tambays and hoping to pick up odd jobs in a harbor in the Philippines, use methamphetamine, locally known as shabu, for strength, confidence, and disinhibition. "We are not educated and we have nothing. Where will we gets the confidence to talk to others, if not from shabu?" they explain (Lasco 2014, p. 85). To help them manage irregular working hours, they use methamphetamines to stay awake, and cannabis and alcohol to fall asleep.

A third, very different set of studies examines substance use as a kind of self-optimization, fueled by pharma campaigns and neoliberal policies that call on citizens to take responsibility for their own well-being (Rose 2007). These studies are interested in how today's youth use "brain chemicals," to manage their feelings (Dumit 2010; Jenkins 2011). Many such studies have examined students' off-label use of prescription drugs to manage attention deficit hyperactivity disorder (ADHD) and to reduce fatigue and improve cognitive functions. For example, fraternity members at a college in the southeastern United States use the ADHD drug Adderall off-label when they have to perform academically even though they have no medical diagnosis, as well as for recreational purposes (DeSantis et al. 2010).

A final group of studies emphasizes the pleasures of taking drugs (Moore and Miles 2004; Hunt et al. 2007; Duff 2008; Martinic and Measham 2008; Shapiro and Kirksey 2017; Bengtsson and Ravn 2018) and the role of social environments in enabling pleasurable substance use (Duff 2011; Keane 2011). For example, weekend raves allow young people to have a break from pressures in their lives (Moore and Miles 2004; Riley et al. 2010). Young people try out new "designer drugs" to experience an intense form of pleasure, especially if users are able to avoid negative effects (Quintero and Nichter 2011; Hunt et al. 2007). Among such studies, Race's (2009) study of ecstasy at queer dance parties has been influential; he argues that it generated pleasure, euphoria, caring, and togetherness, facilitating a form of bonding that enabled gay communities to confront homophobia and the challenges of the HIV epidemic.

ChemicalYouth

The project that this book is about, ChemicalYouth, made a case for examining a broader range of chemicals that young people use in their everyday lives. It focuses not just on psychoactive substances—the use of which is viewed with concern by parents, educators, and policy-makers—but all other chemicals that young people use to boost pleasure, mood, vitality, appearance, and health, more general dynamics that have received far less scholarly attention. It approaches the use of chemicals as situated practices that are embedded in social relations and that generate shared understandings of efficacy. More specifically, it seeks to answer the question: how do young people balance the benefits and harms of chemicals in the quest for a good life?

In our inquiries into young people's chemical practices, we have aligned ourselves with social analyses that approach social life as 'doing' rather than being (Nicolini 2013). Following Schatzki (2001), we define chemical practices as "embodied, materially mediated arrays of human activity centrally organized around shared practical understandings" (p. 2). This analytical approach encompasses the wide-ranging multitude of chemical practices, and the diverse situations and concerns that fuel these practices in everyday life. Focusing on practices, we find out what young people do with chemicals and why. Our approach overcomes the limitations of the youth drug-use studies that we reviewed above, which focus on the role risk environments in drug use and on particular kinds of reasons for taking drugs (survival, self-optimization, pleasure).

Approaching chemical practices as embodied arrays of human activity further provides insights into how chemical effects are experienced and the shared understandings that emerge through the exchange of experiences and practices.[1] We thus uncover the diverse pragmatic reasons why people use chemicals,[2] and the trajectories through which some chemicals become "routinized way of engaging with the world," reproduced through "repeated performances of everyday actions" (Bengtsson and Ravn 2018, p. 41). We show how over time, chemical experimentation can develop into more habitual and individualized use of chemicals, as Mimi Nichter (2015) also observes in her ethnography of smoking on a college campus. Young people may start smoking cigarettes together, but they often end up also smoking on their own to relax after a hard day's work. When chemical use is routine, concerns about balancing safety and harm become less prominent. Users find their "hiyang," a Filipino term used to indicate that a user and a product are compatible (Hardon 1992).

These fine-grained ethnographies of situated chemical practices, provide profound understandings of the everyday dynamics through which youth mitigate chemical harm and navigate risk and uncertainty across diverse social worlds, contributing to a growing body of critical studies that examine the complex webs of social practices, power dynamics, gender and race relations, and inequalities that shape risk (Zinn and Olofsson 2019; Nygren and Olofsson 2014).

The ChemicalYouth project examined chemical practices in great detail. We observed how young people chewed, snorted, injected, and ingested diverse chemicals; how they applied them to their skin; and how they mixed and carefully dosed drugs to optimize effects. We asked why chemicals were used in specific ways, which led to insights into the diverse aspirations that youth try to achieve by doing chemicals as well as the conditions of precarity that fuel their use. We also probed into how they sought to prevent harm, which led to insights into how they adjusted dosages, mixed substances, and sought substitutes to balance benefits and harms.

We found that benefits and harms are not only physical. Youth also seek social efficacies, such as having the confidence to connect with clients, while seeking to avoid negative social effects, such as being stigmatized by peers for not moderating their intake of drugs. Such balancing acts are rarely individual. Rather, as demonstrated by the ethnographies undertaken as part of the ChemicalYouth project, young people try out and tinker with chemicals together, a process we have labeled "collaborative experimentation" (Hardon and Idrus 2014). The collaborative nature of chemical use may come as a surprise, as young people might be expected to compete with each other for educational opportunities and jobs. But fieldwork suggests that desires for social bonding are stronger than competition, driving chemical use.

In the ChemicalYouth project, we examine young people's chemical practices as collaborative experiments that involve strategies to try out new chemicals, enhance efficacies and mitigate both bodily and social harms, and to share understandings and experiences. A key insight is that youths' collaborative experimentation with chemicals involved connecting to people across generational, professional, and spatial divides to learn about the effects of chemicals. Our observations resonate with the analysis of Callon and colleagues (2001), who point out that in an uncertain world characterized by rapid technological change, the division between professional and laypeople is outdated. They emphasize the importance of collective experimentation and learning in hybrid forums, in which professionals, experts, and ordinary citizens come together, to discuss the risks of GMO, mobile phones, and asbestos. "Everyone contributes information and knowledge that enrich the discussion" (Callon et al. 2001, p. 9). Our interlocutors consulted and contributed to online forums and websites, scrutinized package inserts and prescription guides, and sought advice from relatives or friends with medical knowledge or pharmacy backgrounds. All this work made us realize that the label "layperson", indeed, does not properly characterize our interlocutors.

The collaborative nature of experiments is highly visible in online drug forums (Berning and Hardon 2016), as illustrated by this exchange, in which a drug user who calls himself GTCharged asks for advice on how to use Soma (a potent painkiller) on the website Drugsandbooze.com, which is dedicated to reduce harm through informed use.

> *GTCharged [1 May 2010 at 20:50]*: I just got prescribed Soma250 mg. It's a muscle relaxant. Can you snort this pill? Will it kick in faster? …
>
> *Robert Poop [answers within 30 minutes]*: I think it burns like a mother fucker if I remember correctly so if you can deal with the pain give it a shot. I personally never felt the need to snort it, just eating them worked great.

We examine how knowledge is generated through such forums, forming the basis of more systematic forms of "evidence" generation on the effects of new designer drugs (see Chapter 8).

Doing Chemicals

In our analysis of how young people do chemicals, and what chemicals do for youth, we took as a point of departure the idea that efficacies are not fixed but fluid (Hardon and Sanabria 2017). Young people through their situated practices and collaborative experiments make chemicals act in specific ways. We began with the premise that chemicals are rendered efficacious in laboratories, manufacturing plants, therapeutic settings where they are prescribed, drug stores where they are sold, and everyday lives where they are used. Medical and toxicological research, commercial interests, and societal concerns all shape the effects that are actualized. Efficacies are thus made and remade in drugs' trajectories from production to use, where young people appropriate them in their quests for the good life. The ChemicalYouth project asks how, at the end of this trajectory, youth generate new understandings of what chemicals can do, by trying them out and tinkering with them to generate specific efficacies that matter in their everyday lives. Many of our interlocutors also sold products in stores or to their peers, or worked as distributors in multilevel marketing schemes. When selling chemicals, they testified to their beneficial effects and tailored products to their clients' needs. Social media influencers, in particular, promoted products and were compensated for their efforts by advertising agencies and manufacturers, thereby amplifying the circulation of positive information on products.

In examining the ever-emergent nature of chemical efficacy, we pay attention not only to how chemicals are made but also how they are made meaningful. In developing this analytical framework, we are inspired by Ingold (2012) who proposes a shift from studying objects to knowing materials, which requires following matter as it flows from one situation to the next. The chemicals used by our interlocutors are derived from plants, mined, or engineered in laboratories and production plants. Manufacturers not only mix them with adjuvants to create attractive taste, color, and texture, and to enable ingestion, inhalation, injection, or application to the skin, but they also "inform" them through labels that declare contents, benefits, and harms, and through advertisements that link products to positive effects and desires. We borrow this idea from Barry (2005), who argues that chemistry is a science of associations in which molecules are "informed." When young people appropriate chemicals in their everyday lives, to achieve their aspirations, they also inform chemicals by producing shared knowledge on what chemicals can do and how best to use them. This shared knowledge contributes to fluid efficacies by arousing expectations of beneficial effects. Consider the packaging of a popular Indonesian energy drink called KukuBima (Fig. 1.1).

The manufacturers package the product as a sachet, containing a very sweet, grape-flavored powder and a combination of active ingredients, including caffeine and ginseng. As we elaborate in Chapter 6, some men working in the port of Makassar use this product to keep up their physical stamina, while others take it after work to enhance their virility (ginseng is known to be a potency-enhancing herbal medicine). Our interlocutors mixed the powder into water (the cheapest option) and

Fig. 1.1 KukuBima Ener-G drink (Picture taken by Anita Hardon, October 15, 2019, Indonesia)

different kinds of drinks. When dissolved in Sprite, they expected the product to kick in quickly; dissolving it in milk was thought to add nutritional content to the drink, a benefit if one suffers from fatigue. Printing virile images on packages, highlighting chemicals that are included in the sachets, and mixing the powders with milk and Sprite to achieve specific effects—all of these can be understood as "informing" the chemicals contained in the sachets.

There is a substantial body of critical social science literature that analyzes how pharmaceutical companies reinform their products to increase the market for their products. Companies link their drugs to the lifestyle desires of new groups of users, rebranding pills and attractively packaging them (Droney 2016; Ecks and Basu 2009; Quintero and Nichter 2011; Wolf-Meyer 2014). Greenslit (2005), for example, describes how Pfizer successfully reinformed its blockbuster drug fluoxetine (the active ingredient of Prozac) for the treatment for premenstrual dysphoric disorder, giving the pill a pink color and calling it Sarafem. Similarly, Hartley (2006) describes how the "pinking" of Viagra expanded the market of this potency drug to female sexual dysfunction. Martin (2006) emphasizes how informing consists of "carefully engineered images and concepts with sparse language designed to capture desires and hopes, while transposing in minuscule font the potential side effects that are not really meant to be read" (p. 282).

Critical social scientists point out that research on pharmaceutical efficacy is generally funded by pharmaceutical corporations and investment banks, which seek to increase sales and maximize profits (Dumit 2012; Healy 2006; Sismondo 2010; Sunder Rajan 2017). This scientific "informing" amplifies positive pharmaceutical potencies, while downplaying risks (Applbaum 2009; McGoey 2012). The ChemicalYouth ethnographies suggest that something similar is going on in the informing of chemicals through collaborative experiments by youth. Positive effects are amplified through face-to-face and online exchanges of experiences, sometimes paid for by manufacturers who see the potential of social media to market their products.

Collaborative Inquiry

Throughout this book, I honor the intensely collaborative inquiry that has characterized this project by referring extensively to our published studies and using the pronoun "we" to refer to our work and our insights. Each chapter provides a box featuring the short biographies of the youth ethnographers whose case studies are highlighted in the chapters. The full studies are available at chemicalyouth.org, the project's website, and we encourage readers to consult it for more specific information.

The research team conducted multisited fieldwork in Amsterdam, Paris, Makassar, Yogyakarta, Cagayan de Oro, Puerto Princesa, and Brooklyn from early 2013 to late 2018, with additional ethnographies conducted by an associated researcher in Addis Ababa. These eight urban centers are magnets for young people who seek to study, work, and make their future; they are "innovative, unchartered borderlands along which the global meets the local" (Comaroff and Comaroff 2000, p. 8). They are spaces of interaction that gather young people, ideas, and material objects and practices from around the world, creating gateways to a wider world of opportunities (Nilan and Feixa 2006; Hansen 2008). Our interlocutors faced diverse challenges and led multifaceted lives—as students, workers, designers, lovers, and social media influencers—that changed over time, along with their educational trajectories, work engagements, migration processes, and social affiliations. They connected to each other and to opportunities through kinship networks and social media, facilitated by mobile phones and their rapidly increasing access to the internet.

A key premise of the project was that, by examining how and why youth "do" chemicals, we could gain insight into the socialities that make up their lives and their shared aspirations for a better future, while also learning about the challenges and vulnerabilities they experience. Following Butler (2004a), we use precariousness to refer to vulnerabilities that emerge from life itself, in the sense that we need others to survive. While precariousness is shared, it is not the same for all. Young people's control over their destinies is affected by poverty, unequal access to education and health systems, the globalization of capitalist production, the rise of information technologies, the flexible labor arrangements that emerge along with these trends, and gender-, sexuality-, and race-based discrimination, which, taken together, are also referred to as "precarity" (Lorey 2015).[3] Precariousness thus refers to the condition of vulnerability shared by youth, while precarity refers to the regulatory, labor, welfare, education and health structures that shape these vulnerabilities (Vallas and Prener 2012; Han 2018).

We examined across our sites, the regulatory structures that do or do not protect young people from chemical harm, gender dynamics and racial inequalities that fuel consumption of hazardous products, and labor policies, all of which render their lives insecure. The differential precariousness of our interlocutors' lives has become painfully clear in the COVID-19 pandemic, which is raging while I am finalizing this manuscript. Across our sites young people are losing their jobs, with huge variations in their capacity to protect themselves and each other from the new coronavirus, and large inequalities in opportunities for government support to mitigate the economic downturn.

Across the urban centers where we did fieldwork, youth encountered a bewildering array of chemical products in drugstores, supermarkets, pharmacies, and online shops, which they strategically used to feel well and remain productive at work. And, they are targeted by advertisements for beauty products, pharmaceuticals, (e-)cigarettes, (energy) drinks, vitamins and supplements through their Instagram and Facebook accounts, TV and radio, and by posters hanging at neighborhood stores. The images that circulate through these media encourage "imagination and consumption" (Appadurai 1996), while at the same time sharpening feelings of exclusion and marginality among those who have not achieved their aspirations and cannot afford the chemical goods (Comaroff and Comaroff 2000; Cole and Durham 2007). The advertising images moreover amplify the potential benefits of chemicals, rendering any toxicities they may entail invisible.

Our interlocutors were roughly between the ages of 18 and 30 when we conducted fieldwork. Born in the late 1980s and 1990s, they grew up in a period when new communication technologies and the gig economy dramatically changed young people's lives throughout the world. Their futures were connected through global markets, exploitative labor arrangements, and "flows of signifiers and practices that make up contemporary youth cultures" (Farrugia 2018, p. 3). Many conducted outsourced labor and work 24/7 through internet technologies and new labor platforms. Their situated chemical practices, movements across literal and imagined spaces, and connections to global markets and commodity chains joined them to global "youthscapes" (Maira and Soep 2004).[4]

Navigating Precarity

Although increased access to education, and images that they view online fuel dreams for a better future, the precariousness of their everyday lives led the youth we spoke with to doubt if their aspirations could really be achieved (see also Butler 2004b; Vallas and Prener 2012; Lorey 2015). Many young people inhabit a commercially mediated "nowhere place" between a devalued local past and an unreachable future (Liechty 2003). The future becomes even more bleak in settings where people are directly affected by the impact of climate change, including Cagayan de Oro and Makassar, where heavy floods have resulted in increased economic insecurity for young people and their kin.

Across the urban sites where we conducted fieldwork, young people have responded to these challenges by seeing themselves as "flexible collection of assets," which they hoped to develop to "position themselves in a rapidly shifting global economy" (Martin 2000, p. 582; see also Gershon 2017; Urciuoli 2008). To increase their chances of success, they were eager to learn new competencies, make new local and global connections, refashion their styles, and groom their faces and bodies (Liechty 2003; Rofel 2007; Lukose 2009; Cole 2010; Newell 2012; Hann 2018). Aware that the world was changing rapidly, they were willing to "sacrifice, work, invent and negotiate for a future different, and better than the one they live in now" (Durham 2008, p. 947). These desires for a better future made them an easy target market for corporations seeking to sell a whole range of chemicals, deploying advertisements to reinforce and fuel desires through an ever-expanding range of communication channels. At the same time their eagerness to succeed in life spurred them to set themselves up as mediators and movers in the same commodity markets, if only to make some money to pay for their chemical needs.

While job prospects differed across the urban sites, our interlocutors shared concerns about precarious labor conditions. Most had to contend with temporary employment, as technological advances have made routine and manual jobs scarce. Across our field sites, the service sector was the largest employer of youth, providing both formal and informal jobs in banks, malls, markets, household services, the emerging wellness industry, transport, restaurants and bars, and more. In the European cities, labor laws and state unemployment benefits offered some protection, while in the Asian cities being jobless or having to tend to family (health) crises could result in acute poverty. As a result, their educational careers and economic aspirations could be seriously disrupted.

Across our ethnographic sites, we explored the situated social and economic dynamics that contributed to youth precariousness. This precariousness concerns existential anxieties about the wellness of their bodies and minds, as well as concrete fears of "politically and economically induced precarization, fear of unemployment or not being able to pay the rent or health care bills even when employed" (Lorey 2015, p. 131). Chemicals provided our interlocutors a sense of control as they faced multiple insecurities and challenges in their everyday lives, which explained why they invested their scarce resources in such products.

We found that many of our interlocutors ended up worse off than when they started their chemical "investments." While our interlocutors thought the products that they bought in supermarkets, pharmacies, and online markets were safe, sadly, all mechanisms over the world to prevent hazardous chemicals from being sold are weak, because the economic interests of pharmaceutical and tobacco corporations, vitamin and supplement manufacturers, and beauty product companies exert a stronghold on regulatory processes. As a result, though it was often not immediately evident, our interlocutors ran health risks due to their long-term exposure to multiple toxic substances (which may interact with each other to cause even more harm), while the benefits they gained from their chemical investments were often minimal.

Regulatory protection from chemical harm was uneven across the research sites. While governments take responsibility for the safety of some chemicals, notably pharmaceuticals and narcotic drugs, we found that beauty products, energy drinks, herbal medicines, food supplements, and vitamins are regulated much less stringently. For these products, pre-market approval is easy to get, as long as the companies avoid including certain chemicals, such as mercury, that are known to cause serious harm. In some countries, there have been regulatory moves toward adopting the "precautionary principle," a cautious strategy of pausing and reviewing before allowing new chemicals on the market (Read and O'Riordan 2017), but implementation of this principle has proven to be difficult for government regulators.

Head to Toe

To ethnographically explore the expansive range of chemicals that matter to youth in their everyday lives, and gain insights in the ways in which the confront existential uncertainty and chemicals risks we started fieldwork with a new research instrument the researchers dubbed the "head-to-toe interview."[5] We asked respondents to take us on a "grand tour" of every chemical they used for their hair, eyes, face, lips, teeth, bodies, ending with their toenails. The systematic treatment of the human body prevented feelings of shame or fear for repercussion when talking about chemical practices and body parts that might be more sensitive. This method helped us tune into the role that chemicals played in our interlocutors' lives, including the social relations in which a given use was embedded, and the aspirations and challenges reflected in the practice. We asked our informants what they sought to achieve through chemical use (also probing into their more general aspirations in life), the advantages and disadvantages of different products on the market, and how they learned about and acquired them. Their responses allowed us to identify themes for further enquiry.

The second phase of the project involved focused ethnographies of specific chemical practices that emerged as central in the everyday lives of particular subgroups of youth. We collected data through interviews, participant observation, and "four-day recalls" in which our interlocutors meticulously tracked the substances they used. We also conducted feedback and validation sessions, where we discussed emergent findings with our interlocutors. Together we identified potential foci for ethnographic observation, based on the findings of the grand tours, thereby co-producing a body of knowledge, as collaborators rather than as field assistants, which is a second way the ChemicalYouth project engaged in collaborative experimentation. The project thus not only described ethnographically our interlocutors' collaborative experiments with chemicals, but it also engaged them in gaining insights into and analyzing these situated practices. The youth ethnographers received intensive guidance during fieldwork and have published their case studies in edited volumes, special issues, and on the project's website; most of their publications are open access (www.chemicalyouth.org).

The feedback and validation sessions were done in karaoke bars or other public spaces that allowed for some privacy. During these, we further explored our interlocutors' engagements with chemicals; we brought samples of commonly used products (only legal ones) and asked our interlocutors to sort them into piles, listening closely as to why products were grouped together. The physical presence of the products in the group discussion signaled to our interlocutors that we knew what mattered to them. On one occasion, one of our informants exchanged a full bottle of vaginal cleansing liquid with a half-empty one from her purse, which led us to ask who else had half-empty bottles in their purses; all of the female participants did. On another occasion we were confronted with the ethically compromising interaction with a heavy drug user taking a tablet of buprenorphine (a heroin substitute) with him to the toilet, despite our entreaties to not do so. When he came back he told us that he had crushed the pill, diluted it in mineral water, and injected the fluid to treat his withdrawal symptoms. This taught us to not bring heroin replacement drugs to these group discussions. The event also led to a discussion on safe injecting practices.

The focused ethnographies described everyday situations in which these young people studied, worked, socialized, sought partners, and engaged in sexual relations. The settings included bars, street corners, nightclubs, music festivals, private homes, shopping malls, construction sites, universities, and the internet. Across the research sites, our core research questions included: When do youth use which chemical substances? How do they use, adjust, and make them? What effects do they seek and why? How do they manipulate chemical substances to modulate their effects? What adverse effects do they experience and what strategies do they use to avoid or lessen drug-related harms?

Collaborative contrasting analysis was a key feature of the project. Anthropology has long been committed to understanding particular practices and beliefs in bounded cultural settings (see, e.g., Abu-Lughod 1991). However, understanding global phenomena, such as the widespread use of chemicals by youth, "requires approaches that can not only identify the effect of the outside on the 'local' but also show that the effects operate differently in various locations" (Besnier and Guinness 2020, p. 201). Documenting these differences allows us to compare "complex and diverse configurations of categories and processes" (Besnier and Guinness 2020, p. 212).

By conducting collaborative ethnographic research across various local sites, we were able to engage in an iterative analysis of similarities and differences in situated chemical practices. This process sharpened the ethnographic inquiries that were done. Together the youth ethnographers examined how phenomena can play out differently in different locales; this we refer to as "collaborative contrasting analysis." Why, for example, were our female Indonesian respondents just interested in whitening their faces, while in the Philippines women wanted to whiten their whole bodies? And why did Filipino men also whiten their skins, a practice most Indonesian men would frown upon (Chapter 5)?

Young people across our field sites used chemicals for three main reasons: to achieve wellness, to enhance work opportunities and capacity, and to try out different kinds gender identities and sexual ways of being in the world. Achieving wellness entailed using products to feel attractive, connected, happy, and healthy, and to experience what we refer to elsewhere as "hassle-free" highs (Hardon and Hymans 2016; van Schipstal et al. 2016; Hardon et al. forthcoming, 2020). We found that it also involved using chemicals to create and enjoy lean and muscular bodies. Trying out different kinds of gender identities and sexual ways of being in the world involved multiple 'chemical sexualities' (Chapter 4), including using hormones to grow breasts and using drugs to enhance sexual experiences. In terms of enhancing work opportunities and capacities, we found that youth across the sites used chemicals to achieve what is euphemistically called a "pleasing personality" (Taqueban 2018), or in other words a physical expression that pleases clients. They used chemicals to feel confident, be creative, have focus, and enhance stamina, and in doing so they built up biocapital, the value generated in capitalist modes of production through investments in biological materials. This investment-oriented logic highlighted the precarious labor arrangements (Hewison and Kalleberg 2013) that shaped young people's use of chemicals to enhance their productivity. In seeking wellness and productivity, our interlocutors joined in the quest for "the good life" (Gregory and Altman 2018), a pursuit that characterizes the everyday lives of so many young people who struggle to make a living in times of precariousness.

Our youth ethnographers did extensive participant observation and semi-structured interviews.[6] All interviews were recorded and transcribed. Transcripts were stored in NVivo and analyzed in teams, with the research team reading each other's interviews in analysis sprints, to jointly generate core themes for analysis. We exchanged notes from our field research in Asia, Europe, and the United States, and read each other's transcripts, seeking core themes for further analysis, and held workshops to interpret the emerging insights. We asked: why are some practices similar and others different? Together we submitted contributions to special issues and edited volumes. In the publishing process, we received editorial support from Takeo David Hymans, a science writer who was involved in the ChemicalYouth project from the beginning.

Our fieldwork was multimodal by design. We engaged youth in photography projects, and we conveyed your insights through documentary films and exhibits. The findings are also available on the project's website, organized by chemical, topic, location, researcher, and methods (Fig. 1.2).

The website displays the full range of chemicals, locations, topics, methods, and researchers that make up the ChemicalYouth project. It enabled contrasting analysis across our sites, as well as the writing of this book. It was made to inspire future researchers by providing access to the multitude of open-access publications that we made together, as well as

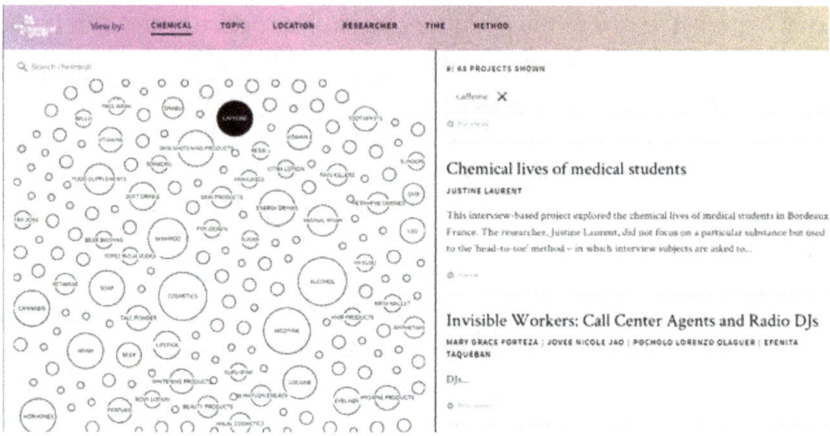

Fig. 1.2 Screenshot of an overview of the chemicals that figure in the reports of the youth ethnographers. Clicking on a bubble calls up the corresponding results for the whole project.

still unpublished work, and the audio-visual arts projects that emerged from the project.

Unevenness of Harm Protection Mechanisms

While studying the chemical lives of young people, we were struck by the unevenness of the regulatory strategies for different kinds of chemical products, not only between the countries where we did fieldwork, but also within countries. In all our sites, consumers were warned about the adverse effects of some substances, while receiving no cautionary information regarding others (Singer 2007; Homburg and Vapeul 2019). Why are some chemicals with exaggerated health claims allowed on the market, while the efficacy claims of others are tightly regulated? Why are some chemicals ruled illegal, while other equally hazardous ones are allowed to seep into our environments?

In the United States, where many cosmetics and food supplements are manufactured, the Food and Drug Administration (FDA) maintains that manufacturers "have a legal responsibility to ensure the safety of their products" (U.S. FDA 2005). All companies are required to do is list the ingredients on packages; they do not need to submit proof of safety to the government. The European Union has adopted the precautionary principle in its Registration, Evaluation, and Authorization of Chemicals (REACH) Policy, which requires manufacturers to provide evidence of a product's safety before it is allowed on the market, and doing so has led to the banning of 1328 chemicals from cosmetics that are known or suspected to cause cancer, genetic mutation, reproductive harm, or birth defects (Homburg and Vapeul 2019). In contrast, the US FDA has only banned or restricted 11 chemicals from cosmetics (Campaign on Safe Cosmetics 2020). In the Asian region, the cosmetic directive (adopted in 2008) regulates the use of only three chemicals: mercury, lead, and arsenic (Milman 2019).

Manufacturers have been successful in preventing the adoption of the precautionary principle in the United States (MacKendrick 2018), despite the 1976 adoption of the Toxic Substances Control Act (TSCA), which assigned the Environmental Protection Agency (EPA) the responsibility to control commercial and industrial chemicals that pose "unreasonable risks of injury to health or the environment," by 2005 the agency had only restricted the use of five chemicals (United States Environmental Protection Agency 2016). The TSCA was toothless from the moment it came into force. It oversees over sixty-two thousand chemicals that were in use prior to the bill being signed into law. Once chemicals are on the market, it is very hard for governments to restrict their use, as they then have to prove the product's adverse effects on human health or the environment.

Narcotic drugs, namely drugs that are potent psychoactive substances, are the most strictly regulated and most aggressively informed substances in all of the countries where the ChemicalYouth project was conducted, which paradoxically gave our interlocutors the impression that legally marketed cosmetics, energy drinks, and supplements are safe. Each country has a list of scheduled drugs. Drugs such as cocaine, heroin, methamphetamine, ecstasy, cannabis, and LSD are often included on such lists. Governments ban these drugs because they are seen to have no medical utility and because they can cause addiction and/or cause serious adverse effects. But the lists change, as regulatory agencies reassess evidence and in response to contestations.

The Independent Scientific Committee on Drugs (ISCD), based in the United Kingdom, scored 20 psychoactive drugs on 16 criteria, nine related to harms to individuals and seven concerning harms related to others. Both categories of harm included physical, psychological, and social dimensions. The experts concluded that the drugs most harmful to individuals were heroin, crack cocaine, and methamphetamine, whereas the drugs most harmful to others were alcohol, followed by crack cocaine and heroin (Fig. 1.3).

The interesting point in this scoring by experts is that alcohol, a legal drug, is scored as the most harmful drug, whereas cannabis, ecstasy, and LSD have relatively low scores for harm to users and others.

Indonesia and the Philippines have declared a War on Drugs, and both users and dealers have been sentenced to the death penalty. In contrast, France and the Netherlands prosecute drug users in less severe ways. The Netherlands stands out with a tolerant drug policy that distinguishes between hard drugs like heroin and ecstasy, which are entirely prohibited, and soft drugs like cannabis, the sales and use of which are tolerated (though commercial production is illegal). Many countries

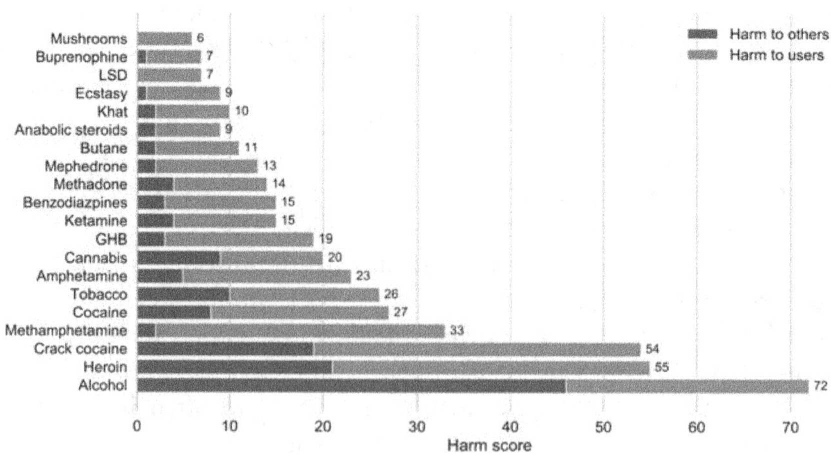

Fig. 1.3 Graph reproduced by Javier Garcia-Bernardo with original data from Nutt and colleagues (2010)

(including Uruguay, Canada, and several states in the United States) have recently taken cannabis off the list of scheduled drugs, based on evidence that it can be used safely. As a result, cannabis products are now being re-classified in many different ways (Caulkins and Kilborn 2019).

Tobacco is also a heavily regulated substance. The global consensus on nicotine's addictive properties and the severe adverse health outcomes associated with (secondary) smoking have led to a global treaty on tobacco control, called the World Health Organization (WHO) Framework Convention on Tobacco Control, which came into effect in 2005. The United Nation's Sustainable Development Goals, adopted in 2015, call on governments to strengthen the implementation of the treaty in all countries, a target that is monitored by measuring the prevalence of current tobacco use among people aged 15 years and older (United Nations 2015). The Philippines, the Netherlands, and France are adopting the recommendations of this treaty, including those that aim to protect youth from tobacco advertising. However, Indonesia (a country with a large tobacco industry) has not signed the treaty, and in that country youth are heavily targeted with advertising for cigarettes (Fig. 1.4). In all countries, e-cigarettes are increasingly used by young

Fig. 1.4 Banner for Surya Pro, which suggests that brave men never quit (Photo taken by Anita Hardon, December 30, 2018, Morotai, Indonesia)

people as a substitute for cigarettes, partially due to advertising that is not constrained by the global tobacco treaty.

If chemicals make medical claims, as is the case with pharmaceuticals, governments demand strong evidence of safety and efficacy before allowing them on the market. The evidence has to involve at least two large-scale clinical trials. The safety-efficacy profile also determines whether a pharmaceutical can be sold over the counter or only by prescription. If a drug is categorized as a prescription drug, it may not be advertised directly to consumers (except in the United States). But the enforcement of these regulations differs wildly. In Indonesia most prescription drugs can be bought over the counter, which is how the young people we conducted ethnography with gained access to a wide range of psychoactive prescription drugs.

Despite the pre-market approval process, adverse effects often only become visible when the products are used in larger populations, and among groups of people who were not included in the clinical trials. In an ideal world, post-market surveillance would pick up these adverse effects, but such studies are rarely conducted in our Asian field sites, and information on adverse effects that are occasionally reported by users and observed by doctors are generally not widely publicized, because drug surveillance systems are not in place or not functioning well.

A pharmaceutical's regulatory status is revisited when adverse effects are reported, and when post-marketing surveillance provides evidence of harm (Abraham and Lewis 2000; Davis and Abraham 2013). Food and drug authorities have standing committees that review new evidence and decide if the regulatory status of a product needs to be revised. One reason for revision can be a drug's potential for abuse. For example, the potent painkiller carisprodol came on the market more than 50 years ago as a pain medication for the treatment of lower back pain and other indications. However, US doctors increasingly reported withdrawal symptoms—including vomiting, anxiety, insomnia, and hallucinations—among patients who discontinued carisoprodol (Substance Abuse and Mental Health Data Archive 2003; DEA 2011). In Europe, a study by Bramness and colleagues (2007) found that carisoprodol was hugely overprescribed and that patients often received their prescriptions from multiple doctors. The drug was subsequently taken off the market in Sweden (2007) and Norway (2008), and the European Medicines Agency recommended that member states stop authorizing carisoprodol for the treatment of acute back pain (Hardon and Ihsan 2014). But often, companies contest the regulatory proposals, making it difficult for regulatory agencies to take action. As this book shows, such an uneven regulatory landscape means that drugs prohibited in some places still circulate widely; indeed, carisoprodol, under the brand name Somadril, was one of the more common drugs taken among the youth we studied in Indonesia.

The ChemicalYouth ethnographies drawn upon in this book reveal that young people use a wide range of chemicals to enhance wellness and enable work, and that they develop elaborate techniques to increase benefits and avoid harms. They do so in an ecosystem that informs different categories of chemicals in very different ways. For some chemicals, warnings about harms are amplified by drug authorities and health educators, while for other kinds of chemicals, such as beauty products and supplements, benefits are overly touted and risks dangerously downplayed.

What Follows

In each of the following chapters, we draw on our collective ethnographic research to show how young people 'do' particular kinds of chemicals and why they do so. Each chapter contrasts ethnographic insights from at least two different countries and multiple focused ethnographies. Our method of following chemicals from one country to another provided insights into the site-specific conditions of everyday life and regulations that shape use. We learned how chemicals are ingested, inhaled, and injected, and how they are also mixed to enhance effects. Across the sites, we examined how shared understandings of efficacy emerged and how knowledge produced in scientific studies intersected with these more popular understandings. We scrutinized safety and efficacy claims made in advertising campaigns and on product packaging. By doing so, we saw firsthand how the amplification of benefits in advertising and social media contributed to the widespread use of more ordinary chemicals, such as food supplements and e-cigarettes, and how the lax regulation of such products amplifies the already existing precarization of young people's lives.

The analysis of young people situated chemical practices presented in this book is located at the intersections of youth studies, anthropology and science and technology studies, disciplines from which we borrow concepts and offer new understandings. More specifically, this book offers an ethnographic contribution to the critical studies of risk and uncertainty (Zinn and Olofsson 2019). Starting from in-depth inquiries into the precariousness of young people's lives and understandings of how chemicals are used tools in their quests for a good life, we examine how youth navigate chemical harms in a social world structured by inequalities and social forces which often keep them in the dark about the toxicities that they face. We contribute to the critical study of risk and uncertainty by ethnographically examining the situated chemical practices of youth, and by building an analytical framework for understanding the risks that they face and the harms that they mitigate, from in-depth understandings of their engagements with chemicals in their everyday lives.

The first empirical chapter in this book, entitled "Chemical Highs," zooms in on the situated practices and techniques that enable some youth to enjoy the positive effects of narcotic drugs while avoiding their adverse events. In Amsterdam, for example, youth invented and employed distinct techniques in their quest for hassle-free highs. These included innovative and precise methods for dosing and administering drugs. Our interlocutors trusted their peers and had confidence in their collective techniques to determine the quality of substances. If they experienced adverse effects, they had confidence that their friends, coworkers, and online acquaintances would watch over them until the effects waned. And we also looked at how trust could be increased between youth and authorities: in Amsterdam, city authorities work with young people to carefully design harm reduction programs, which earn the participation of partying youth.

We contrast the quest for hassle-free highs in Amsterdam with the situation in Indonesia, where a severe drug war is being waged by the government that involves a different kind of risk. In Indonesia, young people commonly use psychoactive prescription drugs to get high, and they consider these safer than illicit drugs, because those can lead to the death penalty. Like their peers in Amsterdam, they seek hassle-free highs, but they lack information to protect themselves against harm—many have become addicted to psychoactive prescription drugs, without knowing that this could happen—and they don't have a trusted partner in government.

Chapter 3, "Chemical Breath," contrasts the smoking practices of young cannabis users in Makassar with those of young people who have turned to e-cigarettes in Paris. In both cases our interlocutors valued the bonding that happens in this shared practice and the gustatory pleasure of inhaling from joints. But in Makassar, the students who consumed cannabis were worried about the risk of attracting police attention and being imprisoned. We observed the introduction of synthetic cannabis-like designer drugs in Indonesia, ordered online, that are mixed into branded cigarettes and smoked with less risk of criminal prosecution, but more severe harm to their health. In France, e-cigarettes are increasingly popular among young smokers who want to avoid tobacco-induced harms, while continuing to enjoy the social relations that are fostered by smoking together.

In both cases, social media amplified the positive effects of the products, while information about their potential harm did not circulate as freely, thus contributing to the precarization of young people's lives. Both cases also point to the need for sensible government regulation. Indonesia's drug policy, which criminalizes cannabis, caused youth to take severe health risks, while the lax regulation of e-cigarettes similarly put youth at risk in Europe.

In Chapter 4, "Chemical Sexualities," we turn to the chemicals used by young people to mold their sexual being in the world. With ethnographic vignettes from six focused ethnographies conducted in the Philippines, Indonesia, Ethiopia and France, we show how chemicals are used to try out sexual identities, enhance sexual experiences, and prevent unwanted pregnancies and sexually transmitted infections. Young women used substances to tighten and cleanse their vaginas; men sought to "last longer" by turning to penile wraps and tissues, and a plethora of virility-enhancing drugs. In Paris, we observed how young gay men engaged in "chem sex," which involves injecting drugs during (often unprotected) sexual encounters. Our interlocutors explained how the practice of injecting drugs was entangled with their search for love. Feelings of euphoria and "love fusion," common when new relationships blossom, often encourage risk taking within couples, where syringe sharing is experienced as a sign of trust (Amaro 2016). Looking through the lens of collaborative experimentation, we see how young people observed effects in their own bodies and then shared their lived experiences. We suggest that sexual health programs should acknowledge the sexual desires and health needs that are reflected in such chemical practices, and develop more chemical products to meet these needs.

Chapter 5, "Chemical Whitening," looks at skin-lightening practices, which we found to be the most prevalent among service-sector workers in the Philippines and Indonesia. Many of our interlocutors explained this practice as a way trying to "please" their clients and employers. By having light skin, service-sector workers aimed to portray the good life that they were selling to their clients, while also performing the "pleasing personality" that their companies expected. Our analyses revealed skin whitening to be an elaborate and expensive process, involving layers of whitening via soaps, scrubs, and lotions. However, the practice differed across sites in the Philippines. While only women used to whiten their skin, more and more young men have begun engaging in this practice. Many do so because they are competing with women for service-sector jobs. Some are also inspired by the androgynous masculinities that have begun circulating in the Philippines, influenced by Korean popular culture. Seeking a lighter skin involves economic costs and has adverse effects as potent and cheap products bought on the black market, often containing banned products such as mercury. The chapter argues that while skin lighteners may be used to increase one's value in the service-sector economy, their use can lead to the further precarization of young people's lives. The chapter ends with a description of initiatives that seek to counter the colorist marketing of skin-whitening products and celebrate skin diversity.

Chapter 6, "Chemical 24/7," presents the chemical lives of night workers—producers, promoters, DJs, hosts, artists, performers, drag queens, musicians, stage managers, bartenders, hospitality girls, and dancers—in Amsterdam (Netherlands), Brooklyn (United States), Bira (Indonesia), and Puerto Princesa (Philippines). In Brooklyn and Amsterdam, young people's work entailed producing the social spaces where partygoers can enjoy themselves. Our interlocutors used stimulants to stay alert at night, to be friendly to customers regardless of their mood, and to engage with audiences when performing on stage. In the karaoke bars of Puerto Princesa and Bira, hospitality girls and dancers were required to consume "ladies' drinks" along with their customers. Our interlocutors employed tactics to prevent becoming drunk, including the covert sharing of drinks and teaming up with barmen to dilute their drinks with water. This chapter also examines the work conditions that perpetuated this chemical use, and the precariousness caused by night work and heavy caffeine use, which can lead to serious health conditions. It ends with a call for occupational health programs to acknowledge the 24/7 demands on workers, to seek to prevent the overuse of stimulants, and prohibit unethical ways of selling beer.

In Chapter 7, "Chemical Supplements," we examine how the demands of service-sector labor, the strain of night work, the excitement of weekend raves, and growing concerns about environmental toxins all result in a sense of vulnerability among youth, fueling a felt need for supplements. Aggressively marketing to young people through online commercials, mass media, and street-level vitamin stores, marketers capitalize on these fears. Youths across our field sites took vitamin C to prevent colds and coughs, and to generate energy; vitamin E to gain radiant skin; and multivitamin capsules for shiny hair. Vitamin-fortified energy drinks are especially popular among construction workers and porters, both engaged in heavy physical work. Our respondent consume more complex food supplements to increase muscle mass, such as fruit shakes that were combined with ginger extract, turmeric, and honey to strengthen immunity. Young people worried about the lack of nutrients in their fast food noodles, burgers, and pizzas, and supplementing was thus a rational strategy when there was rarely time to cook. Two contrasting ethnographic vignettes—of youth who sold supplements in a multilevel marketing sales pyramid in Puerto Princesa and a young woman in Amsterdam who sold vitamins and protein powders to female body builders—show how young people co-created products to alleviate this perceived vulnerability, how they tailored products to their clients' needs in face-to-face and online interactions, and how they consumed the products that they sold and created in order to be able to personally testify to their effects. This chapter reflects on the economic costs of supplement use in young people's lives, and the exploitative labor arrangements that drew youth to participate in multilevel marketing.

In Chapter 8, "Chemical Creativities," we discuss how, using novel virtual ethnography techniques, the ChemicalYouth project examined popular online drug forums where users, mostly men, share their experiments with chemicals. In this chapter, we zoom in on the online discussions about microdosing of LSD and psilocybin to enhance creativity, a common practice among young people in creative, academic, and tech environments. We present users' narratives which show how they "do" microdosing, what they want to achieve by using these substances, and what they do to prevent or reduce harm. Collaborations between researchers and users aggregate users' experiences online, which form the basis for clinical trials that compare the effects of psychoactive substances with those of placebos.

"Chemical Futures," the concluding chapter, shows how young people mobilize to reduce the adverse effects of chemicals in their everyday lives. Here, we focus on a group of activists in France called Générations Cobayes (Guinea Pig Generations) and their campaigns on endocrine-disrupting chemicals. Building on this case, we take stock of the ways that young people across our field sites sought to mitigate chemical harm, showing how, unlike the Cobayes, they generally did not realize how toxicities can compound one another or act slowly, over time. We further describe how youth in their everyday lives sought to mitigate harm "from below," though constrained by industrial strategies that amplify chemicals' benefits through marketing and render risks invisible (Proctor 2011; Healy 2012). We propose the more widespread adoption of the precautionary principle before allowing chemicals on the market, and for building on and supporting young people's collaborative experiments in harm reduction. Young people have been induced by manufacturers to believe in and promote the benefits of many chemicals, and governments have allowed these products on the market. When adverse effects become apparent, they tend to be dealt with one chemical at a time. Can academics, policymakers, and the concerned public all engage with youth to spread precautionary tales beyond those related to narcotic drugs, while attending also the combined risks of chemicals and slow toxicities to enhance the safer use of chemicals?

International ChemicalYouth Research Coordinators

Michael Tan was the Principal Investigator for the ChemicalYouth project in the Philippines. In this role, Michael conducted the analysis of skin whitening practices, supervised one ChemicalYouth PhD project, organized the site visits, and co-edited and book launch of *Making bodies work: Young people's everyday body management in urban Mindanao* in the Philippines. He is a Professor of Anthropology at the University of the Philippines Diliman. He also served as the Chancellor from 2014 to 2020 (Fig. 1.5).

Fig. 1.5 Michael Tan

Emilia Sanabria was the Principal Investigator for the ChemicalYouth project in France and co-supervisor to two ChemicalYouth PhDs. She is a Senior Researcher at the Centre National de la Recherche Scientifique in Paris. She has worked at the intersections of the anthropology of health, care, and the body and science and technology studies (STS) on topics ranging from sex hormones, menstruation, and pharmaceutical cultures to obesity, nutrition, non-ordinary states of consciousness, and the psychedelic renaissance. Emilia is currently the Principal Investigator of a project on the new therapeutic uses of the Amazonian psychoactive brew ayahuasca (Fig. 1.6).

Fig. 1.6 Emilia Sanabria

Nurul Ilmi Idrus was the Principal Investigator for ChemicalYouth in Indonesia and coördinated the Grand Tour there, as well as the students' fieldwork and reporting. She is a Professor of Anthropology at the Hasanuddin University in Indonesia. Her areas of interest for research include health, gender, and sexuality. Idrus has collaborated with Anita Hardon both in the field and writing, and several of these publications are essential to this book and presented throughout (Fig. 1.7).

Fig. 1.7 Nurul Ilmi Idrus

Notes

1. See Nichter (2003) for an incisive analysis of risk taking, vulnerability and harm reduction among people in diverse cultural settings, who confront different kinds of health issues.
2. Thevenot (2001) points to the importance of 'pragmatic regimes' in every day life. He invites scholars to empirically differentiate between kinds of material engagements between agents and their environments in order to

gain insights into the concept of good that underlies practice. This is an analytical strategy that inspired me in developing the ChemicalYouth project.

3. The term emerged in the 1980s in Europe to describe moves towards more flexible, globally connected labor arrangements and weakening labor protection mechanisms and welfare provisions. The term indexes a loss of labor security and stable jobs, which arguably 'only certain countries, at certain historical periods, and certain workers had in the first place (Allison 2013, p. 5). Our respondents grow up without the expectation that employers will care for them. Standing (2011) refers to the people affected by these trends as 'the precariat'.
4. The European Research Council's ethics board demanded that if respondents were younger than 18, we obtain their parents' permission for them to engage in the research. This was not practical, as many youth live away from their families We also did not consider it ethically appropriate to do so, given the nature of some of their chemical practices and our commitment to anonymity. However, the European Research Council's ethics committee demanded that we did not analyze the fieldnotes that concerned youth below the age of 18.
5. This interview tool can be found on the ChemicalYouth website (chemicalyouth.org) under the methods section.
6. Because of the risks related to the illegal use of drugs in most of our study sites, the ChemicalYouth project adopted anonymity procedures. Informants were assured that their participation was both completely voluntary and anonymous. Before conducting any interviews in the GrandTours, PhD field researchers and junior researchers in all four countries were trained by their respective PI's in keeping and maintaining a vigorous commitment to the anonymity of participants. For example, interviewers made sure to inform participants that any and all identifying details that they gave (such as name, address, date of birth, place of birth) would be removed from their transcripts, that a pseudonym would be given, and that interviews would take place in public spaces that allowed for private discussions. Furthermore, researchers were trained on using a system of acronyms to title their interview transcripts and other documents that did not contain the name of the respondent. Anonymity was of particular importance in our focused ethnography of an online forum of drug users reporting and sharing their experience with new psychoactive substances (see Berning and Hardon 2016). In order to safely report on their online data, and not have their quotes be traceable on search engines, their online pseudonyms were

pseudonymized again and the names of the fora were not revealed. These safeguards were approved by an independent ethics advisor. One exception to adhering to our anonymity guidelines is the focused ethnographies discussed in chapter seven with supplement creator and vitamin shop owner. Upon consideration, it was concluded that they were well-known internet personalities, therefore their names were easily identifiable. Moreover, the products that they sell are legal and thus sharing their real identity or their company did not pose a risk as it would have, had they been selling illegal products.

References

Abraham, J., & Lewis, G. (2000). *Regulating medicines in Europe: Competition, expertise and public health.* London: Routledge.

Abu-Lughod, L. (1991). Writing against culture. In R. Fox (Ed.), *Recapturing anthropology: Working in the present* (pp. 50–59). Santa Fe, NM: School of American Research Press.

Allison, A. (2013). *Precarious Japan.* Durham, NC: Duke University Press.

Amaro, R. (2016). Taking chances for love? Reflections on love, risk, and harm reduction in a gay slamming subculture. *Contemporary Drug Problems, 43*(3), 216–227. https://doi.org/10.1177/0091450916658295.

Appadurai, A. (1996). *Modernity at large: Cultural dimensions of globalization.* Minneapolis: University of Minnesota Press.

Applbaum, K. (2009). Getting to yes: Corporate power and the creation of a psychopharmaceutical blockbuster. *Culture, Medicine and Psychiatry, 33*(2), 185–215.

Assanangkornchai, S., Pattanasattayawong, U., Samangsri, N., & Mukthong, A. (2007). Substance use among high-school students in southern Thailand: Trends over 3 years (2002–2004). *Drug and Alcohol Dependence, 86*(2–3), 167–174. https://doi.org/10.1016/j.drugalcdep.2006.06.001.

Barry, A. (2005). Pharmaceutical matters: The invention of informed materials. *Theory, Culture & Society, 22*(1), 51–69. https://doi.org/10.1177/0263276405048433.

Bengtsson, T., & Ravn, S. (2018). *Youth, risk, routine: A new perspective on risk-taking in young lives.* Oxfordshire: Routledge.

Berning, M., & Hardon, A. (2016). Educated guesses and other ways to address the pharmacological uncertainty of designer drugs: An exploratory study of experimentation through an online drug forum. *Contemporary Drug Problems, 43*(3), 277–292. https://doi.org/10.1177/0091450916662164.

Besnier, N., & Guinness, D. (2020). Global sport industries, comparison, and economies of scale. In M. Schnegg (Ed.), *Comparing cultures: Innovations in comparative ethnography* (pp. 201–222). Cambridge: Cambridge University Press.

Bourgois, P. (1998). The moral economies of homeless heroin addicts: Confronting ethnography, HIV risk, and everyday violence in San Francisco shooting encampments. *Substance Use & Misuse, 33*(11). https://doi.org/10.3109/10826089809056260.

Bramness, J. G., Furu, K., Engeland, A., & Skurtveit, S. (2007). Carisoprodol use and abuse in Norway: A pharmacoepidemiological study. *British Journal of Clinical Pharmacology, 64*(2), 210–218. https://doi.org/10.1111/j.1365-2125.2007.02847.x.

Butler, J. (2004a). *Undoing gender*. Oxfordshire: Routledge.

Butler, J. (2004b). *Precarious life: The powers of mourning and violence*. New York: Verso.

Callon, M., Lascoumes, P., & Barthe, Y. (2001). *Acting in an uncertain world: An essay on technical democracy*. Cambridge, MA: Massachusetts Institute of Technology Press.

Campaign for Safe Cosmetics. (2020). *Campaign for safe cosmetics: International laws*. Campaign for Safe Cosmetics. http://www.safecosmetics.org/get-the-facts/regulations/international-laws/. Accessed on November 5, 2019.

Caulkins, J. P., & Kilborn, M. L. (2019). Cannabis legalization, regulation, & control: A review of key challenges for local, state, and provincial officials. *The American Journal of Drug and Alcohol Abuse, 45*(6), 1–9. https://doi.org/10.1080/00952990.2019.1611840.

ChemicalYouth. (2020). *ChemicalYouth*. Chemical Youth. www.chemicalyouth.org. Accessed on November 5, 2019.

Cole, J. (2010). *Sex and salvation: Imagining the future in Madagascar*. Chicago: University of Chicago Press.

Cole, J., & Durham, D. (2007). *Generations and globalization: Youth, age, and family in the new world economy*. Bloomington: Indiana University Press.

Comaroff, J., & Comaroff, J. (2000). Millennial capitalism: First thoughts on a second coming. *Public Culture, 12*(2), 291–343. https://doi.org/10.1215/08992363-12-2-291.

Davis, C., & Abraham, J. (2013). *Unhealthy pharmaceutical regulation: Innovation, politics and promissory science.* New York: Palgrave Macmillan.

DEA. (2011). *2011—Final rule: Placement of Carisoprodol into schedule IV*. US Department of Justice. https://www.deadiversion.usdoj.gov/fed_regs/rules/2011/fr1212_10.html. Accessed on November 5, 2019.

DeSantis, A., Noar, S. M., & Webb, E. M. (2010). Speeding through the frat house: A qualitative exploration of non-medical ADHA stimulant use in fraternities. *Journal of Drug Education, 40*(2), 157–171. https://doi.org/10.2190/DE.40.2.d.

Droney, D. (2016). Networking health: Multi-level marketing of health products in Ghana. *Anthropology and Medicine, 23*(1), 1–13. https://doi.org/10.1080/13648470.2015.1057104.

Duff, C. (2008). The pleasure in context. *International Journal of Drug Policy, 19*(5), 384–392. https://doi.org/10.1016/j.drugpo.2007.07.003.

Duff, C. (2011). Networks, resources and agencies: On the character and production of enabling places. *Health and Place, 17*(1), 149–156. https://doi.org/10.1016/j.healthplace.2010.09.012.

Dumit, J. (2010). Inter-pill-ation and the instrumentalization of compliance. *Anthropology & Medicine, 17*(2), 245–247. https://doi.org/10.1080/13648470.2010.493708.

Dumit, J. (2012). *Drugs for life: How pharmaceutical companies define our health.* Durham, NC: Duke University Press.

Durham, D. (2008). New horizons: Youth at the millennium. *Anthropological Quarterly, 81*(4), 945–957.

Ecks, S., & Basu, S. (2009). The unlicensed lives of antidepressants in India: Generic drugs, unqualified practitioners, and floating prescriptions. *Transcultural Psychiatry, 46*(1), 86–106. https://doi.org/10.1177/1363461509102289.

Farrugia, D. (2018). Youthfulness and immaterial labour in the new economy. *The Sociological Review, 66*(3), 511–526. https://doi.org/10.1177/0038026117731657.

Gershon, I. (2017). *Down and out in the new economy: How people find (or don't find) work today*. Chicago: University of Chicago Press.

Greenslit, N. (2005). Depression and consumption: Psychopharmaceuticals, branding, and new identity practices. *Culture, Medicine and Psychiatry, 29*(2), 477–502.

Gregory, C., & Altman, J. (2018). *The quest for the good life in precarious times: Ethnographic perspectives on the domestic moral economy.* Canberra: Australian National University Press.

Hartley, H. (2006). The "pinking" of Viagra culture: Drug industry efforts to create and repackage sex drugs for women. *Sexualities, 9*(2), 363–378.

Han, C. (2018). Precarity, precariousness, and vulnerability. *Annual Review of Anthropology, 47,* 331–343.

Hann, M. P. G. (2018). *Sporting aspirations: Football, wrestling and neoliberal subjectivity in urban Senegal* (Doctoral dissertation). Anthropology department, Amsterdam: University of Amsterdam. https://pure.uva.nl/ws/files/30399861/Thesis.pdf.

Hansen, K. T. (2008). Introduction: Youth and the city. In K. Hansen (Ed.), *Youth and the city in the global South* (pp. 3–23). Bloomington: Indiana University Press.

Hardon, A. (1992). That drug is hiyang for me: Lay perceptions of the efficacy of drugs in Manila, Philippines. *Central Issues in Anthropology, 10*(1), 86–93. https://doi.org/10.1525/cia.1992.10.1.86.

Hardon, A., & Hymans, T. D. (2016). Guest editors' introduction: Harm reduction from below. *Contemporary Drug Problems, 43*(3), 191–198. https://doi.org/10.1177/0091450916663247.

Hardon, A., & Idrus, N. I. (2014). On coba and cocok: Youth-led drug-experimentation in eastern Indonesia. *Anthropology & Medicine, 21*(2), 217–229. https://doi.org/10.1080/13648470.2014.927417.

Hardon, A., & Ihsan, A. (2014). Somadril and edgework in South Sulawesi. *International Journal of Drug Policy, 25*(4), 755–761. https://doi.org/10.1016/j.drugpo.2014.05.012.

Hardon, A., & Sanabria, E. (2017). Fluid drugs: Revisiting the anthropology of pharmaceuticals. *Annual Review of Anthropology, 46*(1), 117–132. https://doi.org/10.1146/annurev-anthro-102116-041539.

Hardon, A., Van Schipstal, I., Mishra, S., Berning, M., & Murray, H. (forthcoming, 2020). Caring for "hassle-free highs" in Amsterdam. *Anthropology and Humanism.*

Healy, D. (2006). The new medical Oikumene. In A. Petryna, A. Lakoff, & A. Kleinman (Eds.), *Global pharmaceuticals: Ethics, markets, practices* (pp. 61–84). Durham, NC: Duke University Press. https://doi.org/10.1215/9780822387916.

Healy, D. (2012). Review of pharmaceutical self: The global shaping of experience in an age of psychopharmacology. *Transcultural Psychiatry, 49*(3–4), 638–640. https://doi.org/10.1177/1363461512437148.

Hewison, K., & Kalleberg, A. L. (2013). Precarious work and flexibilization in south and southeast Asia. *American Behavioral Scientist, 57*(4), 395–402. https://doi.org/10.1177/0002764212466235.

Hibell, B., Guttormsson, U., Ahlstrom, S., Balakireva, O., Bjarnason, T., Kokkevi, A., & Kraus, L. (2009). *The 2007 ESPAD report: Substance use among students in 35 countries.* Stockholm: The Swedish Council for Information on Alcohol and Other Drugs.

Homburg, E., & Vapeul, E. (2019). Conclusion. In E. Homburg & E. Vapeul (Eds.), *Hazardous chemicals: Agents of risk and change, 1800–2000* (pp. 376–393). New York: Berghahn Books.

Hunt, G. P., Evans, K., & Kares, F. (2007). Drug use and meanings of risk and pleasure. *Journal of Youth Studies, 10*(1), 73–96. https://doi.org/10.1080/13676260600983668.

Ingold, T. (2012). Toward an ecology of materials. *Annual Review of Anthropology, 41*(1), 427–442. https://doi.org/10.1146/annurev-anthro-081309-145920.

Jenkins, J. H. (2011). *Pharmaceutical self: The global shaping of experience in an age of psychopharmacology.* Santa Fe, NM: School for Advanced Research Press.

Jovic, S., Genolini, C., Delpierre, C., Spilka, S., Ehlinger, V., Ross, J., Arnaud, C., & Godeau, E. (2014). Socialization instances linked to cannabis experimentation among French teenagers. *Substance Use and Misuse, 49*(13), 1808–1819. https://doi.org/10.3109/10826084.2014.935788.

Keane, H. (2011). The politics of visibility: Drug users and the spaces of drug use. *International Journal of Drug Policy, 22*(6), 407–409. https://doi.org/10.1016/j.drugpo.2011.09.006.

Kokkevi, A., Richardson, C., Florescu, S., Kuzman, M., & Stergar, E. (2007). Psychosocial correlates of substance use in adolescence: A cross-national study in six European countries. *Drug and Alcohol Dependence, 86*(1), 67–74. https://doi.org/10.1016/j.drugalcdep.2006.05.018.

Lasco, G. (2014). Pampagilas: Methamphetamine in the everyday economic lives of underclass male youths in a Philippine port. *International Journal of Drug Policy, 25*(4), 783–788. https://doi.org/10.1016/j.drugpo.2014.06.011.

Legleye, S., Janssen, E., Beck, F., Chau, N., & Khlat, M. (2011). Social gradient in initiation and transition to daily use of tobacco and cannabis during adolescence: A retrospective cohort study. *Addiction, 106*(8), 1520–1531. https://doi.org/10.1111/j.1360-0443.2011.03447.x.

Liebregts, N., van der Pol, P., Van Laar, M., de Graaf, R., van den Brink, W., & Korf, D. J. (2013). The role of study and work in cannabis use and dependence trajectories among young adult frequent cannabis users. *Frontiers in Psychiatry, 4*(85). https://doi.org/10.3389/fpsyt.2013.00085.

Liechty, M. (2003). *Suitably modern: Making middle class culture in a new consumer society*. Princeton, NJ: Princeton University Press.

Lorey, I. (2015). *State of insecurity: Government of the precarious*. New York: Verso.

Lukose, R. (2009). *Liberalization's children: Gender, youth, and consumer citizenship in globalizing India*. Durham, NC: Duke University Press.

MacKendrick, N. (2018). *Better safe than sorry: How consumers navigate exposure to everyday toxins*. Berkeley: University of California Press.

Maira, S., & Soep, E. (2004). United States of adolescence? *Young, 12*(3), 245–269. https://doi.org/10.1177/1103308804044508.

Martin, E. (2000). Mind body problems. *American Ethnologist, 27*, 569–590.

Martin, E. (2006). The pharmaceutical person. *BioSocieties, 1*(2), 273–287.

Martinic, M., & Measham, F. (2008). *Swimming with crocodiles: The culture of extreme drinking*. New York: Routledge.

McGoey, L. (2012). Strategic unknowns: Towards a sociology of ignorance. *Economy and Society, 41*(2), 1–16.

Milman, O. (2019). US cosmetics are full of chemicals banned by Europe—why? *The Guardian*. https://www.theguardian.com/us-news/2019/may/22/chemicals-in-cosmetics-us-restricted-eu. Accessed on November 5, 2019.

Moore, K., & Miles, S. (2004). Young people, dance and the sub-cultural consumption of drugs. *Addiction Research & Theory, 12*(6), 507–523. https://doi.org/10.1080/1606635041233l323083.

Nasir, S., & Rosenthal, D. (2009). The social context of initiation into injecting drugs in the slums of Makassar, Indonesia. *International Journal of Drug Policy, 20*(3), 237–243. https://doi.org/10.1016/j.drugpo.2008.02.001.

Newell, S. (2012). *The modernity bluff: Crime, consumption, and citizenship in Cote d'Ivoire*. Chicago: University of Chicago Press.

Nichter, M. (2003). Harm reduction: A core concern for medical anthropology. In B. Herr-Harthorn & L. Oaks (Eds.), *Risk, culture, and health inequality: Shifting perceptions of danger and blame* (pp. 13–33). Westport, CT: Praeger.

Nichter, M. (2015). *Lighting up: The rise of social smoking on college campuses*. New York: New York University Press.

Nicolini, D. (2013). *Practice theory, work, and organization: An introduction*. Oxford, UK: Oxford University Press.

Nilan, P., & Feixa, C. (2006). *Global youth? Hybrid identities, plural worlds*. Oxfordshire: Routledge.

Nutt, D. J., King, L. A., & Phillips, L. D. (2010). Drug harms in the UK: A multicriteria decision analysis. *The Lancet, 376*(9752), 1558–1565. https://doi.org/10.1016/S0140-6736(10)61462-6.

Nygren, K. G., & Olofsson, A. (2014). Intersectional approaches in health-risk research: A critical review. *Sociology Compass, 8*(9), 1112–1126.

Pilkington, H. (2007). Beyond "peer pressure": Rethinking drug use and "youth culture". *International Journal of Drug Policy, 18*(3), 213–224. https://doi.org/10.1016/j.drugpo.2006.08.003.

Proctor, R. (2011). *Golden holocaust: Origins of the cigarette catastrophe and the case for abolition.* Berkeley: University of California Press.

Quintero, G., & Nichter, M. (2011). Generation RX: Anthropological research on pharmaceutical enhancement, lifestyle regulation, self-medication and recreational drug use. In M. Singer & P. Erickson (Eds.), *A companion to medical anthropology* (pp. 339–357). Oxford: Wiley-Blackwell.

Race, K. (2009). *Pleasure consuming medicine: The queer politics of drugs.* Durham NC: Duke University Press.

Read, R., & O'Riordan, T. (2017). The precautionary principle under fire. *Environment, 59*(5), 4–15. https://doi.org/10.1080/00139157.2017.1350005.

Rhodes, T. (2002). The "risk environment": A framework for understanding and reducing drug-related harm. *International Journal of Drug Policy, 13*(2), 85–94. https://doi.org/10.1016/S0955-3959(02)00007-5.

Riley, S. C. E., Griffin, C., & Morey, Y. (2010). The case for 'everyday politics': Evaluating neo-tribal theory as a way to understand alternative forms of political participation, using electronic dance music culture as an example. *Sociology, 44*(2), 345–363. https://doi.org/10.1177/0038038509357206.

Rofel, L. (2007). *Desiring China: Experiments in neoliberalism, sexuality and public culture.* Durham, NC: Duke University Press.

Rose, N. (2007). Molecular biopolitics, somatic ethics and the spirit of biocapital. *Social Theory & Health, 5*, 3–29. https://doi.org/10.1057/palgrave.sth.8700084.

Schatzki, T. (2001). Practice minded orders. In K. Cetina & E. von Savingy (Eds.), *The practice turn in contemporary theory* (pp. 42–55). Oxfordshire: Routledge.

Shapiro, N., & Kirksey, E. (2017). Chemo-ethnography: An introduction. *Cultural Anthropology, 32*(4), 481–493. https://doi.org/10.14506/ca32.4.01.

Singer, M. (2007). *Drugging the poor: Legal and illegal drugs and social inequality.* Longrove, IL: Waveland Press.

Singer, M. (2008). Drugs and development: The global impact of drug use and trafficking on social and economic development. *International Journal of Drug Policy, 19*(6), 467–478. https://doi.org/10.1016/j.drugpo.2006.12.007.

Sismondo, S. (2010). Linking research and marketing, a pharmaceutical innovation. In V. Quirke & J. Slinn (Eds.), *Perspectives on twentieth century pharmaceuticals* (pp. 241–256). Bern, Switzerland: Peter Lang.

Standing, G. (2011). *The precariat: The new dangerous class.* London: Bloomsbury.

Substance Abuse & Mental Health Data Archive. (2003). *Drug abuse warning network US*. Substance Abuse & Mental Health Data Archive. https://www.datafiles.samhsa.gov/study/drug-abuse-warning-network-us-dawn-ns-1997-nid13592. Accessed on November 5, 2019.

Sunder Rajan, K. (2017). *Pharmocracy: Value, politics, and knowledge in global biomedicine*. Durham, NC: Duke University Press.

Taqueban, E. M. M. (2018). *Lipstick tales: Beauty and precarity in a southern Philippine boomtown.* Anthropology department, Amsterdam: University of Amsterdam. https://pure.uva.nl/ws/files/27042354/Front_matter.pdf.

Thevenot, L. (2001). Pragmatic regimes governing the engagement with the world. In T. R. Schatzki, K. Knorr Cetina & E. van Savigny (Eds.), *The practice turn in contemporary theory* (pp. 56–73). London: Routledge.

Urciuoli, B. (2008). Skills and selves in the new workplace. *American Ethnologist, 35*(2), 211–228.

United Nations. (2015). *United Nations Sustainable Development Goal 3: Good health and well-being*. United Nations Sustainable Development Goals 2015. https://sustainabledevelopment.un.org/sdg3. Accessed on November 5, 2019.

United States Environmental Protection Agency. (2016). *Summary of the Toxic Substances Control Act*. United States Environmental Protection Agency. https://www.epa.gov/laws-regulations/summary-toxic-substances-control-act. Accessed on November 5, 2019.

U.S. Food and Drug Administration. (2005). *FDA authority over cosmetics: How cosmetics are not FDA-approved, but are FDA-regulated*. U.S. Food and Drug Administration. https://www.fda.gov/cosmetics/cosmetics-laws-regulations/fda-authority-over-cosmetics-how-cosmetics-are-not-fda-approved-are-fda-regulated. Accessed on November 5, 2019.

Vallas, S., & Prener, C. (2012). Dualism, job polarization, and the social construction of precarious work. *Work and Occupations, 39*(4), 331–353. https://doi.org/10.1177/0730888412456027.

van Schipstal, I., Mishra, S., Berning, M., & Murray, H. (2016). Harm reduction from below: On sharing and caring in drug use. *Contemporary Drug Problems, 43*(3), 199–215. https://doi.org/10.1177/0091450916663248.

Wolf-Meyer, M. (2014). Therapy, remedy, cure: Disorder and the spatiotemporality of medicine and everyday life. *Medical Anthropology, 33*(2), 144–159. https://doi.org/10.1080/01459740.2013.792812.

Zinn, J. O., & Olofsson, A. (2019). Introduction. In A. Olofsson & J. O. Zinn (Eds.), *Researching risk and uncertainty: Methodologies, methods and research strategies* (pp. 1–28). London: Palgrave Macmillan.

2

Hassle-Free Highs and Adverse Events

This chapter is written in the midst of the US opioid crisis, which is an extreme challenge for families and policymakers there, and causing astounding numbers of deaths across the country. In the wake of the crisis, anthropologists are revisiting themes of structural violence and pharmaceutical malpractice, both of which fuel the addiction crisis (Hansen 2017). Talking to colleagues at the 2019 conference of the American Anthropological Association, I had a hard time explaining why, in the Netherlands, levels of opioid addiction are very low, despite widespread use of recreational drugs. Young people in my country seem to be able to regulate their drug use to achieve relatively "hassle-free highs." Part of the reason for fewer drug-related deaths and drug-related problems in the Netherlands is the government's decision, in the late 1970s, to make a distinction between "hard" drugs like heroin that are highly addictive and criminalized, and "soft" drugs such as cannabis, the recreational use of which is permitted. As a result, Amsterdam youth have tended to stay away from the hard stuff.

But this is not the full answer. Much has to do with a more subtle regulation of drug use by governmental health programs in Amsterdam. This is a city that annually hosts the world's most extensive electronic dance festival, the five-day Amsterdam Dance Event; attendees of these events widely use ecstasy and amphetamines for their stimulating effects. This is also a city that appointed the world's very first "Night Ambassador" to monitor drug use during this citywide festival and conference, in order to intervene if substandard drugs are found on the dancefloor. In doing so, the city authorities have presented themselves as pragmatic harm reduction agents, who have earned the trust of partying youth. They provide the youth information, and they also call on youth to take responsibility for their drug use and for one another.

This chapter describes how young people in current-day Amsterdam self-regulate to achieve hassle-free highs, using strategies that elsewhere we have referred to as "harm reduction from below" (Hardon and Hymans 2016; Van Schipstal et al. 2016). In our research in Amsterdam, we found that our interlocutors came to trust harm reduction workers as sources of accurate information on drugs, even as such workers sought to support youth in self-regulation and keep track of new trends in drug use. We contrast these harm reduction dynamics in Amsterdam with the drug-use situation in Indonesia, where a draconian drug war has been raging over the past decade. Like their peers in Amsterdam, Indonesian youth self-regulated their substance use to avoid harm. But, in contrast, they fear the authorities, which means they did so with limited information on the potential harmful effects of the drugs they used (Idrus and Hardon 2019).

"At Risk Youth"

There is a large body of social and behavioral research, briefly discussed in the introduction, that aims to understand why young people take drugs and what determines addiction trajectories. In such studies, youth are usually approached as individuals who are affected by "risk factors," such as having experienced adverse childhood events or growing up in low-income neighborhoods where they may be seduced into taking drugs. Researchers then propose to intervene at the level of these risk factors to prevent drug use problems. This youth-at-risk paradigm is being challenged by social scientists who point to the ever-changing nature of drug use, and to the social—not just individual—pleasure that young people experience when taking drugs with their friends (Duff 2004).

Drug use indeed shapes friendship groups, which Pilkington (2007) refers to as "bonds of emotionality and mutual accountability about acceptable and unacceptable drug use and a secure and supportive environment in which to enact the ensuing drug decisions" (Pilkington 2007, p. 222). Because of these shared norms, being surrounded by friends can reduce the risks of taking drugs while at the same time increasing pleasure (Hunt et al. 2007). Risks can further be mitigated when the group shares a value that Riley and colleagues (2010) call the "duty of care" (Riley et al. 2010, p. 43).

The duty to care found within friendship groups who take drugs together often involves a strong social etiquette in which clubbers regulate each other's behavior on the dancefloor or smoking room, and this also happens between strangers at house parties (Moore and Miles 2004). An example of this etiquette is young women refusing drinks from strangers. If they do, their friends will chastise them, as doing so puts one at risk of being drugged and raped. When we were doing fieldwork in Amsterdam there were several stories circulating of young women who had ended up in intensive care after being drugged with what became known as the "rape drug," formally called flunitrazepam or Rohypnol.

Our fieldwork in Amsterdam sought to understand how the city's harm reduction policies intersected with young people's strategies to achieve hassle-free highs. A team of youth ethnographers conducted fieldwork at festivals, clubs, and private after-parties (Van Schipstal et al. 2016). We identified four ways that our respondents sought to achieve hassle-free highs, all of which were acknowledged and reinforced by the city's harm reduction workers: (1) testing the content of substances, (2) cautious consumption, (3) peer support, and (4) balancing acts. In the second half of this chapter we contrast these self-regulation practices with those observed in our Indonesian field sites, where the government has been imprisoning people caught with drugs.

Self-Regulation in Amsterdam

Our interlocutors in Amsterdam confronted uncertainty about the contents of recreational pills and powders, by acquiring them from friends and trusted connections. Generally, more experienced users were responsible for buying drugs and sharing them at parties, clubs, and festivals (Hardon et al. forthcoming, 2020). Often youth consulted online drug forums, such as Pill Report (www.pillreports.net), a user-driven site that reports the quality of the wide range of ecstasy pills found in the market.

Amsterdam's harm reduction initiatives recognize these youth-led quality assurance mechanisms and offered help in the form of drug-testing facilities. Young people can bring their purchased drugs to testing sites throughout the Netherlands, where they are asked a few questions on the source of the drugs and past experiences. During the visit, a simple test is done to determine the MDMA (3,4-methylenedioxymethamphetamine, the active ingredient) content of ecstasy pills. Other drugs, such as lysergic acid diethylamide (LSD) or gamma hydroxybutyrate (GHB or G), which require more detailed equipment, are sent to a laboratory for further testing. Young people often post the test results on the Pill Reports website, along with pictures of the drugs for identification (see Fig. 2.1).

Fig. 2.1 A compilation of pictures of ecstasy pills posted online, prepared by the Utrecht Data School for the ChemicalYouth project, November 2017

The government-sponsored harm reduction programs do not endorse pillreports.net, as they cannot guarantee the quality of the posts. They warn that drug content can change with each new batch of pills and online reports may therefore be inaccurate. To meet the need for information, they have developed a smartphone application called Red Alert, through which they can instantaneously inform drug users of substandard pills when these are identified in the pill-testing facilities. Alongside notes of caution about risky substances entering the Dutch drug market, the Red Alert app also provides information, for example, on the increasingly high dosages of MDMA found in ecstasy pills, noting that high dosages can cause adverse effects such as anxiety and insomnia (Hardon et al. forthcoming, 2020).

Sometimes, the city also uses billboards to alert youth. For example, in December 2014, after several tourists died after consuming cocaine cut with heroin, purchased from street dealers, the municipality placed billboards in the center of the tourist district warning tourists about contaminated cocaine (see Fig. 2.2). Harm reduction workers had realized that tourists would not have received Red Alerts on their phones.

A similar situation occurred during the festivities of 2016's Amsterdam Dance Event, where an ecstasy pill that someone brought into one of the

Fig. 2.2 Warnings on billboard in a popular nightlife area (Photo taken by Anita Hardon, December 2014, Amsterdam)

several testing sites turned out to be adulterated with PMMA, which is toxic at high levels. Attendees were alerted via several media: push notifications went out to users of the RedAlert app, posts were shared via several harm reduction organizations via their Facebook pages, and warning signs were posted at the entrance of clubs and bars (Fig. 2.3).

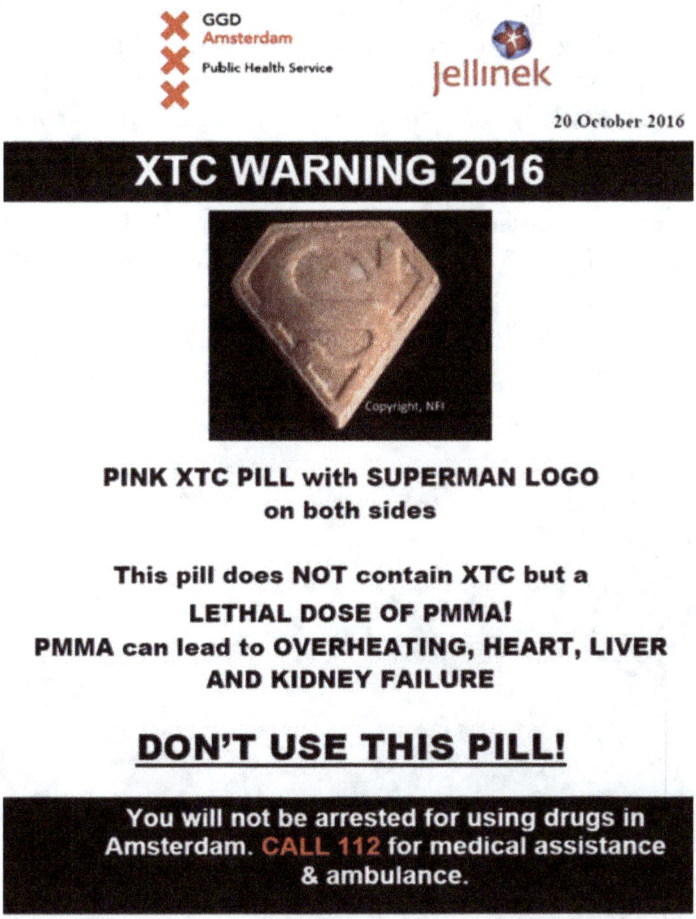

Fig. 2.3 Government released "Superman" warning during Amsterdam Dance Event 2016 (Photo taken by Hayley Murray, October 2016, Amsterdam)

In addition to making sure drugs are of good quality by buying from trusted sources, and in turn having the substances tested, our interlocutors sought to achieve hassle-free highs by taking the right dosage of drugs. However, different drugs require different dosing techniques. MDMA, the active component of ecstasy pills, can be purchased as a powder; because of this, it is weighed. Dennis, an experienced user, who was responsible for giving out MDMA at a party told his friends: "So, here we go! I am going to measure the exact dose of MDMA for everybody. One by one you can tell me how much you guys weigh and the rule of thumb basically is 1.5 times the bodyweight" (Van Schipstal et al. 2016, p. 204). GHB, on the other hand, comes as a fluid and is dosed with a syringe, see Fig. 2.4.

At one party we observed Heleen, also known as "Mama G," keeping a logbook (see Fig. 2.5) listing the number of milliliters of GHB that she had given to the attendees of an after-party and the time of ingestion (Van Schipstal et al. 2016). This detailed approach helped the partiers feel safer in their GHB use, as this substance is notoriously difficult to dose.

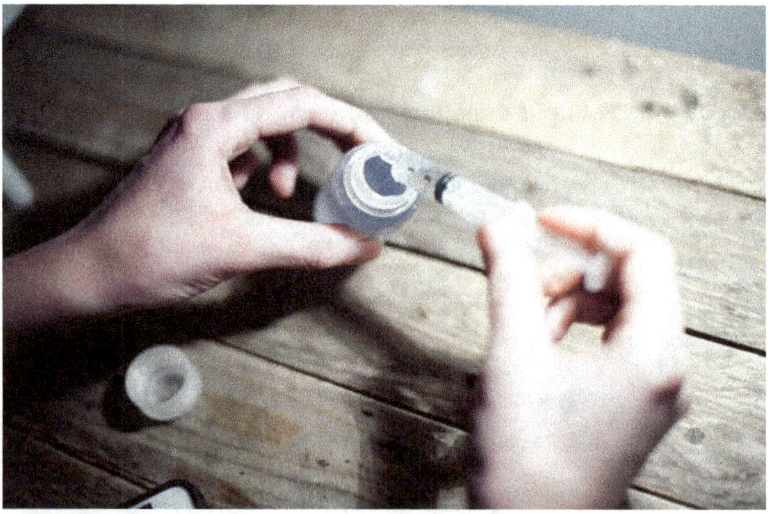

Fig. 2.4 Dosing GHB with a syringe (Photo taken by Romy Kaa, July 2014, Amsterdam)

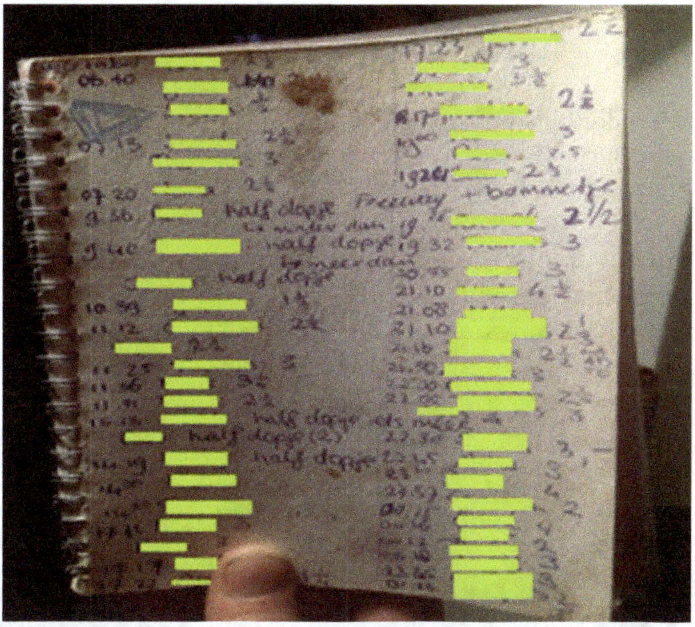

Fig. 2.5 Heleen's GHB logbook. The notebook lists the time of intake very precisely and the volume of GHB used, measured in "*dopjes,*" or bottlecaps (Photo taken by Inge van Schipstal, 2015, Amsterdam)

Our researchers identified a third technique from our online fieldwork among young people taking new kinds of drugs, also known as "designer drugs," for which the optimal dose remains unknown. This technique for dosing these new psychoactive substances is called "allergy dosing." The idea is to begin with a very small amount to avoid adverse events (Hofmann et al. 2009). The online drug forum we examined gives the following instructions:

> Measure out approximately 5 mg of your material. … Dissolve your 5 mg in 1 litre of distilled water and allow to go into solution. Your solution should now have a concentration of approximately 5 μg./ml. Measure out 1 ml of water and hold it in your mouth for 5-10 minutes to see if any reaction occurs. If not, swallow and wait 1 hour to see if any reaction occurs. If no reaction has occurred, repeat the same operation with 2 ml of water. At the end of that hour repeat with 5 ml of water.

> This can continue along until you reach a level where you are satisfied that you will not have an extreme anaphylactic reaction. Ideally you probably would want to go up to about 1/10th of an active dose or so. The amount required to do this will of course depend on the compound in question and its presumed active dose. (Baloo on Forum Y, retrieved 3 April 2015, in Berning and Hardon 2016, p. 284)

These cautious dosing strategies are reinforced by educational materials circulated by Amsterdam-based harm reduction programs. Unity, a nonprofit peer-run organization funded by the government of Amsterdam, created a five-year campaign called "Celebrate Safe." Their mandate was to be present at Dutch music events to encourage young partiers to take care of each other and to educate them on the risks involved with partying. Their website for example states: Be warned that 'less is more.' Better to take one less than one more. One too much can

Fig. 2.6 Celebrate Safe's 10 commandments banner found at one of the entrances to an event at Amsterdam Dance Event (Photo taken by Hayley Murray, October 2016 Amsterdam)

make you feel bad, and ruin the party. That would be a shame. Realize that when you take too much you will also ruin the evening for your friends who are partying with you (Celebrate Safe 2017).

Self-regulation, as seen in the strategies outlined above, is all about taking care, by buying good quality drugs and using appropriate dosages together with friends. This includes not accepting drinks from strangers. Young people are assertive in enacting and requesting this social support. For example, Nina told us how she asked for support from a friend, saying to her:

> Tonight I want to test my limit of sanity. I want to try and go crazy and come back, and see what this world looks like. I am going to try at least double the dose of LSD I have taken [before], and maybe a little bit more. And then come down with MDMA. You be here with me, OK? (Van Schipstal et al. 2016, p. 208)

Others say they look for online advice, which we also observed in our ethnography of online drug forums (Berning and Hardon 2016). We for example found this post by Blanka, in which she asked for advice on a new kind of drug she was researching:

> I am getting ready to research allylescaline … and will write up a Trip Report afterwards but does anybody know if I can research [use] allylescaline while still having residual kratom under the microscope [under the influence of kratom]? I can't find anything on these two interacting and really don't want some chemical reaction from researching too close together. Also does anyone know of other substances interacting with allylescaline? And yes I have tried Google and looking here for the answer. (Van Schipstal et al. 2016, p. 210)

Blanka, in this case, is engaging in "edgework," a concept introduced by Lyng (1990) and applied by Quintero and Nichter (2011) to young people's recreational use of psychoactive drugs. Quintero and Nichter (2011) explain that an edgeworker, "is at once attracted by the sensation of being on the edge as an intense form of pleasure, and the accomplishment of being able to avoid a bad or disastrous effect" (p. 347; cf. Hunt et al. 2007). In trying out new substances, edgeworkers face the "pharmacological uncertainty" (Berning and Hardon 2016) of ingesting novel substances for which there is still little information on their efficacies and adverse effects. Our use of the concept of "pharmacological uncertainty" is inspired by Zinn (2008), who argues that people "working on the edge" cope with high levels of uncertainty and risk in different ways. When youth try out new chemicals, with advice from their online peers, they trust in the testimonials of others and in the suppliers of chemicals, while also doing online research and carefully weighing and dosing, together comprising what Zinn (2008) refers to as an "in-between strategy" of risk-mitigation.

Our interlocutors both on- and offline further sought to achieve hassle-free highs by using "balancing" techniques. For example, users know that they should drink water when taking ecstasy, but not too much. In addition to water, some of our interlocutors took magnesium pills before ingesting ecstasy to reduce the uncontrolled jaw movements caused by the drug. And they also paid attention to the spaces in which they used drugs. MDMA can be used at dance parties or at home; one person explained it was best to do so:

> …in a nice comfy environment with people you love. If you like other types of trips you can also go to the countryside, out in nature. There you can mediate or take a walk to calm yourself before it begins. (Van Schipstal et al. 2016, p. 207)

Sunday and Monday tend to be recovery days, designated to recharge for the coming work or study week. Young people who worked in the nightlife industry reported difficulties with the transition. They used stimulants such as amphetamines or cocaine to stay up very late, and then came home "hyped up," exhausted, yet unable to sleep. Smoking cannabis was a balancing act for them, which they did to prepare their bodies for sleep, sometimes along with melatonin to reset their biological clocks. Many of our respondents also took food supplements, vitamins, and serotonin boosters such as 5-HTP, sometimes combined in fruit and vegetable smoothies, to recuperate (Van Schipstal et al. 2016).

Dutch harm reduction programs highlight this need for self-regulation. Celebrate Safe advises youth to drink enough water, use earplugs, wear comfortable shoes, avoid the sun, keep an eye on each other, and help peers who don't feel well (Hardon and Hymans 2016). Their materials give the following advice: "Pace Yourself: Eat, Sleep, Rave." The campaign also emphasizes the need to recuperate: "Sleeping is also great and needed. Catch up with sleep so you are ready for the next party: eat a good breakfast. You deserve it after the party" (Celebrate Safe 2017).

These self-regulation techniques are not static but evolve through collaborative experimentation with substances and shared evaluation of results. When self-regulation is encouraged and reinforced by local harm reduction programs, it can contribute to a highly informed drug use culture that is oriented toward the prevention of adverse events and overdoses, while jointly crafting "hassle-free" highs. This culture has been referred to as "calculated hedonism" (Measham 2004), an apt concept for the strategies used in Amsterdam. The calculation is literal in young people's tailoring of dosages to users' body weight and in the method of allergy dosing unknown substances. The city's harm reduction workers support these strategies by providing pill-testing services, which allow users to determine the exact content of their drugs. The city thus supports sensible self-regulation by being alert to new trends and responding rapidly when problems occur.

Such a pragmatic approach to harm reduction generates trust in the government-sponsored testing facilities and information sources, enabling rational strategies to confront the uncertainty of consuming illegal drugs. In Amsterdam, young people know that they will not be arrested if they turn to the police or security officers for drug-related help, and they value the "red alerts" that help them take drugs more safely. They also trust each other and the techniques that they have developed to avoid bad trips. Perhaps most surprising of all, they trust online drug forums, where they consult and follow the advice of complete strangers. In the eyes of the harm reduction programs, this trust in strangers and online reports is unsettling. The Dutch Trimbos Institute, a government-sponsored agency responsible for testing services and the Red Alert App, advises against using information from Pillreports.net to check drug quality because of the anonymous nature of the website (Hardon et al. forthcoming, 2020).

Self-Regulation in a Drugs War

When I present this case of Amsterdam at panels and conference, my audience is often surprised and puzzled, yet they quickly assert that this co-production of safer drug use cannot work in their country, where young people are less responsible and authorities don't have a history of pragmatic harm reduction. We turn now to self-regulation in Indonesia, where young people are experiencing an intensification of the ongoing drug war. Across our field sites, we observed that young people were turning away from illegal narcotic drugs and toward psychoactive prescription drugs (PPDs), which they were able to access easily through street dealers and pharmacies. They were not aware that some of the PPDs they were taking can cause addictions.

President Jokowi, shortly after being elected in 2014, reinvigorated the drug war. He reintroduced the death penalty for drug traffickers, which soon after led to the execution of the Dutch citizen Ang Kiem Soei for his alleged involvement in producing ecstasy. The drug authorities also clamped down on the trafficking of methamphetamines (locally known as *shabu*), reporting nearly every day on raids on meth laboratories and seizures by the police (United Nations Office on Drugs and Crime 2018).

Amphetamines, ecstasy, cocaine, and marijuana are all classified as Group 1 narcotics in Indonesia on the basis that they are therapeutically useless and have a high potential for addiction. Since 2015, possession of these drugs can lead to life imprisonment and the death penalty for drug traffickers and users. Group 2 drugs include opioids such as morphine, oxycodone, and the opioid-replacement drug methadone. These drugs, according to the 2009 narcotics law, have some therapeutic value as well as a potential for addiction. Street sellers and users caught taking these drugs can also end up in prison.[1]

Our fieldwork in Indonesia revealed that many of our drug-using respondents were struggling to make a living and had a limited education. Needing to work in the informal sector, they turned to drugs to induce confidence and increase stamina, selecting combinations that did not make them feel too disoriented. On other occasions, they sought to escape from the stresses of daily life by taking extreme dosages that made them "fly." They sought to achieve hassle-free highs by using psychoactive prescription drugs, which they viewed as "legal" and safe because they can be bought in pharmacies.

PPD use in Indonesia is facilitated by processes of "pharmaceutical leakage," a term Lovell (2006, p. 146) uses to refer to the circulation of PPDs outside of therapeutic settings. Such leakage occurs in many settings in the global South where drug regulations are weak and/or not fully implemented (Ecks and Basu 2009). It is also facilitated by physicians, who like their colleagues in the United States, prescribe PPDs without sufficiently recognizing the capacity of the substances to cause dependence.

The Indonesian health and drug authorities are only recently beginning to realize how widespread the off-label use of PPDs is. In 2018, the nation's child protection agency reported that one out of every 15 children—a staggering 5.9 million children—are using drugs; prominent among them are the opioid painkiller tramadol and the cough medication dextromethorphan (Rakhmat and Tarahita 2018). Our ethnographic studies confirm the popularity of these PPDs.

Our informants in Indonesia, whose friend and acquaintance groups regularly take drugs, told us that PDDs were cheaper and easier to obtain than the Group 1 narcotic substances. They encouraged each other to try out different kinds of PPDs in order to find out which (combinations) worked best for them. See Table 2.1 for a list of commonly used PPDs and their medical indications.

In our focus group discussions, respondents noted that PPDs have different, sometimes contradictory, effects on individuals. Tramadol, for example, made Zaky sleepy, while it made Amir awake and alert. For Mamat, the drugs did not work well at all, as they made him itch and gave him ulcers. To achieve these stronger highs, our respondents mixed different PPDs, mixed PPDs with alcohol, and combined PPDs

Table 2.1 Commonly used PPDs and their medical indications

	Content	Indication
Methadone	Methadone	Heroin substitution
Subutex	Buprenorphine	Heroin substitution
Suboxone	Buprenorphine with naloxone	Heroin substitution
Alprazolam	Alprazolam	Sleeping problems, anxiety
Calmlet	Alprazolam	Sleeping problems, anxiety
Dextromethorphan	Dextromethorphan	Cough
Kode-15	Dextromethorphan	Cough
Tramadol	Tramadol	Pain
Somadril	Carisoprodol	Pain

with hot food or drinks, and also experimented with diverse ways of administration (oral, injection, inhalation of crushed oral tablets).

Much of the discussion in our interviews and focus groups with young people revolved around their experiences in finding the best PPDs, by which they meant drugs that generate a good high without unwanted effects such as dizziness or nausea. For example, one of our informants in Gowa, Broken, a 17-year-old, said that he first relied on the painkiller tramadol, an opioid pain killer, to feel high. But after trying Somadril, another pain killer, it became his drug of choice. He liked Somadril better because it not only made him feel high, it also made him feel more confident and increased his appetite. When we spoke, he was taking Somadril every day. If he wanted the effect to kick in rapidly, he combined it with spicy food. He usually did this when informally performing music on Saturday nights (Idrus and Hardon 2019). In Maros, Romo, a 14-year-old, named Somadril and tramadol as his favorite PPDs. Taken on its own, the former can produce a strong effect, so Romo did not combine Somadril with other drugs. He felt that Tramadol had a more pleasant, mellow effect on him.

Much of the discussion revolved around whether the (combinations of) PPDs are *cocok* (compatible) with their bodies. Finding a *cocok* substance involved trying out and combining drugs for different purposes. Dirham, a 23-year-old, took Riklona and/or Calmlet to feel strong while at work, and when he was done for the day, he combined marijuana with beer to make him feel happy. Yayan, an 18-year-old street singer in Yogyakarta who previously favored marijuana and heroin, subsequently tried out two different brands of cough tablets to replace these illegal drugs. He had begun taking 50 tablets of dextromethorphan and 40 tablets of Kode-15 together to achieve a strong effect. He had tried combining 20 tablets of Kode-15 and 10 tablets of trihexyphenidyl, but this combination made him feel sleepy; it was not *cocok*. Once, he mixed tramadol, Calmlet, and a local traditional drink, but this combination made him vomit and cough up blood.

The dosages depended on the costs of the pills and young people's financial resources. Dextromethorphan is a cheap drug and is generally taken in large quantities. It also does not have euphoric effects in lower dosages. Depending on whether one bought it in the pharmacy or from a street dealer, tramadol, the cheapest of the PPDs, cost around Rp 2000–3000 per tablet (US $0.13–0.19), while Xanax, Calmlet, and Somadril cost much more. Jono, a 13-year-old, told us he had been using PPDs since his first year of high school. He became a dealer so he could use the profits to buy school supplies, snacks, clothes, and more PPDs, which he and his friends sold. He bought tramadol for Rp 1500–2000 per tablet and then resold it for Rp 3000–5000 per tablet. The money earned was shared among his friends, and used to buy drugs again.

We found PPD use patterns to be temporally structured. In Gowa, we encountered intense PPD use by high school students on Saturday nights. One group of friends drank and popped extreme quantities of PPDs to get high and feel courageous for motorbike races, a popular activity among Indonesia youth. Zaky, a 17-year-old, told us that he took up to 10 tramadol tablets per day on a weekday, but increased his dose to 40 tablets on Saturday nights. Similarly, Mamat, a 16-year-old, took 15 tablets of tramadol on weekdays, but to prepare for the motorbike racing, he took 7 tablets in the morning, 15 tablets in the afternoon, and 7 tablets or more in the evening. Harianto, a 16-year-old, combined 10 tramadol tablets with five bottles of Topee Rioja beer. When racing, the boys often bumped into curbs and cars, but they didn't feel it as tramadol is a strong pain medication.

Another focused ethnography was conducted in high-end clubs in Makassar (Amelia 2019). There, cocaine and ecstasy had been the drugs of choice, but the young partygoers had turned to the use of poppers, which they claimed were not (yet) illegal; see Fig. 2.7 for some of the more popular brands. Note that one of the brands is named "The Real Amsterdam," suggesting that partying in Amsterdam is a source of inspiration for Makassar clubbers.

Nightclub visitors found it safer to bring poppers when clubbing than other club drugs (such as ecstasy, meth, and marijuana) because poppers had not yet been included by the National Narcotics Agency (BNN) on its list of narcotics, psychotropics, and addictive substances. Rani, who

Fig. 2.7 Popular brands of poppers. Note the Real Amsterdam brand, which reflects the circulation of imaginations globally (Photos taken by Lia Amelia, 2018, Indonesia)

sold poppers in a club, said she preferred to use poppers because of its immediate effects: "You use it and right away you get high … no need to wait. Inhale it, get high, and dance, really perfect" (Amelia 2019, p. 7). Like Rani, Cindy preferred to use poppers rather than other drugs for clubbing, even though she had previously used ecstasy. This was because poppers also brought her an immediate "high," and also she felt it was safer because it was rather new and was not being policed.

Rani and her friends did not immediately use poppers on arriving at the club. They usually sat on the couch and ordered a few bottles of vodka, Jägermeister, whiskey, and cognac, all of which are expensive in Makassar. When the DJ started, it was time to use the poppers. The dance beats made them excited and poppers were especially complementary for such moments. Moreover, the substance gave them confidence to connect with others on the dance floor.

Cindy and Rani are referred to as "experimental women" in Indonesia. These are highly educated women, who have careers of their own, and who don't see their future primarily as an *ibu* (the mother of the household) responsible for housekeeping while supporting a husband who operates in the outside world (Hardon and Idrus 2015; Yeom et al. 2002). Rather, they experiment with sexual enjoyment with multiple partners. Cindy explained:

> You could say it's cheating, that's true. … I am not divorced yet. But I do not feel anything when doing it with my husband. Well, it's like my obligation. I enjoy it more with my date, especially with poppers, they understand more what I want. … When I do it with my husband, it is flat. (Amelia 2019, p. 12)

Cindy and her friends worried that taking poppers was not healthy. When using them, Cindy suffered from insomnia, and others reported experiencing dizziness and headaches. To combat this fear, they eat healthily, go to the gym, and do yoga during the week. The small 10 ml bottles of poppers used by clubbers did not list any contents. They were labeled as cleaners, with warnings that they should not be swallowed. Mina, one of our informants at the Makassar health office, said that it was hard to check the contents of poppers, but once, when she had one of the liquids sent for lab testing, she was told that it contained morphine.

Risks of PPDs are bigger when they are used daily, as was the case for a group of sex workers who worked along Losari Beach. They told us they used Somadril every day to bolster their confidence when approaching prospective clients. The three male and three female sex workers filled out four-day recalls for us, in which they reported using between 6 and 24 pills a day, far above the recommended daily maximum. (See Table 2.2 for more details on the dosages and the effects of Somadril.) They explained that they craved Somadril if they take it, suffering all kinds of aches and pains, anxiety, and insomnia, and they acknowledged that they had become dependent on the drug. While they initially took the drug to enable their work, they said that they now had to work to be able to buy the drug (Hardon and Ihsan 2014).

Across our Indonesian field sites, we encountered young people who felt that they had become addicted to PPDs. Jack, a 21-year-old student in Makassar, for example, told us that he had been taking tramadol since high school:

> Initially it was because of my friends. ... Later on I got hooked and addicted. ... It's difficult to kick the habit, just like cigarettes. ... It depends, usually I take one strip a day, but if I am really upset I could take five strips. (Idrus and Hardon 2019, p. 83)

In Maros, Aco told us that he started using PPDs in order to be accepted by his peers, but he came to need the drugs daily, just like food. Similarly, Romo told us:

> It's hard. It's very difficult to stop. Even if I were paid any amount I would not stop. I just have a different feeling if I don't take the drugs. If the drug is no longer available, I would maybe make it myself. (Idrus and Hardon 2019, p. 84)

Harm reduction programs in Indonesia have only recently acknowledged that young people are at risk of becoming addicted to PPDs, and that they might be facing an epidemic similar to the opioid crisis in the

Table 2.2 Somadril daily dosages and reported effects among sex workers

Informant	Pills per day	Reported beneficial effects	Reported adverse effects	Reported withdrawal effects
Mira female, 24	3–10, average 7	Confidence, increased sexual desire	Dizziness, falls asleep with too many pills, headache	Neck and shoulder pain
Naimah female, 22	3–10, average 5	Feels comforted, less shy, more happy, less resistance to sex with clients	None reported	Throbbing eyes, crying, bad mood, insomnia
Rina female, 20	8–16, average 10	Confident, less shy, happy, stays awake and flies high	Dizziness	None reported
Hasan male, 22	7–23, average 16	Confident, more talkative, can stay up late; fly high; feels less stress, enjoys himself more and has more sex; weight loss	Nausea, makes you stupid, thinking too much, hard to move; insomnia or sleepy (depending on dose)	Headache and bad mood
Udin male, 24	5–10, average 8	Confident, less shy, happy, stronger	Feels sick and hungry, vomiting, If too much: angry, delirious, cannot walk, stomach problems	Sleepy, anxious, sad, crying
Rudi male, 23	21–31 average 24	Confident, calm, sleepy	Diarrhea, trembling	Headache, thinks a lot

United States. Local-level health officials and drug policymakers have responded to problematic PPD use by limiting access to these drugs, but our ethnography suggests that young people can easily find pharmacies or street dealers who are willing to sell them the drugs, or psychiatrists who are willing to prescribe them (Idrus and Hardon 2019).

This contrasting analysis shows that youths' self-regulation efforts in Amsterdam and our Indonesian field sites were remarkably similar. They involved cautious dosing and careful assessments of effects. However, in Amsterdam, young drug users turned to the government to check the quality of the drugs that they were taking, and they were regularly provided up-to-date information on substandard drugs that were circulating on the market. They also received medical advice on possible adverse effects and how to prevent them. For youth in Amsterdam, "balancing" involves taking a rest after party weekends, eating good foods, and taking vitamins and supplements.

Self-regulation for our Indonesian respondents, in contrast, meant refraining from illegal drugs to avoid being incarcerated, and relying on the use of prescription drugs, which were seen to be safe. It also involved mixing drugs to get desired effects, while ensuring that such effects were also compatible with other elements, like needing to approach clients to earn a living as sex worker, or singing on the streets, or specificities of individual bodies. A key framework for our interlocutors was compatibility, which each drug user sought to achieve by observing effects, mixing PPDs with food and drinks, and finding the right combination of PPDs and the right dosage. Such balancing involved moderating use to not feel too high, and, for some of our financially better-off interlocutors, taking vitamins and eating good food. For others, balancing also involved using more PPDs to ease the withdrawal effects from not using other drugs. However, despite their caution and these balancing acts, many of our interlocutors became addicted to PPDs. While they initially experimented with PPDs for pleasure, over time they came to crave the drugs and suffer withdrawal effects. Finally, the number of pills taken per day increased, which could also become an economic problem.

Changing Regulatory Regimes

Thus far, our discussion of self-regulation has focused on the most common recreational chemicals found in the field. In this section we now turn to the history, regulatory status, and adverse effects of commonly used drugs and chemicals, highlighting how new understandings of efficacies emerge over time (Hardon and Sanabria 2017). Specifically, we do this for MDMA and GHB in the Netherlands, and the commonly used PPDs in Indonesia, showing how the regulatory status of both legal and illegal drugs is ever-changing in relation to dynamic safety and efficacy profiles, and in response to how young people appropriate and experience the substances.

Perhaps surprisingly, in light of the above ethnographic descriptions of drug use, MDMA is still classified as a hard drug in Amsterdam while cannabis or magic mushrooms, are classified as soft drugs and sold in small quantities in coffeeshops (Uitermark and Cohen 2005). Our fieldwork revealed that while bars and festival organizers are expected to prevent MDMA from entering their sites, young people could consume these drugs without repercussions at festivals and in bars. MDMA use is very common in the Netherlands; a 2016 Trimbos Study on recreational drug use ($N = 4.905$ respondents, recruited online), reveals that 37% of young adults (15–35 years old) had used MDMA in the past year (Monshouwer et al. 2016). In response to this widespread use, Dutch politicians, especially younger ones, regularly call for the legalization of MDMA. Often cited is an analysis conducted by a team of researchers in the United Kingdom that found MDMA safer than nicotine and alcohol (Nutt et al. 2010). But to date, the policy has not changed. In the meantime, clinical trials have shown that MDMA has beneficial effects in the treatment of trauma in clinical trials (Feduccia et al. 2019; Mithoefer et al. 2018), which may lead to its legalization as a prescription drug.

But MDMA can be used in many ways. Reports from pill-testing facilities show that the MDMA content of ecstasy pills used by young people has been increasing, which seems to be leading to increased rates of adverse events, more specifically, increased heartbeat, difficulty sleeping, and panic attacks. Brain imaging studies suggest that ecstasy depletes serotonin in the brain and increases the stress hormone cortisol, which causes disruptions in sleep patterns (Reneman et al. 2001; Parrott et al. 2002).

While studying parties and festivals in Amsterdam, we became concerned that the culture of calculated hedonism, in which self-regulation and responsible drug use is the norm, may suppress narratives on adverse drug-related events. Our worries increased after reading a 2017 report by the Trimbos Institute that analyzed the clinical reports of 116 patients who had reported to an addiction care center with strange neurological symptoms. Given the huge number of MDMA users in the Netherlands, the number may be small, but is it perhaps the tip of an iceberg?

The report describes the neurological problems as hallucinogen persisting perception disorders (HPPD) and as depersonalization syndrome (DPS) (Croes et al. 2017), and points out that the symptoms started to appear after using ecstasy, often following a "bad trip." The researchers considered that the adverse events were perhaps being reported by relatively naïve users, that is users who had only ever used a few pills of the drug. The problem with the symptoms reported to the addiction center is that they don't go away. It's hard to draw conclusions from these case reports, because the patients often had also used other drugs, but it does make one wonder how safe MDMA really is. Adverse effects of substances often only become known when large populations use them.

In the above description of self-regulation in Amsterdam, we also mentioned the use of GHB. This drug is a relative newcomer to the party scene. A *Vice* blog notes its emergence in Amsterdam nightlife in 2009, describing its efficacy as a combination of ecstasy and beer: "Lately when someone is puking in a club in Amsterdam, the relevant question is no longer 'Too much booze?' but 'Too much G?'" While MDMA is produced in illegal laboratories all over the country, a key characteristic of GHB is that it can be made at home by mixing typical cleaning products found in the kitchen. The *Vice* blogger interviewed an anonymous GHB user who explains that the most important ingredient is gamma butyrolactone (GBL), which is a chemical used as a paint thinner and floor stripper, which can easily be bought in hardware stores. GBL is then mixed with drain cleaner, which, the anonymous GHB user clarifies, is done to adjust the pH of the mixture. Other ingredients are demineralized water and concentrated acetic acid. The anonymous source stresses,

> Proportion is very important, that's why a decent measuring cup and balance are crucial. Adding too much water, for instance, might result in very poor GHB, and you don't want that. Anyway, with pH level test strips I check the acidity of the substance, depending on which I add a little more GBL or sodium hydroxide. After that, I always take half a dose to test the effects myself. (Vice 2009)

Adverse events emerged quite soon after GHB became a popular party drug. It became clear that the substance is easily overdosed and, if that happens, people become unconscious and can end up in coma (Trimbos-Instituut 2020). Responding to many young people ending up in ICUs after a night out, the harm reduction programs in Amsterdam tried to discourage GHB use through a campaign warning that it can cause you to pass out, and advising friends to bring an unconscious person to the hospital as soon as possible.

It also became clear very quickly that some young people who use GHB frequently become seriously addicted to the substance, and that this is an addiction that is very hard to overcome. Because of the severe adverse effects and addiction risk, the national drug authorities decided in 2012 to include GHB in the list of hard drugs, alongside MDMA and heroin. Many establishments in Amsterdam now have a zero-tolerance policy on GHB. While MDMA use is accepted, GHB use is not.

In Indonesia, we found a limited number of psychoactive prescription drugs to be used commonly across our field sites; interestingly, PPDs did not figure in the drug use narratives of our recreational drug users in Amsterdam, probably because it's hard to obtain them over the counter in the city. The PPDs used by our informants in Indonesia have diverse efficacies and regulatory statuses. They include heroin substitution drugs, potent painkillers containing tramadol or carisoprodol (the active ingredient of Somadril), sleeping pills and anti-anxiety drugs (containing alprozalam), and cough medicines (containing dextromethorphan), see Table 2.1.

While the heroin substitution drugs methadone and buprenorphine were developed to counter addiction, we observed that in Indonesia these drugs have become part of the pharmacopeia for drug users. Sometimes these drugs are bought on the streets or obtained over the counter at "naughty" pharmacies. But we also found that some doctors were willing to prescribe them, along with other PPDs, to ease users' mental health problems, many of which are related to their dependence on the drugs.

PPDs containing the anti-anxiety medicine alprozalam were also popular among our respondents. This drug is not primarily used to feel high; indeed it does not cause euphoria according to the pharmacological handbooks. Rather, it is used to self-medicate panic attacks or general malaise caused by the other PPDs used, or to dampen the pain that comes with not using drugs one has come to depend on. What our respondents didn't realize is that these drugs are also known to cause dependence.

The Indonesian authorities have forbidden sales of single-ingredient dextromethorphan pills to prevent misuse by youth. But the active ingredient is still on the market, in the form of syrups and combination drugs, which can thus be used as substitution drugs for those who want to continue taking the drug to feel high. PPDs are manufactured by large pharmaceutical companies that set the parameter of efficacy used in clinical trials. Independent studies are rare in the field of pharmaceuticals, if only because they are very expensive. What's more, these trials often have skewed study populations, favoring healthy white men and women. When problems occur, they are often only noticed once the products have been out on the market for a long time, and post-market surveillance picks them up, or when addiction problems become hard to ignore, as in the opioid crisis.

Aware that potent pain killers can cause addiction, following a ban of carisoprodol by the European Medicine Authority (EMEA) and responding to reports of overuse of Somadril for recreational use, the Indonesian Food and Drug Authority canceled the distribution permit for the drug.[2] At the time, Somadril was registered in Indonesia as a "strong medicine" (*golongan keras*). When we asked about the drug in pharmacies, we were referred to the 2010 Indonesian pharmaceutical compendium *Informasi Specialite Obat*, which lists Somadril for all kinds of aches and pains: lower back pain, muscle spasms, tension headache, painful menstruation, and other ailments such as chronic arthritis (Ikatan Sarjana Farmasi Indonesia 2010). The guide does not warn of the risk of addiction.

Carisoprodol entered the global market in the 1960s. Wallace Laboratories (the US company that still produces the Soma brand), claimed that Carisoprodol had superior muscle-relaxing properties and less potential for misuse than meprobamate, the tranquilizer that it replaced (Berger et al. 1960). Marketed as Miltown, Meprobamate was the first tranquilizer to appear on the American market. It was prescribed as treatment for mental disorder, and was used off-label in the 1960s Hollywood party scene, mixed in a dry martini cocktail that people called a "Miltini". But, Meprobamate turned out to be habit-forming (Tone 2009; Herzberg 2011).

It later became apparent that carisoprodol did so too, because it metabolized into meprobamate in the body (Olsen et al. 1995), leading to the same withdrawal effects (Reeves and Burke 2010). When Soma started being prescribed to increasing numbers of patients, US doctors encountered withdrawal symptoms—including insomnia, vomiting, muscle twitching, anxiety, and hallucinations—among patients who stopped taking the drug (DEA 2011; Substance Abuse & Mental Health Data Archive 2003). Nevertheless, it is still on the market in the United States as a Class IV drug, meaning that it is accepted for prescribed medical use but its use can lead to physical or psychological dependence. In Europe, a post-market study (Bramness et al. 2007) found that 14% of carisoprodol users in Norway had been prescribed more than 75 times the recommended daily dose, suggesting that it was overused for non-medical reasons. Carisoprodol was subsequently taken off the market. In the European Union, the EMEA recommended member states suspend carisoprodol's authorization for the treatment of acute (but not chronic) back pain.

Drug regulation in Indonesia, as elsewhere, is based on an evaluation of a drug's therapeutic benefits versus its potential harms. The PPDs used by our Indonesian respondents are legal because they are seen to have therapeutic use in the treatment of pain, anxiety, heroin addiction, and insomnia. But this does not mean that they are safe. Pharmaceutical drugs are tested in clinical trials before they come on the market;

however, in such trials the parameters of safety and efficacy tend to be determined by the companies that sponsor the trials. Evidence of adverse effects often only emerges once the drugs are on the market (Healy 2012; Medawar and Hardon 2004). Norwegian post-market surveillance for example revealed that carisoprodol causes dependence (as do tramadol and alprazolam). In contrast, MDMA is not a legal drug in the Netherlands, because it is seen to be a dangerous drug with no therapeutic indications. But this assessment is being questioned by studies that suggest that MDMA is safer than nicotine and alcohol and by new clinical trials that show that the substance can have therapeutic use. At the same time, addiction clinics are reporting rare adverse effects among MDMA users that need to be taken into consideration in future use of the substance.

Co-Creating Harm Reduction

How to reduce the harm caused by the ever-changing drug use practices of youth? The Amsterdam approach, as we have seen, has made recreational drug use safer by providing services to test drugs and observing drug-use patterns at festivals, with an aim of supporting self-regulation and providing users up-to-date information. In doing so, Dutch government-sponsored health programs co-produce a drug-use scene in which addiction is rare and adverse events quickly addressed.

In thinking through what drug-related harm can be prevented, the ChemicalYouth collaborative proposed a more radical, deliberative approach (Wardman 2008). Such an approach would go further in co-producing knowledge on safety and efficacy of commonly used recreational chemicals, by using the tools of artificial intelligence to generate evidence from drug experimentation forums on the effects of chemicals. When we proposed this approach to the European Union's Research Area on Illicit Drugs (ERANID) program, we were denied funding in favor of studies that instrumentally seek to identify risk factors for heavy drug use. We still are convinced that those contributing to such forums could be productive collaborators, and are working to demonstrate how this might be done. In Chapter 8 we present some results from our ethnographies of online knowledge production, reflecting more on how virtual spaces could be used as sites for joint learning.

In Conclusion

Focusing on chemical practices generates insights into how youth appropriate diverse chemicals to feel good and how they seek to mitigate harm. In Amsterdam, young people manage risks by frequenting government-sponsored testing facilities to assess the quality of illegal drugs, while in Indonesia they reduce harm by substituting illegal drugs with psychoactive prescription drugs to limit the risk of being incarcerated. Government regulators respond to shifting drug use patterns by changing the regulatory status of drugs and curtailing drug supply. In the Netherlands, for example, GHB was classified as a hard drug, following reports that young people were becoming heavily addicted to the drug, while in Indonesia the government discontinued the sale of cough tablets when they found that young people were using them to get high.

Youth drug use practices are highly dynamic. New ways of using drugs are tried out and effects evaluated. Self-experimenting online communities exchange information on new kinds of drugs and rapidly adapt to the challenges posed by new compounds, for instance, through substance warnings and immediate, practical peer support for members experiencing problems. The international character of such forums and the large number of participants means that there are always people online to help.

One of the central arguments of this book is that the collaborative experiments of young people lead to shared understandings of chemical efficacy; as a corollary, we argue that closely examining how young people manage uncertainty and risks can contribute to novel ways to reduce harm "from below" (Hardon and Hymans 2016; Van Schipstal et al. 2016). Harm reduction from below builds on young people's existing interest in mitigating the risks of chemicals, the hybrid nature of the networks in which they experiment with chemicals, and the protective nature of the social networks in which they experiment with drugs. It amplifies the cautionary tales shared by young people online and supports their modes of self-regulation. But it cannot prevent harm on its own. As exemplified by the Amsterdam case study presented in this chapter, harm reduction from below needs to be enabled by harm reduction from above, which facilitates young people's search for hassle-free highs. How this co-production of safer drug use can take place is further elaborated in the concluding chapter of this book, "Chemical Futures."

Chemical Youth Ethnographers

Inge van Schipstal was a junior researcher and former coordinator for ChemicalYouth project. Trained as an urban sociologist with a liking for ethnography, she studied the social aspects of drug use among young adults. Her focus was on processes of social bonding, collective action, and the intention that precedes drug use. She observed a gradual transformation from recreational, hedonistic intentions toward more profound goals of self-realization and collective evolution, wherein socialities continue to play a major role (Fig. 2.8).

Fig. 2.8 Inge van Schipstal

Moritz Berning focused on mixing classical and virtual ethnographies, trying to balance the limitations that come with each approach. For the ChemicalYouth project, he explored ways that risk is approached and dealt with, in regard to old and new psychoactive substances. These could be situational practices at festivals or clubs, as well as refined social mechanisms of testing substances in virtual spaces (Fig. 2.9).

Fig. 2.9 Moritz Berning

Swasti Mishra is an anthropologist with an interest in the intersection of health, drugs, biomedicine, and society. She completed her PhD under the ChemicalYouth project. Her doctoral research focused on the generation and circulation of knowledge regarding psychedelic drugs, ranging from clinical trials, psychiatric practices, and public health centers, and non-medical use in office spaces or festival venues, primarily situated in the United States and the Netherlands. She is currently part of a research project on the assessment of public health emergency preparedness across the European Union Framework contract with European Centre for Disease Prevention and Control (Fig. 2.10).

Fig. 2.10 Swasti Mishra

Hayley Murray is a medical anthropologist, drug researcher, and project coordinator of the ChemicalYouth project. She is energized by talking to young people about their substance use and has had the privilege to do so with recreational drug users in the Netherlands, Germany, Poland, and the United Kingdom. Her contribution to the ChemicalYouth project was her fieldwork in the Dutch music festival scene, where she explored how recreational drug users perceive, manage, and legitimize the risks and harms related to their drug use in a festival setting. This project reflects her interests in harm reduction and risk practices (Fig. 2.11).

Fig. 2.11 Hayley Murray

Lia Amelia was a researcher for the ChemicalYouth project who conducted research on alkyl nitrites (poppers) use among middle-class teenagers in Makassar. She is a student at Hasanuddin University.

Notes

1. See Law Number 35 of 2009 concerning narcotics (hereinafter referred to as the Narcotics Law).
2. Decree of the Head of the Republic of Indonesia Food and Drug Supervisory Agency Number HK.04.1.35.06.13. 3535, 2013.

References

Amelia, L. (2019). *Poppers: Sex after clubbing among middle class adolescents in Makassar* (Unpublished report). Hasanuddin University.

Berger, F. M., Kletzkin, M., Ludwig, B. J., & Margolin, S. (1960). The history, chemistry, and pharmacology of Carisoprodol. *Annals of the New York Academy of Sciences, 86*(1), 90–107. https://doi.org/10.1111/j.1749-6632.1960.tb42792.x.

Berning, M., & Hardon, A. (2016). Educated guesses and other ways to address the pharmacological uncertainty of designer drugs: An exploratory study of experimentation through an online drug forum. *Contemporary Drug Problems, 43*(3), 277–292. https://doi.org/10.1177/0091450916662164.

Bramness, J. G., Furu, K., Engeland, A., & Skurtveit, S. (2007). Carisoprodol use and abuse in Norway: A pharmacoepidemiological study. *British Journal of Clinical Pharmacology, 64*(2), 210–218. https://doi.org/10.1111/j.1365-2125.2007.02847.x.

Celebrate Safe. (2017). *Celebrate safe recommendations.* Celebrate Safe. https://celebratesafe.nl/en/recommendations. Accessed on November 12, 2019.

Croes, E., Vreeker, A., Ruiter, N. De, & Alderliefste, G. (2017). *Langdurige klachten na ecstasygebruik.* Utrecht: Trimbos Instituute.

DEA. (2011). *2011—Final rule: Placement of Carisoprodol into schedule IV*. Drug Enforcement Agency. https://www.deadiversion.usdoj.gov/fed_regs/rules/2011/fr1212_10.htm. Accessed on November 12, 2019.

Duff, C. (2004). Drug use as a "practice of the self": Is there any place for an "ethics of moderation" in contemporary drug policy? *International Journal of Drug Policy, 15*(5–6), 385–393. https://doi.org/10.1016/j.drugpo.2004.06.010.

Ecks, S., & Basu, S. (2009). The unlicensed lives of antidepressants in India: Generic drugs, unqualified practitioners, and floating prescriptions. *Transcultural Psychiatry, 46*(1), 86–106. https://doi.org/10.1177/1363461509102289.

Feduccia, A. A., Jerome, L., Yazar-Klosinski, B., Emerson, A., Mithoefer, M. C., & Doblin, R. (2019). Breakthrough for trauma treatment: Safety and efficacy of MDMA-assisted psychotherapy compared to Paroxetine and Sertraline. *Frontiers in Psychiatry, 10*. https://doi.org/10.3389/fpsyt.2019.00650.

Hansen, H. (2017). Assisted technology of social reproduction: Pharmaceutical prosthesis for gender, race, and class in the white opioid "crisis". *Contemporary Drug Problems, 44*(4), 321–338.

Hardon, A., & Hymans, T. D. (2016). Guest editors' introduction. *Contemporary Drug Problems, 43*(3), 191–198. https://doi.org/10.1177/0091450916663247.

Hardon, A., & Idrus, N. I. (2015). Magic power: Changing gender dyanamics and sex-enhancement practices among youth in Makassar. *Indonesia. Anthropology & Medicine, 22*(1), 49–63. https://doi.org/10.1080/13648470.2015.1010114.

Hardon, A., & Ihsan, A. (2014). Somadril and edgework in South Sulawesi. *International Journal of Drug Policy, 25*(4), 755–761.

Hardon, A., & Sanabria, E. (2017). Fluid drugs: Revisiting the anthropology of pharmaceuticals. *Annual Review of Anthropology, 46*(1), 117–132. https://doi.org/10.1146/annurev-anthro-102116-041539.

Hardon, A., Van Schipstal, I., Mishra, S., Berning, M., & Murray, H. (forthcoming, 2020). Caring for "hassle-free highs" in Amsterdam. *Anthropology and Humanism.*

Healy, D. (2012). Review of pharmaceutical self: The global shaping of experience in an age of psychopharmacology. *Transcultural Psychiatry, 49*(3–4), 638–640. https://doi.org/10.1177/1363461512437148.

Herzberg, D. (2011). Blockbusters and controlled substances: Miltown, Quaalude, and consumer demand for drugs in postwar America. *Studies in History and Philosophy of Science Part C: Studies in History and Philosophy of Biological and Biomedical Sciences, 42*(4), 415–426. https://doi.org/10.1016/j.shpsc.2011.05.005.

Hofmann, A. M., Scurlock, A. M., Jones, S. M., Palmer, K. P., Lokhnygina, Y., Steele, P. H., et al. (2009). Safety of a peanut oral immunotherapy protocol in children with peanut allergy. *Journal of Allergy and Clinical Immunology, 124*(2). https://doi.org/10.1016/j.jaci.2009.03.045.

Hunt, G. P., Evans, K., & Kares, F. (2007). Drug use and meanings of risk and pleasure. *Journal of Youth Studies, 10*(1), 73–96. https://doi.org/10.1080/13676260600983668.

Idrus, N. I., & Hardon, A. (2019). Experimental trajectories of young users of psycho-active prescription drugs in urban Indonesia. *Journal of Extreme Anthropology, 3*(2), 72–93.

Ikatan Sarjana Farmasi Indonesia. (2010). *Aplikasi mobile katalog iso (informasi spesialite obat) pt. isfi penerbitan jakarta berbasis android sebagai media informasi obat bagi masyarakat*. Ikatan Sarjana Farmasi Indonesia. https://www.academia.edu/7449057/Aplikasi_mobile_katalog_iso_informasi_spesialite_obat_pt_isfi_penerbitan_jakarta_berbasis_android_sebagai_media_informasi_obat_bagi_masyarakat. Accessed on November 12, 2019.

Lovell, A. (2006). Addiction markets: The case of high-dose buprenorphine in France. In A. Petryna, A. Lakoff, & A. Kleinman (Eds.), *Global pharmaceuticals: Ethics, markets, practices*. Durham, NC: Duke University Press.

Lyng, S. (1990). Edgework: A social psychological analysis of voluntary risk taking. *American Journal of Sociology, 95*(4), 851–886. https://doi.org/10.1086/229379.

Measham, F. (2004). The decline of ecstasy, the rise of 'binge' drinking and the persistence of pleasure. *Probation Journal, 51*(4), 309–326. https://doi.org/10.1177/0264550504048220.

Medawar, C., & Hardon, A. (2004). *Medicines out of control? Antidepressants and the conspiracy of goodwill*. Groningen: Aksant.

Mithoefer, M. C., Mithoefer, A. T., Feduccia, A. A., Jerome, L., Wagner, M., Wymer, J., et al. (2018). 3,4-methylenedioxymethamphetamine (MDMA)-assisted psychotherapy for post-traumatic stress disorder in military veterans, firefighters, and police officers: A randomised, double-blind, dose-response, phase 2 clinical trial. *The Lancet Psychiatry, 5*(6), 486–497. https://doi.org/10.1016/S2215-0366(18)30135-4.

Monshouwer, K., van der Pol, P., Drost, Y. C., & van Laar, M. W. (2016). *Het grote uitgaanonderzoek 2016*. Trimbos Instituute. https://www.trimbos.nl/aanbod/webwinkel/product/af1494-het-grote-uitgaansonderzoek-2016. Accessed on November 12, 2019.

Moore, K., & Miles, S. (2004). Young people, dance and the sub-cultural consumption of drugs. *Addiction Research & Theory, 12*(6), 507–523. https://doi.org/10.1080/16066350412331323083.

Nutt, D. J., King, L. A., & Phillips, L. D. (2010). Drug harms in the UK: A multicriteria decision analysis. *The Lancet, 376*(9752), 1558–1565. https://doi.org/10.1016/S0140-6736(10)61462-6.

Olsen, H., Koppang, E., Alvan, G., & Morland, J. (1995). Carisoprodol elimination in humans. *Therapeutic Drug Monitoring, 16,* 337–340.

Parrott, A. C., Buchanan, T., Scholey, A. B., Heffernan, T., Ling, J., & Rodgers, J. (2002). Ecstasy/MDMA attributed problems reported by novice, moderate and heavy recreational users. *Human Psychopharmacology: Clinical & Experimental, 17*(6), 1–7.

Pilkington, H. (2007). Beyond "peer pressure": Rethinking drug use and "youth culture". *International Journal of Drug Policy, 18*(3), 213–224. https://doi.org/10.1016/j.drugpo.2006.08.003.

Quintero, G., & Nichter, M. (2011). Generation RX: Anthropological research on pharmaceutical enhancement, lifestyle regulation, self-medication and recreational drug use. In M. Singer & P. Erickson (Eds.), *A companion to medical anthropology* (pp. 339–357). Oxford: Wiley-Blackwell.

Rakhmat, M., & Tarahita, D. (2018). *Drug use among Indonesian children is pervasive.* International Policy Digest. https://intpolicydigest.org/2018/11/08/drug-use-among-indonesian-children-is-pervasive. Accessed on November 12, 2019.

Reeves, R. R., & Burke, R. S. (2010). Carisoprodol: Abuse potential and withdrawal syndrome. *Current Drug Abuse Reviews, 3*(1), 33–38. https://doi.org/10.2174/1874473711003010033.

Reneman, L., Booij, J., Majoie, C. B. L. M., van den Brink, W., & den Heeten, G. J. (2001). Investigating the potential neurotoxicity of ecstasy (MDMA): An imaging approach. *Human Psychopharmacology: Clinical and Experimental, 16*(8), 579–588. https://doi.org/10.1002/hup.347.

Riley, S., More, Y., & Griffin, C. (2010). The 'pleasure citizen'. *Young, 18*(1), 33–54. https://doi.org/10.1177/110330880901800104.

Substance Abuse & Mental Health Data Archive. (2003). *Drug abuse warning network US*. Substance Abuse & Mental Health Data Archive. https://www.datafiles.samhsa.gov/study/drug-abuse-warning-network-us-dawn-ns-1997-nid13592. Accessed on November 12, 2019.

Tone, A. (2009). *The age of anxiety: A history of America's turbulent affair with tranquilizers.* New York: Basic Books.

Trimbos-Instituut. (2020). *GHB risico's.* Drugs En Uitgaan. https://www.drugsenuitgaan.nl/middelen/ghb/risico-ghb. Accessed on November 12, 2019.

Uitermark, J., & Cohen, P. (2005). A clash of policy approaches: The rise and (fall?) of Dutch harm reduction policies towards ecstasy consumption. *International Journal for Drug Policy, 16,* 65–72.

United Nations Office on Drugs and Crime. (2018). *World drug report 2018.* United Nations Office on Drugs and Crime. https://www.unodc.org/wdr2018/. Accessed on November 12, 2019.

Van Schipstal, I., Mishra, S., Berning, M., & Murray, H. (2016). Harm reduction from below: On sharing and caring in drug use. *Contemporary Drug Problems, 43*(3), 199–215. https://doi.org/10.1177/0091450916663248.

Vice. (2009). *How to make your own drug supply.* Vice.https://www.vice.com/en_au/article/yvnnjv/amsterdam-how-to-make-your-own-drug-supply. Accessed on November 12, 2019.

Wardman, J. K. (2008). The Constitution of risk communication in advance liberal societies. *Risk Analysis, 28*(6), 1619–1637.

Yeom, M., Acedo, C., Utomo, E., & Yeom, M. (2002). The reform of secondary education in Indonesia during the 1990s: Basic education expansion and quality improvement through curriculum decentralization. *Asia Pacific Education Review, 3*(1), 56–68. https://doi.org/10.1007/bf03024921.

Zinn, J. O. (2008). *Social theories of risk and uncertainty: An introduction.* Oxford, UK: Blackwell Publishing.

3

Smoking Practices: A Comparative Study

James Monsees and Adam Bowen, two product design students at Stanford University, California, met each other while taking smoke breaks 15 years ago. Their failed attempts to quit inspired them to develop a vaping device that could help people stop smoking. Studying at a Silicon Valley university that encourages entrepreneurship, they soon set up their own company, Ploom, Inc. (later Pax Labs), where they designed a new slick device that worked by heating tobacco in a small, very hot oven, creating a vapor that could be inhaled. Monsees, CEO of Ploom, stated that the product offered a "premium luxury vape experience" (Abrahamian 2014). By 2015, the company had developed JUUL, a slim, rectangular vaping device, which can be charged via a USB port. Monsees points out that the combustion mechanisms of the e-cigarette creates a physiological "buzz," similar to the sharp peak of nicotine after the first puff of a cigarette (Tiku 2019).

The focused ethnographies presented in this chapter show how young people inhale tobacco and new kinds of synthetic cannabinoids in the form of e-cigarettes or vape devices. Our team found that they turn to these new products in groups, exchanging experiences and trying out new tastes. The inherently social character of these collaborative experiments with new products lends support to the observations of social scientists who have studied young people's inhaling habits (Nichter 2015; Dennis 2006).

Mimi Nichter (2015), in an elaborate ethnographic study conducted at a university campus in the United States shows that many students start to smoke for social reasons, and that they usually do so at social events such as parties or get-togethers. Smoking—used often together with alcohol—acts as a social lubricant, and it helps users communicate their emotions. Following more than 900 participants over time, Nichter found that students considered their smoking "no big deal" because they expect to quit when they leave campus and have a job. However, quitting often turned out to be harder than they expected. Some of her interlocutors transitioned to smoking regularly, including when they are alone, to reduce stress or overcome unpleasant life events such as relationship break ups.

We begin here by examining the evolution of smoking devices and regulations, and how these were attractive to Parisian youth, who started using e-cigarettes because they wanted to avoid the stigma of smoking ordinary cigarettes. And then we turn to a group of young smokers in Indonesia, who substituted cannabis with new kinds of synthetic cannabinoids, which they mixed with ordinary tobacco, to avoid being caught by the police (cannabis smoke is easily detected because of its strong, recognizable smell). Being caught smoking cannabis in Indonesia is a serious crime that leads to imprisonment—possibly even the death penalty—while tobacco smoking is promoted heavily through advertising, and is highly acceptable (nearly the norm) for men. Our interlocutors in both settings sought to reduce harm, but they did so in different ways, and were encouraged in their efforts by different perceptions of risk. In this chapter, we also track the rising popularity of JUUL in US high schools among boys and girls who have not yet smoked regular cigarettes, and we show how JUUL hired young social media influencers to promote their product.

New Ways of Inhaling Chemicals

There has been a surge in new inhalation devices in the past 20 years, which analysts suggest is related to the increased regulation of ordinary cigarettes (Russel 2019). In 2003 the World Health Organization's Framework Convention on Tobacco Control, or FCTC, was adopted by 160 nation states. The treaty calls on signatories to regulate advertising and labeling of tobacco, increase the price of and taxation on cigarettes, and implement cessation programs. Faced by increasingly constrained markets for ordinary cigarettes, tobacco companies have embraced e-cigarettes as next-generation "safer nicotine products" (SNP), which they market as a way to reduce the harm caused by cigarette smoke (Russel 2019). There are many different kinds of e-cigarettes. Some come in the form of pens or pipes, while others look more like cigarettes or USB sticks. "Open" vaping systems can be used to vaporize any kind of fluid, while others, such as JUUL, are designed for specific liquid cartridges or dry material pods. The liquids and pods may contain nicotine as well as flavorings, and other ingredients.

Recently, the legalization of cannabis in Canada and parts of the United States have led to new lines of e-cigarettes. Young people now inhale marijuana not from "joints" but from novel devices and cartridges filled with cannabis extracts and flavored oils. The *New York Times* reports an estimate that vaping products account for 30% or more of the business of the legal cannabis industry, pointing out that the products attractive alternatives to joints, because they don't produce ash, are easy to hide, and don't have a strong smell (Richtel 2019).

Data from the National Youth Tobacco Survey 2016 show that in the United States among e-cigarette users aged 9–19 years, 33% of boys and 27% of girls had vaped cannabis (Trivers et al. 2018). That so many young people have inhaled vaporized cannabis is not surprising, given that media expressions tend to emphasize positive effects of the products: an analysis of YouTube videos portraying the vaping of marijuana found that only 2% of media expressions noted the potential for harm, while 68% pointed to positive effects (Yang et al. 2018) (Fig. 3.1).

Fig. 3.1 Screenshot of different kinds of e-cigarettes (*Source* Photo taken by Anita Hardon, January 2020, the Netherlands, US Food and Drug Admininstration (FDA) [2020])

The Turn to Vaping in Paris

Imogen Bevan did a focused ethnography of vaping in Paris, in the same year that JUUL was designed by the Stanford graduate students. At the time of her fieldwork, a leading e-cigarette company in France was Gaiatrend, whose founder, Didier Martzel, like the JUUL inventors, declared that he had a harm reduction aim: to stop his sons from smoking tobacco. According to the company's website, it intends "to offer smokers a completely new alternative and a solution to stop smoking on a long-term basis while responding to a real challenge in terms of public health" (Gaiatrend 2020).

The efficacy and safety of e-cigarettes as a way to quit smoking was heavily contested in French regulatory and health circles. France's Public Health Council (Haute Autorite de Sante 2014) has focused on companies attracting youth into unhealthy nicotine consumption by means of e-cigarettes, while a study by the French Monitoring Center for Drugs and Addiction (Observations Francaise des Drogues et des Toxicomanies 2014) suggested (as JUUL's designers emphasize) that e-cigarettes may be a "way out of smoking" (p. 8). In late 2014, Minister of Health Marisol Touraine declared that anything that can help smokers to stop smoking is worth taking. Even so, the government announced a ban on vaping on public transport, in offices, and in schools (Bevan 2016; Boudet 2014). Joining the chorus in 2015, a UK government health committee estimated that e-cigarettes are 95% safer than smoking (Public Health England 2015; see also Britton et al. 2014).

Many of Bevan's interlocutors said they used e-cigarettes as a way to smoke less conventional cigarettes, which they kept for "special" moments. Using this strategy, they hoped to prevent the accumulation of tar in their lungs. Vendors in dedicated shops played a key role in the promotion of e-cigarettes and other substitutes for ordinary cigarettes by offering a wide range of attractive flavors (Bevan 2016) (Fig. 3.2).

The shops generally use a loyalty system that rewards clients with "gifts" (generally e-liquids) and retains a buyer's history. The vendors advised customers to first replace cigarettes with e-cigarettes, and then to gradually lower the amount of nicotine they were consuming. The vendors calculated the nicotine consumed via ordinary cigarettes (nicotine volume multiplied by the number of cigarettes smoked per day), and advised consumers how much nicotine was contained in the available e-cigarettes. Bevan's young informants were well aware of the dangers of smoking, and even before they switched to e-cigarettes, they did all kinds of things to reduce risks, including using disinfectants to remove carbon monoxide from their hands and switching to organic tobacco. In

Fig. 3.2 Examples of dedicated vaping shops (*Source* Photos taken by Imogen Bevan, September 2015, Paris. Note that the Clop and Shop vendor [left] offers 100 aromas and that the Foch Vapote shop [right] uses the tagline "*un nouveau plaisir sain et economique*" [a new pleasure, healthy and economical])

this sense, e-cigarettes were a welcome replacement device for what were perceived as risky and toxic cigarettes (Bevan 2016).

Bevan observes that, at least in Paris, taste was a key driver of vaping. Young people who smoked e-cigarettes compare their hobby to wine tasting and called themselves "flavor junkies". Social gatherings where young people vaped together evolved into spaces of sensory exploration, as users passed e-liquids from hand to hand and shared experiences and tastes—the shared "gustatory pleasure" fostered feelings of community (Bevan 2016).

Bevan (2016) points to the emergence of vaping support groups and social media sites for e-cigarette users, where people share their experiences and promote products. The forums share more than an intention to stop smoking: they help vapers learn how to use e-cigarette devices (McQueen et al. 2011). Members of such groups regularly come together to explore new possibilities and enjoy their practice. The homepage of one vaping forum reads: "We are a big family. We intend to provide continuous support, from the discovery of e-cigarettes to the evolution of confirmed vapoteurs" (Bevan 2016, p. 237). Users' profiles on the forum identify their status, such as "beginner" or "expert." Members bear witness on the sites, enumerate how many toxic ordinary cigarettes they have avoided since they started vaping, and declare their vaping history in great detail.

In these vaping forums, users discuss a variety of issues, including technical issues related to the devices, such as a leaking or dead device, and laws and regulations. But conversations also include more personal concerns, such as having problems with one's partner or wanting to lose weight. Health warnings are posted by members when news emerges on adverse effects of specific kinds of liquids or devices. One section of one of the forums announces in-person gatherings, called "vapodays," and information about where they are to be held. Bevan describes a July "vap-nique" (a combination of "vape" and "picnic") she observed in a city park in Paris:

> On one side of a tartan picnic rug dappled in sunlight, a man asks quietly around him whether anyone else had changed weight when they had stopped smoking. He had put on 5 kg. What is he on? One man asks. Pausing to draw on an intricate wooden e-cigarette and exhaling a large cloud of apple and cinnamon vapor, he replies: 0 mg of nicotine. "It's the nicotine, it makes you burn calories. It affects the brain," a second man ventures. Well, he had had nicotine in it before and it made absolutely no difference, he was putting on weight anyway. The four of us shift position and recline to enjoy the now bearable late afternoon sunshine, slowly absorbing each other's smoking histories, tales of transition and experience of e-cigarettes.
>
> Seated nearby in a circle in the shade, a larger group is leaning over a pile of small bottles of different colors, shapes and sizes. A woman in her forties is interested in how long e-liquids should be kept. The younger woman on her right answers "Officially, a year, but I think you can keep them a bit longer than that." While passing around a plastic tub overflowing with homemade brownies, the group goes on to discuss their preferred brands of e-liquid and to question the traceability of e-liquid

> contents. The five members converge on a general aversion to Chinese liquids as lacking sufficient safety regulations. (Bevan 2016, p. 238)

What stands out in Bevan's ethnography is that one of the attractions of e-cigarettes was the social bonding that comes with the devices, bonding that was facilitated through social media. E-cigarettes allowed youth to experiment with different dosages of nicotine and align their vaping tastes to specific social settings and particular foods. Jem, a 25-year-old employee in a sports shop, explained that he had really suffered when he tried to quit smoking:

> There was something missing from my life. And it's funny, I felt like I wasn't the same person anymore. I was sharing a flat with a friend, and strangely, when I stopped smoking, our relationship was a bit different. It was a bit tenser. Since I wasn't smoking, we couldn't share that moment together anymore. For me, smoking is a kind of sharing. When I had friends who quit, I was—I didn't like it. I felt like I had lost something we had in common. (Bevan 2016, p. 237)

An analysis by Euromonitor (2019) notes that the higher costs of cigarettes due to higher taxes (as proposed in the FCTC) in France encouraged users to adopt vaping products, which were much cheaper. Statistics show that prevalence of smoking among men is gradually declining in France: 40% of adult males smoked in 2000, and this dropped to 35% in 2016 (World Data Bank 2020). Rates for women have stayed the same. A survey conducted in 2019 found that 6% of adults vaped regularly, with health, wanting to quit smoking, wanting to find an alternative to tobacco, and cost listed as the most important reasons to vape (Statista 2019).

Inhaling Sinte in Indonesia

Indonesia is one of the countries that has not signed the FCTC. Cigarettes are extremely cheap throughout the country and advertising is omnipresent and aggressive. Not surprisingly, e-cigarettes are not popular in the country. On weekends and holidays, young girls in sexy outfits offer people in bars and restaurants free samples of cigarettes. The country is home to many tobacco companies that cater to the local market, producing cigarettes that contain a combination of tobacco and cloves (*kretek*). The lack of tobacco control policy is reflected in increasing smoking rates among men. In 2000, a reported 60% of adult men smoked, while in 2016 this percentage was up to 76%; in contrast only about 3% of women smoke in the country (World Data Bank 2020). It's almost impossible to not see tobacco advertisements in Indonesia given that most grocery stores have a banner sponsored by a cigarette company, see below picture taken during a field visit to the remote island of Morotai (Fig. 3.3).

Gudang Garam, the company that products Surya PRO, chose "NEVER QUIT" as its tagline. An analysis of advertising conducted by Mimi Nichter and colleagues (2009) shows how manufacturers present smoking as a way to relax, control emotions, and enjoy social gatherings. As is the case for JUUL marketing in the United States, youth are an important target for advertisers. Marlboro and Star Mild use advertisements designed to attract young men, emphasizing masculinity and

Fig. 3.3 Cigarette banner (*Source* Photo taken by Anita Hardon, December 2018, Indonesia)

sports. A Class Mild advertisement targets young women who want to be modern, with an image showing a young woman with a cell phone wearing a sleeveless top, which "is noteworthy in a country where women are expected to dress modestly and may wear headscarves" (Nichter et al. 2009, p. 103). The text, written in English, reads: "Yesterday is gone. Class Mild is today" (Nichter et al. 2009, p. 102).

In a fascinating historiography of tobacco in China, Matthew Kohrman (2018) argues that tobacco companies strategically "go with the times" in the images they use to promote smoking. Visuals during the reign of Chairman Mao showed men smoking only during political study and work; women were not portrayed with cigarettes, as it was seen to be synonymous with bourgeois decadence (Benedict 2018). China, like Indonesia, has a powerful state-run tobacco industry, and while China has signed the FCTC it is not taking strong measures to implement the treaty (Kohrman 2018).

In Indonesia, cigarette smoking is ubiquitous among men, who often also smoke cannabis. One of the ChemicalYouth ethnographers, Akbar Alamsyah, described how a group of students from the University of Makassar often met to smoke cannabis together. Most of them started using cannabis out of curiosity, when they were still in high school. They touted its relaxing effects, while also pointing to its creative potentials. They consumed it mainly when hanging out with friends, and when they needed to, they pooled their money to buy it. Because it is a plant, they considered cannabis to be harmless and natural—a valuation that meshed with their experience that, while the substance caused them to feel mellow and relaxed, they didn't "go out" (black out, pass out, become unconscious) completely, as has happened with some of the other substances they have used. Some informants, though, said that they had experienced emotional turbulence and even paranoia when smoking cannabis. The effects, they explained, depend on whether the substance is "*cocok*" (compatible) with you.

These interlocutors insisted that they really did not understand why cannabis was included in the list of narcotics in Indonesia, and they complained that heavy policing had driven up the price and that smoking cannabis was now more dangerous (in terms of legal repercussions) than ever. They tried to conceal their use by blending cannabis with tobacco from commercial cigarettes, but feared being caught because of cannabis's strong odor. For this reason, students used synthetic cannabis (referred to as "*sinte*" in Makassar), which could easily be bought via Twitter or Instagram; just type the hashtag "#tembakausuper" (#supertobacco) into Instagram and you will see more than 100,000 posts from users and vendors.

Like Bevan's respondents in France, our informants in Indonesia enjoyed trying out different products with other users. But they also observed serious adverse effects of these synthetic products. Sinte is sold under various names: Hanuman, Ganesha, Temchin, Nataraja, and Cap Gorilla (the last allegedly making users crazy as a gorilla, which the users found humorous) (Fig. 3.4).

Our interlocutors explained that *sinte* contains ordinary tobacco (and sometimes other plant fibers, such as tea) and synthetic cannabis (that is sprayed on the plant material). Sometimes synthetic flavors (such as banana, strawberry, or chocolate) are added, which add to its attraction.

The first time Basaka, one of our key informants, used *sinte*, he was 18 years old and still in high school. He was watching basketball in a

Fig. 3.4 Screenshots of different kinds of Sinte advertised through Twitter and Instagram (*Source* Photo taken by Anita Hardon, January 2018, Indonesia)

local park and his friend offered him a puff of what he thought was ordinary ganja (slang for marijuana). After the first puff, he asked his friend, "Why is it like this?" His friend replied that it was Temchin (a *sinte* imported from China). Bakasa really liked the effect: it worked faster than ordinary ganja.

Our interlocutors emphasized that you can recognize a *sinte* user because his eyes are red and his lower eyelids are puffy. They said that the benefits of *sinte* are that it makes you feel relaxed and that you have fun with your friends. Another advantage is that is does not smell like ganja, so it is safer to use in public. But *sinte* also made some users feel nervous and they found it hard to communicate. As well, they could become thin, because it made them too lazy to prepare food and eat.

Usually Basaka and his friends smoked *sinte* in the afternoons and evenings, when they have finished school or work, to relax and enjoy time together. It made them feel refreshed, even more so when they watched the sunset. The locations where they gathered to use *sinte* were relatively private spaces, such as rooms in their homes, cars, rooftops, and islands (Makassar is a harbor town, with easy access to many small and isolated islands that are secure places to smoke, the breeze making it even more pleasant). Basaka hadn't told his family members that he smoked *sinte*, as he was afraid they might judge him or confiscate his supply. He was also afraid of being arrested by the police. He did, however, confide in his niece, who he could tell by her reddish eyes, also was using *sinte*. She was also afraid of being arrested by the police.

Our interlocutors bought *sinte* from dealers they contacted via text message. In their communications, they used code words, for example asking "*ada bahanmu*?" (do you have stuff). They met the dealers in their homes, in the homes of friends, or on the street; this often involved taking some puffs together to gain the dealer's trust. The process of ordering and consuming was also referred to as "having a snack." The costs of *sinte* varied from 100,000 to 350,000 IRP (US $7–25) for a sachet, which can be used for six or so cigarettes—usually our interlocutors blended it into pre-rolled cigarettes to not make it look like a joint. Unlike ordinary cigarettes, *sinte* was shared, making it affordable for a group of friends. Basaka also said that he had bought it in bulk, making small sachets himself to make some profit to finance his own use.

Mixing *sinte* into cigarettes is a craft, one our interlocutors enjoyed doing. They tinkered with dosages to create the optimal effect. They each had their own preferred brands of cigarette tobacco with which they cut the *sinte*. Basaka preferred red of white Marlboros. Sampoerna (a *kretek* cigarette), which others used, was too sweet, he said. Some of his friend used menthol cigarettes as a base. To remake the cigarettes, after mixing tobacco with *sinte*, our interlocutors used rolling paper, which also came in different brands (and at different prices). Raw paper was more expensive, as it is made out of cannabis fibers. Marsbrand was cheaper, and therefore used more often. Sometimes the youth simply reused the paper of the cigarettes from which they took the tobacco. To these crafted joints they added a cigarette filter, to make inhaling easier. Or they rolled up tax-stamps found on cigarette boxes to make a filter. Others used pens or water bottles to help inhale the tobacco.

Bakasi said he was tapering his use. He would smoke a joint if invited to by a friend, because smoking joints together was highly valued. But overall, he tried to avoid *sinte*. He explained, "I want to keep having fun, but … it's not good for my future."

Karina Maharani (2017), a writer for the online news forum Rappler, reported how a 24-year-old tech worker she calls "Jay" used *sinte* in Jakarta:

> The gold-foiled packet that Jay holds up is small—about 10×10 cm—and innocuous-looking. You could stow it easily in your pocket, or your wallet. When opened, the contents seem similarly harmless. To the naked eye it looks just like ordinary tobacco, a familiar sight in a country of 61 million smokers. He takes a pinch or two from the packet and puts it on rolling paper. The resulting cigarette looks pretty much like a joint of marijuana. Sitting cross-legged on the floor of a dim apartment in Jakarta, he lights it up and takes a drag, and then another one. The effects are almost instantaneous, within a minute. His hands tremble, his eyes redden, and his body slackens. "Two drags are enough to get high," he murmurs, his eyes half-closed. "Your head feels heavy and your body feels limp." The high won't last long, Jay says, maybe 20 or 30 minutes. He doesn't want to take another drag, because he has seen what overuse looks like. "A friend of mine, it was as if he was possessed by a demon."

> Convulsions, hallucinations, yelling. Jay's friend … 30, says he experienced something similar when he had too much—7 drags to be exact. "I felt like I was possessed," he says. "I started getting very aggressive, like I wanted to fight everyone." … "When you smoke weed the effect is stable," he says. "This synthetic stuff is not stable. It's weird."
>
> "When I smoke this, I feel like I'm being brought very high, and then not long after, I fall back down."
>
> As a regular drug user, Jay says he'd prefer marijuana, which he says is cheaper and "healthier," but that he buys super tobacco because of its convenience ("It's so easy to get") and its efficiency ("The high is so much higher"). Dwi, a marketing professional, holds up Jay's unfinished joint. "Can I light this spliff first?" he asks. "To make it more soulful." He takes a drag before speaking to us. Dwi, who like Jay uses drugs regularly, waxes a little poetic about marijuana, calling it God's creation and comparing it unfavorably to the synthetic version.
>
> "You can be creative on weed, productive," he says. "On this stuff," he holds up the joint. "You're just a consumer." He adds that his heavy user friends refuse to smoke super tobacco because "it's always a bad trip." Like Jay, Dwi says that if he could choose between marijuana and super tobacco, he would pick the former. But these days with the marijuana supply dwindling, he's smoking more of the latter, mainly because it's so easy to get. "It's just like ordering fast food." (Maharani 2017)

Indonesian *sinte* smokers are concerned about adverse effects, which is to be expected, according to Michael White, a professor of pharmacy at the University of Connecticut, who explains:

> There are several hundred synthetic cannabinoids in existence, and they all stimulate cannabinoid type 1 receptors (CB1), just like the active component in natural marijuana, THC, that provides the high. But they do so with different intensities and for differing periods of time. There is no way to know which synthetic cannabinoids are actually in the product you purchase. (White 2018)

White explains further that natural cannabis not only contains THC but also has cannabidiol, which actually helps to temper the negative impact of THC. Synthetic cannabinoids do not contain cannabidiol. Moreover, they are often mixed with other chemicals, ranging from opioids to rat poison, which makes their effects even more unpredictable. It is unjust that, in an era when natural cannabis is being legalized in so many places in the world, our interlocutors in Indonesia were turning to more dangerous substitutes from unknown sources.

Our ethnographic research suggests that the War on Drugs in Indonesia actually fueled the use of synthetic cannabis in Jakarta. Super tobacco was easy to get and was seen as safer by the young people who used it as a form of harm reduction. But, as the above observations suggest, adverse effects can be severe. Users cannot tell from the outside how much or what kind of synthetic chemicals have been sprayed onto the tobacco.

In 2019, Indonesian drug authorities made 25 synthetic cannabis compounds illegal (scheduled as Class 1 Narcotics), which means that drug enforcers are now free to crack down on the use and sale of synthetic cannabis. But our fieldwork suggests there will remain a high demand and continuous supply of new kinds of *sinte*, which given the informal networks through which the products are distributed, will be hard for authorities to control.

Meanwhile, in the USA

While quitting smoking appears to be an important reason to start vaping in France, in the United States, concern arose about the popularity of JUUL among youth who had never smoked before. A research project entitled "Stanford Research into the Impact of Tobacco Advertising," based at the Stanford University School of Medicine, connected the surge in the e-cigarette's popularity to JUUL's marketing strategy, which was emphatically youth oriented. Its "Vaporized" campaign, which started in 2015, featured male and female models in their 20's in casual dress, along with bright colors. The researchers note that "the central message seems to be that if you try JUUL you will be blown away (i.e., vaporized) by the wonderful new vapor product" (Jackler et al. 2019, p. 7). Embedded in the campaign was the slogan "smoking evolved." Along with this media campaign, the company offered free

Fig. 3.5 Youth-oriented launch parties (*Source* Photos taken from Jackler et al. [2019, p. 4])

samples of JUUL flavors at youth-oriented music events and movie nights (Fig. 3.5).

The Stanford researchers describe how JUUL strategically sought out social media influencers as brand ambassadors, creating several Twitter hashtags, such as #Juul and #juulvapor, to promote the products. This social approach appears to be one of the key reasons for the popularity of the devices: young people like exchanging their experiences with each other.

Since its inception, flavors have also played a key role in the marketing of JUUL, with mango being the most frequently tweeted flavor. Figure 3.6 shows a 2018 JUUL advertisement for this flavor. Note how the advertisement cites users, with "YOU SAID IT" in capital letters, and then a quote, like this one from Melanie S., reading "LOVE, LOVE, LOVE the Mango Pods!!"

Jackler and colleagues (2019) also observe that, during its launch in 2015 and early 2016, JUUL did not warn young people about the nicotine content of its pods. This was a glaring omission given the considerable nicotine content of JUUL pod, each of which lasts around 200 puffs and contains 40–59 mg of nicotine, which is equal to the nicotine content of an entire pack of cigarettes. This marketing strategy

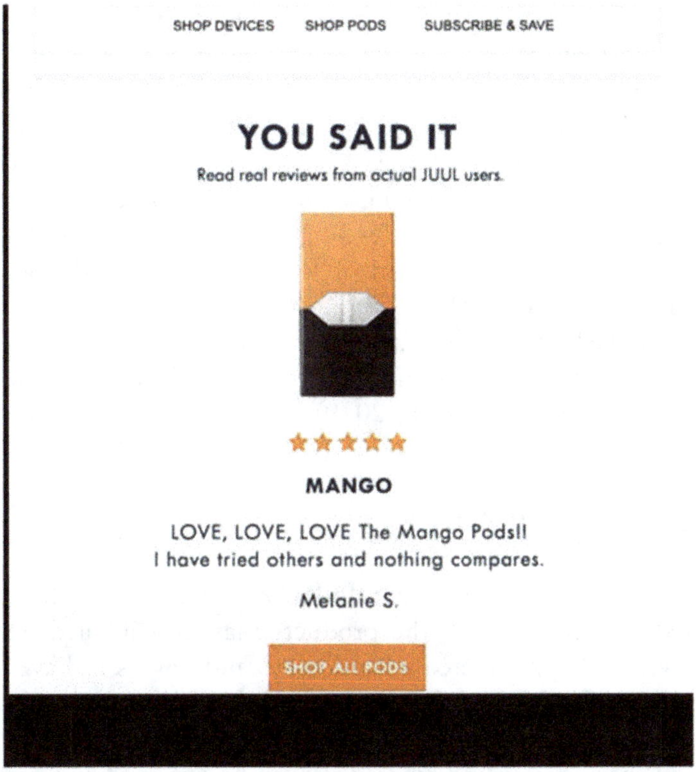

Fig. 3.6 This 2018 advertisement was part of a JUUL promotion for mango pods (*Source* Photo taken from Jackler et al. [2019, p. 11])

is also very different from that chosen by Gaiatrend in France, where slowly reducing nicotine levels through company-provided software was one of the selling points. The Stanford medical researchers conclude that the company's declared aim of "improving the lives of the world's one billion adult smokers" did not align with its actual marketing practices. Two rationales—switching from ordinary cigarettes to e-cigarettes, and adult-use only—became prominent themes in advertisements after JUUL's youth-oriented marketing campaign was criticized by US regulators and parent groups, as well as several class action lawsuits (Jackler et al. 2019).

In November 2018, the US Centers for Disease Control and Prevention reported that current e-cigarette use among American high school students had reached 20.8%, representing a 78% increase from 2017 (Cullen et al. 2018). A 2018 survey among 14,379 teens and young adults (15–34 years old) revealed that use of JUUL was three times higher in teenagers than in young adults: 9.5% for teens aged 15–17, but only 3.2% for those aged 25–34 (Cullen et al. 2018). The CDC researchers found that the appeal of JUUL was threefold: the device's resemblance to a USB stick, making it easily and discreetly used without parents and teachers noticing; its character as technological innovation; and its youth-friendly flavors, including mango, mint, crème brulee, and fruit medley (Ramamurthi et al. 2019).

Unrecognized Harm

Our interlocutors in France and Indonesia shared with their friends their lived experiences with the products that they inhaled, including adverse events. They tinkered with dosages and flavors to have optimal experiences in "do-it-yourself" communities. Marketing *sinte* is illegal in Indonesia, and manufacturers do not advertise the products much, other than sharing how and where they can be obtained and how much they cost. Users posted images of the products on their social networks, but information on how to use and craft *sinte* cigarettes occurred in face-to-face gatherings.

The positioning of e-cigarettes as safe alternatives is fueled by the big tobacco companies, who see a new opportunity to sell nicotine (Elam 2015). Big Tobacco's interest is evident from the establishment of the Foundation for a Smoke-Free World (FSFW) in 2017. The large tobacco company Philip Morris International funded FSFW with a substantial grant of US $80 million. In a press release celebrating this event, Philip Morris International (2020) announced that it intended to "build" its "future on smoke-free products that are a much better choice than cigarette smoking."

The FSFW appointed Derek Yach, who had formerly directed the Tobacco Free Initiative at WHO, as its first CEO. One of FSFW's first actions was to commission a study entitled the "Global Status of Tobacco Harm Reduction 2018." This report categorizes e-cigarettes as "safer nicotine products" (SNP), arguing that to encourage people to quit smoking:

> the new devices need to be easy to use and cost-effective, but must also offer choice. These days, choice is what people expect—of beer in a pub, coffee in cafes, or butter in the supermarket. And just as design is critical to the marketing of smart phones, wearables and similar technologies, the design of new nicotine devices is important. SNP design needs to fit into the modern technological zeitgeist; indeed, the look and feel of many SNP is light years away from dried leaves wrapped in bits of paper. (Shapiro 2018, p. 23)

The report reviews evidence on potential harm from SNP and concludes that public health researchers and medical professionals who warn against e-cigarettes mislead the public by adhering to the precautionary principle. The authors argue that that position is misguided, because "there is a potentially huge saving in mortality and morbidity to be made by actively encouraging persistent smokers to switch to SNP," and that there is a danger from the "global drive to over-regulation and control" (Shapiro 2018, p. 77).

While e-cigarette manufacturers (and government policy makers) suggest that vaping is a safer administration route, given it avoids the tar and other toxins associated with the burning of tobacco leaves, many medical specialists have raised concern about the safety of the adjuvants and flavors included in e-cigarette liquids and pods. A 2014 contribution to the *Journal of the American Medical Association* argues that flavorings are "a largely unrecognized potential hazard" (Barrington-Trimis et al. 2014, p. 2493). The flavors have been mainly evaluated for their safety in food, which is ingested, and such evidence is thus not relevant to the inhaling of the substances. They point to the risk of irreversible obstructive lung disease associated with diacetyl (Kreiss 2014), which was found in 69% of sweet-flavored vaping solutions examined in a recent study (Farsalinos et al. 2015).

As of the writing of this chapter in 2020, five years after the early warnings of harms associated with vaping chemicals were reported, JUUL is front-page news following an outbreak of severe lung illnesses which has left 1479 people sick and 33 dead. The health authorities found that the e-cigarettes that caused the illnesses contained THC (Ritchel 2019), and that the ingredient linked to the lung disease appears to be vitamin E acetate (which is used as a filter in THC containing e-cigarettes). Until more information is known, the US National Institute on Drug Abuse have warned young people not to vape THC containing products (NIDA 2020a). In September 2019, the US FDA sent a warning to JUUL to urge them not to market e-cigarettes as a safe alternative to ordinary cigarettes. A few days later President Trump said he planned to withdraw flavored e-cigarettes from the market and in October 2019 JUUL announced that it would stop selling flavored vaping pods in the United States. In February 2020, the FDA followed suit and banned all flavors except menthol and tobacco in pod-based e-cigarettes. However, the ban doesn't cover e-liquids, which youth can use as alternative to JUUL (Sindelar 2020).

Recognizing these problems, JUUL's chief executive, K.C. Crosthwaite, said in a statement, "We must reset the vapor category by earning the trust of society and working cooperatively with regulators, policymakers, and stakeholders to combat underage use, while providing an alternative to adults smokers" (Wells 2017, p. 1). At the same time, JUUL is gearing up to expand its market in Indonesia, using a US $12 billion investment from Altria, the manufacturer of Marlboro cigarettes, a powerful brand in the country (Tiku 2018). The company plans to sell JUUL in two popular grocery stores, Alfamart and Minimart, which can be found on every street corner in urban areas, ensuring that this brand of e-cigarettes will be more accessible than other brands sold mainly online and at dedicated vape shops.

In countries where cannabis is legal, vaping liquids are on the market and can be used in vaping devices. Faced with the uncertain content of the *sinte* products used by our respondents in Makassar, this would appear to be a safer alternative. Indeed, medical evidence suggests that vaporizing cannabis is safer than combustion, as the temperatures reached in vaping devices are lower, which means that fewer carcinogens and irritants are produced and inhaled (Earleywine and Barnwell 2007). However, in assessing safety, it is important to also consider the thinning agents added to e-cigarettes: propylene glycol and polyethylene glycol 400 (petroleum-based liquids) and vegetable glycerin (also called glycerol), a sugar derived from plant oils. Like flavors, these adjuvants are considered safe for use in the food industry, but when heated to vaporizing temperatures, carcinogenic substances such as formaldehyde are produced. Formaldehyde can also cause watering and burning eyes, and burning sensations in the throat (Troutt and DiDonato 2017).

Changing Regulatory Regimes

In July 2019, the Philippines secretary for health, Francisco Duque III, followed the stance of the French minister of health in forbidding the use of e-cigarettes in public spaces. President Duterte, himself an ardent smoker, had banned cigarette smoking in public spaces two years earlier; taxes on cigarettes (in the category of "sin taxes") are very high in the country (Philippines CNN 2019). In the Netherlands, a country without a substantial tobacco industry, the government is similarly committed to a smoke-free generation. Speaking at the 2018 biannual meeting of the World Health Organization Convention on Tobacco Control, Paul Blokhuis, the Netherlands's state secretary for health, welfare, and sport, declared:

> We have a clear goal: to raise a generation without tobacco—to ensure that children born today will never touch a cigarette... Our mission will require raising children in smoke-free environments. This means smoke-free homes, smoke-free schools, smoke-free public areas. If we want to prevent young people from taking up a smoking habit, we will need to help adults who smoke to quit. (World Health Organization 2018)

While Blokhuis's compliance with the global treaty on tobacco control is commendable, he may appear to be missing an important new trend. A survey of a representative sample of 6718 youth in the Netherlands found that 36% of 16-year-old youth and 39% of 15-year-old youth had tried an e-cigarette (Utrecht University 2018). In 2017, Philip Morris Holland introduced an e-cigarette called IQOS, accompanied by an advertising campaign that claimed that the device has 90% less nicotine. And in 2018 the first JUUL pods entered the country (Euromonitor International 2019).

While global health policymakers have joined forces in the FCTC to reduce harm from nicotine addiction, our ethnographic research shows that many youth are engaging with these novel devices, which can be used as substitute for ordinary cigarettes. It is worrying that despite declaring a commitment to promoting e-cigarettes to adults, for the purpose of quitting ordinary cigarettes, companies are targeting youth through social media. It is also worrying that the products contain a wide variety of flavors and active ingredients, the safety of which has not been sufficiently studied, and that regulators appear to be taking for granted manufacturers' claims that e-cigarettes are a safe alternative to smoking tobacco.

It seems a ripe time to apply the precautionary principle to this new chemical market, as also suggested by Gotts and colleagues (2019), who recently published a review of 193 studies in the *British Medical Journal*. They conclude that because no long-term research on toxicity has been done in humans, it is too early to say "with certainty" that e-cigarettes are safer. Their review found that e-cigarettes can cause increased symptoms of respiratory disease and negatively affect lung physiology and immune function. Gott, who is a pulmonologist at the University of California San Francisco, is quoted in *New York Magazine* as stating:

> People are conducting a huge experiment on themselves about what kind of lung disease you can produce from all these different chemicals that you're putting into the lungs. … And the bulk of the evidence is increasingly that these devices have new and unpredicted toxicity. (Hall 2020)

We propose that tobacco control programs start discouraging the use of e-cigarettes as a means to quit smoking, as there are better methods to quit smoking with proven success. We also propose that programs that seek to achieve a "smoke-free generation" expand their scope to discourage the use of e-cigarettes as well. This is even more urgent now the world is confronted with COVID-19, a viral disease that causes serious lung disease. The US NIDA warns youth "Now more than ever, it's important to be smart about your health. Take care of your lungs: Avoid smoking or vaping any substance" (NIDA 2020b, p. 1).

Similar educational efforts are needed to discourage the use of *sinte* as an alternative to smoking cannabis, a message that is likely to be understood in Indonesia, as our interlocutors recognized the potency and health risks of substitution products. A challenge in such health education messages is that social media are full of positive accounts of vaping and *sinte*, which raises the question: How should we regulate online marketing of products to prevent harm? We think one way is to engage youth who act as influencers, and hope that they are willing to share cautionary tales.

In Conclusion

This chapter provides insights into how young people seek substitutes to mitigate the risks of smoking cigarettes and cannabis. The harms that they seek to avoid differ. In the focused ethnography conducted in France, young people seek to avoid the risks of inhaling cancer-causing chemicals via cigarettes, while in Indonesia they fear being incarcerated because of being caught smoking cannabis. Harm reduction programs tend to overlook such substitution practices by youth. As we elaborate in Chapter 9, they tend to be designed to prevent harmful practices, one chemical at a time (Hardon and Hymans 2016). Failing to acknowledge the dynamic nature of young people's chemical practices means that new risks remain under the radar.

Young people share their experiences with substitutes both face-to-face and online. Our ethnographies show how these interactions tend to amplify the beneficial potentials of the new products, especially when youth are encouraged to do so by manufacturers' deliberate marketing strategy, as we illustrated in the case study on JUUL.

We describe in this chapter how tobacco companies "re-inform" (Barry 2005) their products into "safer nicotine products," in the form of e-cigarettes with a variety of chemical tastes and a diversity of inhaling devices.[1] An epidemic of vaping-related lung disease occurred, which appears to have been caused by the chemical adjuvant used in the devices, an epidemic that could have been prevented if the precautionary principle—a cautious strategy of pausing and reviewing before allowing new chemicals on the market—had been adopted by governmental food and drug agencies for this new category of chemical device (MacKendrick 2018; Read and O'Riordan 2017). Young people value the new vaping technology because it allows for a continuation of social bonding through shared substance use (Duff 2004; Pilkington 2007; van Schipstal et al. 2016), the opportunity to experiment with new kinds of inhaling techniques and devices, and the opportunity to experience different flavors. They trust that the products that they can buy at their corner store are safe and this trust is further fostered by the face-to-face interactions through which information on the benefits of vaping are exchanged (Brown and Calnan 2012).

ChemicalYouth Ethnographers

Imogen Bevan is a social anthropologist at the University of Edinburgh. She has carried out ethnographic research in France on smoking and vaping, and in Scotland on sugar consumption and the social meanings of sugar. As a researcher for the ChemicalYouth project, Imogen examined young people's lived experiences of smoking and e-cigarette use, and the socialities that emerge through non-medicalized forms of substitution. Her study used sensory and creative visual methods to explore what these technologies and substances might do for their users in social context. Imogen's research interests include the anthropology of the body, morality, and kinship; the boundaries between food, drugs, and medicine; sensory anthropology; and visual methods (Fig. 3.7).

Fig. 3.7 Imogen Bevan

Akbar Alamsyah was a researcher for the ChemicalYouth project and conducted fieldwork on synthetic cannabis smoking practices amongst students in Indonesia.

Note

1. In Chapter 1 we explain in detail what informing chemicals entails. We borrow this concept from Barry (2005) who argues that chemistry is a science of associations in which molecules are "informed." We cite literature on how pharmaceutical companies reinform their blockbuster drugs to expand markets, and show how when young people appropriate chemicals in their everyday lives, they inform chemicals by producing shared knowledge on how best to use chemicals, and what chemical can do for them.

References

Abrahamian, A. (2014, April 29). Vaping for yuppies. *The New Yorker*. https://www.newyorker.com/business/currency/vaping-for-yuppies. Accessed on December 20, 2019.

Barrington-Trimis, J. L., Samet, J. M., & McConnell, R. (2014). Flavorings in electronic cigarettes: An unrecognized respiratory health hazard? *Journal of the American Medical Association, 312*(23), 2493–2494. https://doi.org/10.1001/jama.2014.14830.

Barry, A. (2005). Pharmaceutical matters: The invention of informed materials. *Theory, Culture & Society, 22*(1), 51–69. https://doi.org/10.1177/0263276405048433.

Bengtsson, T., & Ravn, S. (2018). *Youth, risk, routine: A new perspective on risk-taking in young lives*. Abingdon, OX: Routledge.

Benedict, C. (2018). Bourgeois decadence or proletarian pleasure? The visual culture of male smoking in China across the 1949 divide. In M. Kohrman (Ed.), *Posionous pandas: Chinese cigarette manufacturing in critical historical perspectives* (pp. 95–132). Redwood City, CA: Stanford University Press.

Bevan, I. (2016). E-cigarettes: Smoking pleasure reinvented? The many faces of harm reduction in France. *Contemporary Drug Problems, 43*(3), 228–241. https://doi.org/10.1177/0091450916657348.

Boudet, A. (2014). Paquet de cigarettes neutre, interdiction de la cigarette électronique… toutes les mesures du plan anti-tabac. *Huffington Post*. https://www.huffingtonpost.fr/2014/09/25/paquet-cigarettes-neutre-interdiction-cigarette-electronique-plan-anti-tabac_n_5880354.html. Accessed on December 12, 2019.

Britton, J., Bogdanovica, I., Ashcroft, R., & Mcneill, A. (2014). Electronic cigarettes, smoking and population health. *Clinical Medicine, 14*(4), 334–337.

Brown, P., & Calnan, M. (2012). *Trusting on the edge: Managing uncertainty and vulnerability in the midst of serious mental health problems*. Bristol: Policy Press.

Cullen, K. A., Ambrose, B. K., Gentzke, A. S., Apelberg, B. J., Jamal, A., & King, B. A. (2018). Notes from the field: Use of electronic cigarettes and any tobacco product among middle and high school students—United States, 2011–2018. *Morbidity and Mortality Weekly Report, 67*(45), 1276–1277. https://doi.org/10.15585/mmwr.mm6745a5.

Dennis, S. (2006). Four milligrams of phenomenology: An anthro-phenomenological exploration of smoking cigarettes. *Popular Culture Review, 17*(1), 41–57.

Duff, C. (2004). Drug use as a "practice of the self": Is there any place for an "ethics of moderation" in contemporary drug policy? *International Journal of Drug Policy, 15*(5–6), 385–393. https://doi.org/10.1016/j.drugpo.2004.06.010.

Earleywine, M., & Barnwell, S. (2007). Decreased respiratory symptoms in cannabis users who vaporize. *Harm Reduction Journal, 4*(1), 11. https://doi.org/10.1186/1477-7517-4-11.

Elam, M. J. (2015). Nicorette reborn? E-cigarettes in light of the history of nicotine replacement technology. *International Journal of Drug Policy, 26*(6), 536–542. https://doi.org/10.1016/j.drugpo.2015.02.002.

Euromonitor International. (2019). *Smokeless tobacco, e-vapour products and heated tobacco in the Netherlands*. Euromonitor International. https://www.euromonitor.com/smokeless-tobacco-e-vapour-products-and-heated-tobacco-in-the-netherlands/report. Accessed on December 12, 2019.

Farsalinos, K. E., Kistler, K. A., Gillman, G., & Voudris, V. (2015). Evaluation of electronic cigarette liquids and aerosol for the presence of selected inhalation toxins. *Nicotine & Tobacco Research, 17*(2), 168–174. https://doi.org/10.1093/ntr/ntu176.

Gaiatrend. (2020). *Gaiatrend: About*. Gaiatrend. https://www.gaiatrend.fr/en/about/. Accessed on December 12, 2019.

Gotts, J. E., Jordt, S.-E., Mcconnell, R., & Tarran, R. (2019). What are the respiratory effects of e-cigarettes? *British Medical Journal, 366*. https://doi.org/10.1136/bmj.l5275.

Hall, S. (2020). How vaping became a public health crisis. *New York Magazine*. https://nymag.com/intelligencer/2020/02/vaping-health-crisis.html. Accessed December 12, 2019.

Hardon, A., & Hymans, T. D. (2016). Guest editors' introduction: Harm reduction from below. *Contemporary Drug Problems, 43*(3), 191–198. https://doi.org/10.1177/0091450916663247.

Haute Autorite de Sante. (2014). *The risks and benefits of electronic cigarettes for the general population*. Haute Autorite de Sante. https://www.hcsp.fr/explore.cgi/avisrapportsdomaine?clefr=591. Accessed on December 12, 2019.

Jackler, R. K., Chau, C., Getachew, B. D., Whitcomb, M. M., Lee-Heidenreich, J., Bhatt, A. M. et al. (2019). *JUUL advertising over its first three years on the market* (pp. 1–48). http://tobacco.stanford.edu/tobacco_main/publications/JUUL_Marketing_Stanford.pdf.

Kohrman, M. (2018). *Poisonous pandas: Chinese cigarette manufacturing in critical historical perspectives.* Redwood City, CA: Stanford University Press.

Kreiss, K. (2014). Work-related spirometric restriction in flavoring manufacturing workers. *American Journal of Industrial Medicine, 57*(2), 129–137. https://doi.org/10.1002/ajim.22282.

MacKendrick, N. (2018). *Better safe than sorry: How consumers navigate exposure to everyday toxics.* Berkeley: University of California Press.

Maharani, K. (2017). *In Indonesia, getting this drug is just a text message away.* Rappler. https://www.rappler.com/world/regions/asia-pacific/indonesia/bahasa/englishedition/158680-super-tobacco-synthetic-marijuana. Retrieved Accessed on December 12, 2019.

McQueen, A., Tower, S., & Sumner, W. (2011). Interviews with "vapers": Implications for future research with electronic cigarettes. *Nicotine & Tobacco Research, 13*(9), 860–867. https://doi.org/10.1093/ntr/ntr088.

Nichter, M., Padmawathi, S., & Thresia, C. (2009). Anthropological contributions to the development of culturally appropriate tobacco cessation programs: A global health priority. In R. Hahn & M. Inhorn (Eds.), *Anthropology and Public Health* (pp. 298–331). Oxford: Oxford University Press.

Nichter, M. (2015). *Lighting up: The rise of social smoking on college campuses.* New York: New York University Press.

NIDA. (2020a). *The latest on vaping-related illness and deaths.* The National Institute on Drug Abuse Blog Team. https://teens.drugabuse.gov/blog/post/latest-vaping-related-illness-and-deaths. Accessed on May 26, 2020.

NIDA. (2020b). *Coronavirus (COVID-19) and Drug Use: What's the Connection?* The National Institute on Drug Abuse Blog Team. https://teens.drugabuse.gov/blog/post/coronavirus-covid-19-and-drug-use-what-s-connection. Accessed on May 26, 2020.

Observations Francaise des Drogues et des Toxicomanies. (2014). *Résultats de l'enquête etincel-ofdt sur la cigarette électronique: Prévalence, comportements d'achat et d'usage, motivations des utilisateurs - note de synthèse - ofdt.* Observations Francaise des Drogues et des Toxicomanies. https://www.ofdt.fr/publications/collections/notes/resultats-de-lenquete-etincel-ofdt-sur-la-cigarette-electronique-prevalence-comportements-dachat-et-dusage-motivations-des-utili/. Accessed on March 10, 2020.

Philip Morris International. (2020). *Delivering a smoke-free future.* Philip Morris International. https://www.pmi.com/our-transformation/delivering-a-smoke-free-future. Accessed on January 30, 2020.

Philippines, C. (2019). *DOH bans use of e-cigarettes, vapes in public.* CNN Philippines. https://www.cnnphilippines.com/news/2019/7/3/DOH-bans-e-cigarettes-vapes.html Accessed on December 12, 2019.

Pilkington, H. (2007). Beyond "peer pressure": Rethinking drug use and "youth culture". *International Journal of Drug Policy, 18*(3), 213–224. https://doi.org/10.1016/j.drugpo.2006.08.003.

Public Health England. (2015). *Health matters: Smoking and quitting in England*. Public Health England. https://www.gov.uk/government/publications/health-matters-smoking-and-quitting-in-england/smoking-and-quitting-in-england. Accessed on March 4, 2020.

Ramamurthi, D., Chau, C., & Jackler, R. K. (2019). JUUL and other stealth vaporisers: Hiding the habit from parents and teachers. *Tobacco Control, 28*(6), 610–616. https://doi.org/10.1136/tobaccocontrol-2018-054455.

Read, R., & O'Riordan, T. (2017). The precautionary principle under fire. *Environment, 59*(5), 4–15. https://doi.org/10.1080/00139157.2017.1350005.

Ritchel, M. (2019). Vaping illnesses increase to 530 probable cases, CDC says. *New York Times.* https://www.nytimes.com/2019/09/19/health/vaping-cdc.html. Accessed on January 31, 2020.

Russel, A. (2019). *Anthropology of tobacco: Ethnographic adventures in non-human worlds*. Abingdon, Oxfordshire: Routledge.

Shapiro, H. (2018). *No fire, no smoke: The global state of tobacco harm reduction 2018*. London: Knowledge-Action Change.

Sindelar, J. L. (2020). Regulating vaping—Policies, possibilities, and perils. *New England Journal of Medicine*. https://doi.org/10.1056/nejmp1917065.

Statista. (2019). *Electronic cigarette: Reasons why French people started 2019*. Statista. https://www.statista.com/statistics/1015706/ranking-reasons-starting-e-cigarette-france/. Accessed on December 13, 2019.

Tiku, N. (2018). *Juul accepts Altria investment and embraces big tobacco.* Wired. https://www.wired.com/story/juul-sheds-anti-smoking-cred-embraces-big-tobacco/. Accessed on January 30, 2020.

Tiku, N. (2019). *Startup behind the lambo of vaporizers just launched an intelligent e-cigarette.* The Verge. https://www.theverge.com/2015/4/21/8458629/pax-labs-e-cigarette-juul. Accessed on January 30, 2020.

Trivers, K. F., Phillips, E., Gentzke, A. S., Tynan, M. A., & Neff, L. J. (2018). Prevalence of cannabis use in electronic cigarettes among US youth. *Journal of American Medical Association Pediatrics, 172*(11), 1097–1099. https://doi.org/10.1001/jamapediatrics.2018.1920.

Troutt, W. D., & DiDonato, M. D. (2017). Carbonyl compounds produced by vaporizing cannabis oil thinning agents. *Journal of Alternative and Complementary Medicine, 23*(11), 879–884. https://doi.org/10.1089/acm.2016.0337.

US Food and Drug Administration (FDA). (2020). *Vaporizers, e-cigarettes, and other electronic nicotine delivery systems.* US Food and Drug Administration. https://www.fda.gov/tobacco-products/products-ingredients-components/vaporizers-e-cigarettes-and-other-electronic-nicotine-delivery-systems-ends. Accessed on December, 20 2019.

Utrecht University. (2018). *Netherlands: Share of youth who have ever smoked an e-cigarette, by age 2017.* Statista. https://www.statista.com/statistics/936221/share-of-youth-who-have-ever-smoked-an-e-cigarette-in-the-netherlands-by-age/. Accessed on January 30, 2020.

Van Schipstal, I., Mishra, S., Berning, M., & Murray, H. (2016). Harm reduction from below: on sharing and caring in drug use. *Contemporary Drug Problems, 43*(3), 199–215. https://doi.org/10.1177/0091450916663248.

Well, P. (2017). JUUL to stop selling flavoured vaping pods in the US. *Financial Times.* https://www.ft.com/content/d96f6354-f104-11e9-ad1e-4367d8281195. Accessed on January 30, 2020.

White, M. C. (2018). *Why synthetic marijuana is so risky.* The Conversation. https://theconversation.com/why-synthetic-marijuana-is-so-risky-102224. Accessed on January 29, 2020.

World Data Bank. (2020). *World development indicators: Indonesia, Philippines, Netherlands, France, US.* World Data Bank. https://databank.worldbank.org/reports.aspx?source=2&series=SH.PRV.SMOK.FE&country=IDN,PHL,NLD,FRA,USA. Accessed on December 13, 2019.

World Health Organization. (2018). *Creating a 'smoke-free' generation: A future without tobacco.* World Health Organization. https://www.who.int/fctc/mediacentre/news/2018/creating-a-smoke-free-generation/en/. Accessed on January 29, 2020.

Yang, Q., Sangalang, A., Rooney, M., Maloney, E., Emery, S., & Cappella, J. N. (2018). How is marijuana vaping portrayed on YouTube? Content, features, popularity and retransmission of vaping marijuana YouYube videos. *Journal of Health Communication, 23*(4), 360–369. https://doi.org/10.1080/10810730.2018.1448488.

4

Molding Sexualities and the Role of Chemicals

Puerto Princesa is known for its tolerance toward non-heteronormative identities, relationships, and practices,[1] which is visible on the waterfront and in the malls, where people wander expressing diverse gender and sexual identities, enjoying the relative peace of the town. We talked to dancers of the Palawan *Sining* (arts) Dance Troupe, a student collective that is linked to the local state university. One of the dancers was Artista, a third-year college student who had moved to Puerto Princesa from a nearby coastal village. His father was a fisherman and his two older brothers, after graduating from college, both worked to augment the family's income. Since high school, Artista had had a summer job in a hotel that paid him US $60 a month. As a dancer for the University dance troupe, he luckily did not have to pay tuition fees.

Artista told us that when he (his preferred pronoun) was still in high school, he wanted to reduce his Adam's apple (which he found too big) and his muscles, and he wanted to have a more androgynous body with somewhat bigger breasts. Advised by a friend, he began taking contraceptives (four tablets of Micropil and two of Diane), which can be bought over the counter in pharmacies in the Philippines. He explained that he refrained from drinking alcohol when using the pills out of fear of drug interactions.

In the beginning, the pills made him feel very dizzy and they made him perspire a lot. He drank a lot of water because he thought that water would help melt his muscles and fill his breasts. When his breasts started growing, he stopped taking the pills for a while, because he feared becoming a man with very big breasts. Then he started using them again, seeking to have breasts that were just the right size.

A few years earlier, when he had enrolled in college, he joined the university dance troupe. In addition to dancing, he was responsible for the maintenance and safekeeping of costumes and accessories and many other objects the troupe used. Carrying these materials around caused his muscles to grow again, so he decided to stop taking contraceptive pills because they no longer were effective in reducing his muscles.

Do-It-Yourself Chemical Sexualities

The focused ethnographies presented in this chapter provide insight into how the young people we spoke with used chemicals to shape sexual bodies, enhance sexual pleasure, foster sexual hygiene, and prevent unwanted pregnancies, all of which we refer to as "chemical sexualities." Some of these chemical practices involved trying different sexual ways of being in the world, as was the case for Artista, while other practices reflected dominant heteronormative gender discourses: men should be virile, and women should be clean, attractive, and take responsibility for preventing unwanted pregnancies.

Our interlocutors used chemicals that are available in pharmacies to achieve their sexual needs and desire. Most of the chemical practices that we describe were "off-label," that is, not in line with a product's formal (that is, approved by the relevant food and drug authority) indication, or purpose. This was the case for the contraceptive hormones that were used by our interlocutors in Puerto Princesa, Jakarta, and Makassar to feminize their bodies and grow breasts, the use of emergency contraceptives as a regular contraceptives by young women in Addis Ababa, and the use of Viagra by young men, who did not suffer from erectile dysfunction, to enhance the duration of their erections (also in Addis Ababa).[2] Our interlocutors turned to pharmacies to obtain tools to augment their sexual health and well-being, because these access points tended to deal with their needs discreetly. No questions asked.

The pharmaceuticals that young people adapted for their own purposes have not been tested in clinical trials for the indications for which they were used, nor for the dosages at which they were taken. In the absence of medical information, our interlocutors developed bodies of knowledge by observing the drugs' effects on their own bodies, and sharing this lived experience with their peers and the medical professionals in their social networks. They tried out different dosing strategies and different brands and compared results, took advice from friends, shared their personal experiences with others. Some of our respondents were "inspired" by circulating (often pornographic) images, which present hyperfeminine and/or hypermasculine sexualities (Jackson 2009; Preciado 2013).

Through these exchanges, which we refer to here as "collaborative experiments" (see also Hardon and Idrus 2014), our interlocutors generated experiential knowledge. In this collective process, youth sought out what worked best for their individual bodies and minds, and they tried out and mixed products until they achieved a good enough match—referred to as "*cocok*" in Indonesia and "*hiyang*" in the Philippines—a match that was further finetuned by combining the chemicals with specific kinds of food and drink.

In these experiments, users determined their own efficacy parameters: growing hard breast tissue, having a longer lasting erection, feeling aroused, having a tight and perfumed vagina, and inducing menstruation (when it was late). These "endpoints" emerged out of the sharing of experiential knowledge on what specific chemicals can do. Users carefully monitored for adverse effects, and shared experiences of them, tinkering with dosages or substituting products to prevent them. But their efforts to avoid harm tended to focus on short-term and visible effects, rather than potential long-term risks.

In this chapter we shed light on these do-it-yourself chemical sexualities with vignettes from six focused ethnographies by ChemicalYouth researchers—though there was so much material about sexualities in our fieldwork that we could have filled a whole book with it. Across our field sites, chemicals made it possible for our respondents to try out different gendered and sexual ways of being in the world. As Butler (1993) incisively puts it: sex is not simply what one has, but what materializes through bodily practices. Here, we show how chemicals provided our young interlocutors with options in terms of the kinds of bodies they wanted to try out, the kinds of sexual experiences they wanted to make happen, and the adverse sexual health conditions they sought to prevent. The vignettes presented here are from the Philippines, Indonesia, Ethiopia, and France.

Sexual Health and Well-Being

Sexual health and well-being entered global policy discourses in the 1990s, when feminist health organizations critiqued the narrow focus of family planning programs that aimed simply to reduce fertility without attending to reproductive rights or well-being (Correa and Reichmann 1994; Eager 2017). The 1994 International Conference on Population and Development developed a declaration that was adopted by 180 countries, which stated that people—including youth—should be able to have "a satisfying and safe sex life" (United Nations ICPD 1994). In 2006, a working group of the World Health Organization built on this agreement to define sexual health as follows:

> a state of physical, emotional, mental and social well-being in relation to sexuality; it is not merely the absence of disease, dysfunction or infirmity. Sexual health requires a positive and respectful approach to sexuality and sexual relationships, as well as the possibility of having pleasurable and safe sexual experiences, free of coercion, discrimination and violence. (World Health Organization 2006)[3]

More recently, in 2017, UNESCO published sexuality education guidelines for youth, which among others teach the learners that "Engaging in sexual behaviours should feel pleasurable and comes with associated responsibilities for one's health and well-being" (UNESCO 2018, p. 72).

Despite such guidance emphasizing that sex should be pleasurable, reproductive health policymakers and health professionals generally approach youth sexuality as a danger zone. They rely on statistics to call for action: about half of the pregnancies among adolescent women aged 15–19 living in developing regions are unintended, and more than half of these end in abortion, often under unsafe conditions (Darroch et al. 2016), and more than 30% of all new HIV infections globally occur among youth aged 15 to 25 years (World Health Organization 2020).

Reproductive health policymakers' solution to these problems has been to offer youth-friendly health services that can provide youth with access to (emergency) contraceptives and condoms. Increasingly, there is a focus on "key populations" (such as people who are gay, transgender, and sex workers), who are at particularly at risk for becoming infected by (and subsequently transmitting) HIV. Because of a failure to increase uptake of condoms, AIDS programs have started providing anti-retroviral drugs through Pre-Exposure Prophylaxis (PrEP) programs to such groups, including young girls who are also considered at risk.

Our ethnographies suggest that these well-intended sexual and reproductive health services are under-used by youth who face cultural barriers when openly seeking such services and/or who fear the side effects of such products. Anthropological research shows that young people may have difficulty communicating with health professionals about contraceptives, preferring to rely on their friends and peers for information and advice (Sweeney et al. 2015). Fine-grained anthropological studies of young women's fertility regulation practices find that they worry that using contraceptive pills every day for preventive purposes increases their risk of infertility (Hardon 1997; Wood and Jewkes 2006). Post-coital methods tend to be preferred, because they can be used after youth have actually had sex and fear becoming pregnant (Hardon 1997; Sobo et al. 2000; van der Sijpt 2012). Interventions targeting high-risk populations also tend to be under-used. In Kisumu, Kenya, a district with a high prevalence of HIV, an evaluation found that only one out of five adolescents and youth who were offered PrEP through youth-friendly services accepted the HIV prevention pills. Their reasons for declining to take the pills included: they were reluctant to take a daily preventive pill, they found the pills too big or difficult to take, they were afraid of side effects, and they wanted to consult with their sexual partners first.

As with all the chapters of this book, we start with youth practices. How did our youthful interlocutors meet their sexual health needs? What were their concerns, and how were their practices shaped by others? By looking closely at their chemical sexualities, we gain a better understanding of what is at stake in their sexual lives. Our ethnographies show how youth across our field sites used chemicals to enact their sexual desires and needs, while at the same time attending to sexual hygiene and pregnancy prevention, and how they sought advice from friends and acquaintances, including nurses and pharmacists.

We describe four kinds of *do-it-yourself (DIY)* chemical sexualities: taking contraceptive pills off-label in order to shape bodies and try out different sexual ways of being in the world, using chemicals to enhance sexual performance, using chemicals for sexual hygiene and STI prevention, and taking substances to abort unintended pregnancies. Each of these do-it-yourself chemical sexualities involves diverse practices, which we compare and contrast across field sites to gain a better understanding of what is at stake in young people's sexual lives.

Shaping Bodies

We observed young people using chemicals to shape their bodies in Puerto Princesa, a provincial town on the Southern Island of Palawan in the Philippines, and in Makassar, Indonesia. In Puerto Princesa, one of our youth ethnographers described how young men appropriated contraceptive hormones to feminize their bodies (Josol 2017). One of her interlocutors was Artista, whom we introduced at the beginning of this chapter. Artista identified as a man, but wanted to have more feminine features. Another dancer whom we interviewed was Queenie, a first-year college student who said she (preferred pronoun) aspired to win gay beauty pageants. Artista and Queenie experimented with hormonal pills to shape their bodies, and they used female skin creams to perform feminine beauty, reflecting what some commentators have called the "commodification of modern norms of feminine beauty" (Jackson 2009).

Queenie used Micropil on the advice of a friend to fill out her thin cheeks. She started with eight pills a day. When this didn't have much effect, she tried combining Micropil with Micropil Plus—four of each at lunch and dinner—for a total of 16 pills a day. The first time she took a dose of eight pills she felt dizzy. Her friend reassured her that this was normal. She also developed a strong appetite and slept a lot. Her breasts started to grow. Her auntie, a nurse, knew that she was taking pills and warned her that she might get cancer if she took such large amounts of pills. "Go slow," her auntie said, so Queenie reduced her daily intake of pills to eight.

In addition to taking hormone pills, Artista and Queenie both used facial cleansers and creams to make their skin lighter and softer. Marketed for women, the feminine images in these products' advertisements added to the femininity Artista and Queenie acquired by applying the products to their skin. Artista used Eskinol Baby Face cleanser and Myra E lotion (on the advice of his sister), though he says that his skin is still quite dark because he does a lot of outdoor activities like swimming. Queenie used Pond's Facial Wash, an upscale brand, along with Myra E lotion.

We also explored feminizing practices in Indonesia, among youth who self-identify as *waria*, which is characterized by the dedicated work that male-born people do to feminize their appearance, referred to locally as "*déndong*" (Hegarty 2018). In Indonesia, the desire of male-born people to perform femininity is said to reflect their having a "woman's soul" (Boellstorff 2007, p. 90). The practice of *déndong* involves a range of bodily practices undertaken on a daily basis, including wearing women's clothing and wigs, extensive grooming, and taking pills or wearing prostheses to have visible breasts. *Waria* often work in beauty salons (ideal places to do feminizing work and practice femininity) and on the streets as informal sex workers or musicians. Their sex work involves male clients who are attracted to their transgender femininity. Most of our *waria* interlocutors confided that their biggest aspiration was to get married in a beautiful white wedding dress, and they proudly showed us pictures in which they had dressed up as brides, stored in their phones.

In Makassar and Jakarta, our *waria* respondents explained how, like Artista and Queenie, they used high dosages of contraceptive pills to achieve a feminine body. The explained that when they took contraceptive pills, a basis of tissue emerged in their breasts, which subsequently became the site for the breast to grow. The first sign of success is a small lump. Like Artista and Queenie, they also valued the other feminizing effects of contraceptive pills. Their hips became rounder and muscle volumes were reduced. And, like Queenie and Artista, they also tinkered with doses and combinations of hormones to limit side effects. For example Rara, a 24-year-old *waria* had been consuming two Andalan tablets twice a day. Her breasts grew, but she felt dizzy, bloated, and irritable. After three months she stopped taking the pills, and her breasts became smaller again, though her nipples stayed enlarged. Ayu, another *waria*, had used five to seven pills of Microgynon per day, but this made her feel sick. On the advice of friends, she switched to Diana at a dose of four tablets a day. But she still felt sick, so she lowered the dose first to two pills a day and finally to one pill a day before going to bed.

These feminizing efforts, undertaken by both our *waria* interlocutors in Indonesia and dancers in Puerto Princesa, show that their chemical practices generated diverse gendered ways of being in the world and of expressing and experiencing sexuality. They also adjusted their chemical practices to mitigate adverse effects and fulfill personal body modification aims.

Our interlocutors in both places were aware of how gender may be transformed abroad. They knew that in gender clinics in the Netherlands and the United States, transgender people seeking a feminine body often "go all the way." Male-bodied clients can have breasts implanted, which frees them from taking hormones every day; this is seen as an advantage. Health workers also expect them to undergo vaginoplasty. When all of this is done, they are expected to have their civil status reassigned to female (van Eijk 2014).

But, our informants confided in us, they were not seeking such absolute transformations. And even if they did, they would not be able to afford it. Talking further about the surgical options, they all said that they didn't necessarily want to have a vagina, which is a common view in Asian settings. Our *waria* interlocutors explained that their penises serve them well in the sex work that many of them did to earn a living; some of their male clients want to be penetrated. One added that they would not want to be buried with a vagina, if only out of respect for their parents who live in a rural village, and are not (yet) aware of their urban life as *waria*. We probed in focus group discussions into our interlocutors' aspirations for the future and found that many of them feared that they would not live long. They had already lost friends due to violence and (sexually transmitted) disease, and they knew that their heavy use of hormones was not healthy.

Enhancing Sexual Experiences

Across the sites, we also encountered DIY chemical practices to enhance sexual performance. We examined these practices in focused ethnographies in Indonesia (Hardon and Idrus 2014; Pakasi 2018) and Ethiopia (Both 2017), countries where prevailing gender norms assign physical strength, sex drive, and bravery to men, and where expectations for these are fueled by pornographic images that circulate online and in print. We found that these are also contexts where young men have difficulty living up to these unrealistic norms. More and more, young women are taking over male roles in the job market, and becoming more assertive (Both 2017; Handajani 2008).

In Indonesia, companies selling herbal medicines, food supplements, and energy drinks promote a wide range of sexual enhancement products through mass media and online. Often these products contain ginseng, a substance that has been clinically proven to improve male sex drive (Kotta et al. 2013). These products are referred to locally as "*obat kuat*" (strength/potency-enhancing medicines (Beers 2001). Hormoviton and Sparta X are two popular herbal preparations, and KukuBima is a popular energy drink. The packaging for KukuBima reflects the bodily strength and virility that young men are expected to perform (Fig. 4.1); the packaging for a Sparta X depicts a man with warrior-like features (see Fig. 4.2). The online site for Sparta X, for example, shows a young woman and a young man in a bed; he appears to suffer from sexual dysfunction and she is not happy.

Fig. 4.1 KukuBima energy drink (*Source* Photo taken by Anita Hardon, October 15, 2019, Indonesia)

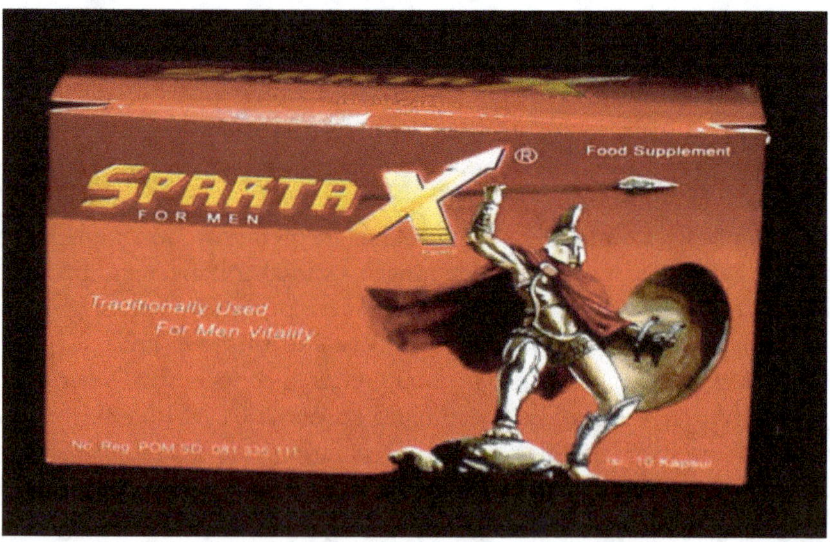

Fig. 4.2 A package of Sparta X, an "herbal Viagra" (*Source* Photo taken by Anita Hardon, October 15, 2019, Indonesia)

The young men whom we interviewed in Makassar drank KukuBima regularly, but they refrained from taking herbal tablets such as Sparta X, as they were worried about side effects. They had heard rumors that the pills were bad for one's heart and can cause black shadows under your eyes. They preferred to use erection-enhancing tissues, with evocative names such as Super Magic Man (see Fig. 4.3) and Magic Power. We only heard about the use of these tissues after several months of fieldwork, when one of our *waria* interlocutor's mentioned that using Super Magic Man during sex work, to enhance the strength of his erection (which was weakened due to her use of hormones to grow breasts). The

Fig. 4.3 Package of Super Magic Man Tissue to control premature ejaculation (*Source* Photo taken by Anita Hardon, October 20, 2016, Indonesia)

tissues are promoted through social media and through online marketing sites selling *obat kuat* (Hardon and Idrus 2015).

One such online store describes Super Magic Man as a tool to enhance (both male and female) sexual pleasure and to prevent sexually transmitted disease: "In addition to creating a long-lasting erection, it is also a product that makes you more hygienic and clean. So you can relax during sex because you are protected with an antibacterial antiseptic against venereal disease." The website provides the following product information:

> Super Magic Man Tissue is a herbal based antiseptic tissue that can be used to refresh and cleanse penis skins effectively, preventing bacterial/antiseptic, increase strength of sexual intercourse and prevent premature ejaculation. It can make you last all night long.
>
> Ingredients: Alcohol, Benzalkonium Chlorida, Triclosan, Cocomidopropyl, Betaine, PEG-78, Glyceryl Cocoate, Purified Water.
>
> Indications:
>
> As an antiseptic, to prevent sex transmitted disease
>
> – Maintain the health of the male organ
> – Extend the penetration
> – Prevent premature ejaculation
> – Powerful erection
>
> Directions: Wipe the entire length of the penis with the Super Magic Man Tissue. Then wrap the tissue around the penis for 5 to 15 minutes. Now you should be ready for sexual intercourse and have better control of ejaculation. (Hardon and Idrus 2015, p. 55; see also Ayden Store 2017)

We bought a packet of these tissues from a local grocery store and had them on the table during a focus group discussion with young men in a karaoke bar. Seeing the product made it easier for them to talk about the way they use it. Mali, a construction worker, said that when using the tissues his erection lasts for about one hour; without tissues he can only keep his erection going for around 15 minutes (Hardon and Idrus 2015).

We realized that many of the young men lacked confidence that they could be good lovers without some help, a finding we also encountered with our interlocutors in Addis Ababa, who worried that their sexual partners may not be satisfied, and might gossip about their less than optimal performance to others. Although the tissues are considered to be safer than virility-enhancing herbal tablets like Sparta X, they are not without side effects. Young men said that the tissues kill the good sensation (*mati rasa*), and/or made their penis feel tender (*perih*) and sore (*pedih*) when having sex. Young women whom we interviewed in Makassar also complained about side effects of the tissues, saying that they made their vaginas feel sore. And despite men's aim to please women by lasting longer, none of our female interlocutors were happy with the longer duration of the erections of their sexual partners (Hardon and Idrus 2015).

We found more elaborate penis-enhancement techniques in Jayapura, West Papua, a region of Indonesia that is known for *bungkus*, the traditional wrapping of leaves around the penis to create a strong and long-lasting erection. Young indigenous men in West Papua grow up with few chances to get ahead in life, as they are oppressed by military forces and outnumbered by men from other regions of Indonesia. Some of our informants echoed our interlocutors from Makassar about wanting to have a long-lasting erection in order to please their sexual partners, but in Jayapura we also found more violent narratives of men seeking to perform "*jago*" (literally fighting cock) masculinity, that is, about being a "virile man, whose penis and sexual prowess are a champion among peers, capable of dominating women sexually" (Pakasi 2018, p. 154).

Apart from wanting to please and/or dominate women, we also observed that young men enjoyed enhancing their erections together. The often lived together in boarding houses in town, where they met up with traditional *bungkus* providers. These practices formed a "collective reinforcement of manhood and sexuality (Pakasi 2018, p. 86). Freddy, for example, told us how he and his high school peers did *bungkus* together, lining up to have their penises wrapped by the *bungkus* doctor. As a result their penises were enlarged, though Freddy is not sure if they were becoming larger than normal. He also said they suffered from adverse effects including rashes and a burning sensation.

In a different setting, in Addis Ababa, Ethiopia, we found that young men preferred using modern pharmaceuticals to enhance sexual pleasure. They stuck to generic and therefore cheaper versions of Viagra, bought over the counter in pharmacies. In Ethiopia, young men are encouraged to engage in sexual encounters to develop their sexual skills for marriage (Tadele 2006). Young men feel frustrated because they are expected to achieve financial or social success, but have a hard time finding jobs (Heinonen 2011; Mains 2013). Unemployed men spend hours chewing *khat,* which is not good for their libido, and the increased circulation of pornographic images and films through social media negatively affects their sexual confidence.

Desta, a 26-year-old college graduate, explained how he met a girl he wanted to have sex with. He was nervous because it was his first time; he believed that men ejaculate too quickly when having sex for the first time and that women dislike this. He voiced his worries to a good friend who not only advised him to use Viagra but also bought the drug for him. Desta was to meet his girlfriend at the guesthouse where he was renting a room. He decided to take the pill several hours before her arrival as he believed the cheap pill could not be strong. But he soon got an erection and had to ask his girlfriend to hurry over. When she arrived they enjoyed sex for several hours. Desta's girlfriend reached orgasm first and was pleased with his performance; he recalled: "My girlfriend cried after the sex. She found it so amazing, telling me *bet'am des yilal*! [I love it!]. But I was tricking her. This was not my own strength, it was artificial" (Both 2015, p. 500). Desta said he experienced tiredness after ejaculating, and his erection did not go away; he had to cool his penis in a bucket. Desti stopped using Viagra after a while, because he didn't like using a medicine with side effects (Both 2015).

Underlying young men's pervasive use of Viagra are the high expectations for "good sex." Without drugs, our interlocutors say they can perform three rounds of sex in a night, with an erection lasting about five to ten minutes each time, while on Viagra they can have five rounds, each lasting 30 minutes. As in Indonesia, our female informants in Addis Ababa did not necessarily value these multiple and extended rounds of sex. They complained that their lovers did not engage in foreplay, just like in the porn clips that men frequently watched. Women also said that they were not interested in the multiple sex positions that their lovers wanted to try out, but rather were seeking compatibility in sex, which they said is achieved when both sexual partners experienced pleasure.

Another chemical sexuality known as "chem sex," has emerged in the gay party scene, which involves, amongst other drug using practices, injecting narcotic substances during sexual activity in order to enhance sexual pleasure. Public health professionals are disturbed about the HIV transmission risks that accompany these chemical ways of relating, while some social analysts have pointed out that these injection parties need to be understood as a form of liberation for gay communities who have been seriously affected by the HIV epidemic (Fournier 2010; Gaissad 2013).

One of our focused ethnographies, a study done in Paris, explored gay men's use of chemicals such as cocaine, MDMA, ketamine, and methamphetamine, as well as newer designer drugs, to enhance sexual pleasure. We observed that many of our interlocutors were especially interested in the bonding effects of shared pleasure. As one man explained:

> My best drug-taking experience was an injection of GBL and Meth, during a duo session we organized ... We thought it out this way: Let's put some music on and light some candles and let's do this really odd thing, a romantic drug-use session. So we injected catheters in our arms, the room was already heated. All we had to do was to put the needle in our arm, that's all. (Amaro 2016, p. 221)

Another informant, a 23-year-old student, described how his "slamming"[4] practice evolved over time:

> We met during a slamming session. And mephedrone [a synthetic stimulant] helped. You're in love with everybody, it may have eased the beginning of our story as a couple, maybe a bit too much? In the beginning, it was my boyfriend who injected me. We began in the evening at six, and told ourselves we would stop at midnight, and we found ourselves still going at ten in the morning, while we were supposed to be at work. (Amaro 2016, p. 222)

Amaro, one of our youth ethnographers, suggests that practices of injecting drug use are entangled with the search for love (see Amaro 2016). Injecting together is experienced as a sign of trust and love, and thereby facilitates bonding between sexual partners.

Enhancing Sexual Hygiene

The third DIY chemical sexuality involves taking substances to enhance sexual hygiene and prevent disease. We have seen how young men in Makassar used tissues to clean their penises before sex, but still, more often than not, we found that, despite changing gender norms, women took more responsibility for hygiene and preventing sexually transmitted diseases. In our fieldwork in Makassar (Indonesia) and Cagayan de Oro (Philippines), our ethnographers found that young women, who were at high risk of acquiring HIV infections due to their sex work, ensured their sexual hygiene by using vaginal washes on a daily basis, just like body soap and toothpaste. In Indonesia, the washes generally contain liquid betel leaves, which have antiseptic properties (Sommer et al. 2016).

Resik-V, with "resik" meaning "tight," is a very popular brand among women who do sex work. The front of the bottle that we bought in a supermarket states: "Fragrant and tight, especially for female areas" (see Fig. 4.4). The back of the bottle states: "Resik-V Feminine contains betel extract and other ingredients that help to reduce odors and clean the feminine area. Use Resik-V feminine wash while bathing" (Hardon and Idrus 2015, p. 55).

Our female interlocutors explained that their clients valued them having tight and fragrant vaginas. They told us that their work makes them feel *kotor* (dirty). They like Resik-V because it comes in different scents (rose, lily, orchid, jasmine), so they can choose the one they like. In addition to using vaginal washes, our informants use antibiotics (such as ampicillin or amoxicillin) before and after sex to prevent infections. They could buy antibiotics without a prescription in pharmacies and market stalls. They said they rarely use condoms, because their clients did not want to use them, and they believed that Resik-V and antibiotics would protect them.

Fig. 4.4 Resik-V feminine wash (*Source* Photo taken by Anita Hardon, October 20, 2016, Indonesia)

Vaginal washes are also popular in the Philippines. They are prominently positioned in drugstores and supermarkets. The ChemicalYouth ethnographers observed the use of vaginal washes in Cagayan de Oro, a city with a thriving sex trade. The city has an estimated 500 registered sex workers who are employed in bars and clubs, and many more informal sex workers on the streets. We contacted street sex workers through a local security guard, Kuya Boy, who also worked as a male sex worker and frequently referred clients to his female peers. We found that many sex workers end up on the streets because of poverty or having lost their virginity due to sexual violence. The sex workers used vaginal washes before sex because their customers usually examined their vaginas before buying their services. The sex workers explained that customers differ in what they want: some want light-colored vaginas, while others demand shaved or fleshy ones. But all men are particular about smell. As one of our interlocutors in Cagayan told us, "It is more important to smell nice, because when a customer uses you and your vaginal smells awful, he will complain and get angry" (Famaloan and Reyes 2018, p. 88). Having a good smelling vagina requires washing it often, as Nenen explains: "I wash my vagina three times a day, morning, afternoon, and evening, to keep it from smelling awful" (Famaloan and Reyes 2018, p. 88). One of her peers, Tata, said she uses a feminine wash every time she urinates. The sex workers in Cagayan de Oro used the Lactacyd pH Care brand; others, who could not afford it, just used Safeguard soap (known for its antibacterial properties) or toothpaste to freshen up their vaginas. The streetworkers invested in their vaginas because, as one of the streetwalkers explained, "The vagina can help you make money" (Famaloan and Reyes 2018, p. 88).

The sex workers in Cagayan de Oro went regularly to the city health clinic for check-ups. The city offers STI tests to prevent the transmission HIV and other sexually transmitted infections. They also give free condoms to sex workers; here, sex workers told us that they refused customers who did not want to use condoms. Sophia, one of the sex workers asserted, "the customer really needs to use a condom always! Never mind if he has a big budget. If you get sick, you lose everything" (Famaloan and Reyes 2018, p. 80).

While global policymakers are concerned about the lack of uptake of condoms, and have started giving women at risk PrEP to protect themselves in some settings, our ethnographies show that women widely use vaginal washes to prevent sexually transmitted diseases. The problem with these washes is that their efficacy in promoting vaginal health and preventing disease is understudied. But some female-controlled methods do indeed prevent infections, such as microbicides and vaginal condoms, which despite much global health investment are not accessible in our study sites. Elsewhere I have argued that more should be done to widely disseminate such methods (Hardon et al. 2012).

Preventing Unwanted Pregnancies

Our ethnographies show that women also took responsibility for avoiding unplanned pregnancies, though across our sites we did see men helping them get ahold of the chemicals to do so. Our fieldwork among students in Makassar found that they used various brands of contraceptive pills and injections to prevent pregnancy. Rossa (24) and her boyfriend were advised to use Andalan birth control pills by a friend who was also a doctor. Mawar's boyfriend bought Microgynon pills for her, which she used before having sex. After sex, she drank Sprite to enhance the pill's efficacy, having heard about this combination from a friend. Ara used Andalan every time she had sex with her boyfriend, without her boyfriend knowing. Her boyfriend did what most young men do in Makassar to prevent conception: coitus interruptus. Ara combined Andalan with *Kiranti Sehat Datang Bulan*, a *jamu* (local term for herbal medication) for healthy menstruation. Young women in Makassar liked using "the pill" to regulate fertility because it came with added benefits. Ika, a 22-year-old, used Microgynon birth control pills to treat her acne, on the advice of a friend who used it for that purpose. Ika not only swallowed the Microgynon pills, but also ground them, mixed the powder with water, and applied the paste to her face (Idrus 2018).

In contrast, our female interlocutors in Ethiopia and the Philippines generally did not use contraceptives, despite being sexually active. They refrained from doing so, they said, because they did not engage in sex frequently and they feared that taking a pill every day would cause side effects, such as headaches and infertility. Also, they preferred not to use contraceptive pills, because they didn't want family members to find out that they were engaging in sex; living in cramped spaces with their parents, they explained, it would be easy for their mothers or siblings to find the pills. This was not a concern among the students we interviewed in Makassar, who were not living at home. Instead, women relied on post-coital methods, which they could use after they had had sex, or if they feared they were pregnant because their menstruation was delayed. They heard about these post-coital methods from friends and siblings, and obtained chemicals for them over the counter in pharmacies.

In Addis Ababa, the preferred fertility-regulating method is Postpill, an emergency contraception that is available over the counter in pharmacies. Emergency contraceptives, similar to regular contraceptives, contain a combination of estrogen and progestin, but at a higher dose than regular pills, and are used within 72 hours after unprotected intercourse.

When talking to young people about Postpill, our respondents pointed to its popularity with comments like: "It will be hard to find a female student who does not carry a Postpill in her bag" and "Postpills are popped like candy" (Both 2015, p. 60). Both's respondents preferred Postpill because they could buy it after sex had occurred. Helen, a 23-year-old female BA student, said, "Postpill is easy to use because you only take it once" (Both 2015, p. 62). Mi'iraf, a 29-year-old female MA student said, "speaking from my experience, Postpills are convenient because I have sex irregularly and you can take it after sex" (Both 2015, p. 62).

In the Philippines, young women do not have access to emergency contraceptives, because the Catholic Church has opposed their distribution. They therefore take action when they find out that their menstruation is delayed, trying all kinds of chemicals, such as mixing pharmaceuticals with Sprite and using herbal concoctions advised by traditional healers. If these did not work, some of them turned to Cytotec, a prostaglandin that is on the market for the treatment of ulcers in both countries. In the Netherlands and France (and elsewhere), the active ingredient of Cytotec, misoprostol, is one of the two active ingredients of the abortion pill. The abortion pill contains both an anti-estrogen (mifepristone) and a prostaglandin (misoprostol), which in combination has proven to be an effective abortifacient if used in the first 40 days after conception. Because mifepristone is a registered abortion drug, its sale and use are not permitted in most countries that have restrictive abortion laws. Misoprostol, however, is also an anti-ulcer medication, which is why it is allowed to be on the market in the Philippines under the brand name Cytotec.

Research has found that misoprostol alone is about 75–85% successful in inducing abortion in the first trimester: four tablets are recommended to initiate an early abortion, and four (or, rarely, eight) more may be required for its completion. It is best to use misoprostol within 63 days counting from the first day of the last regular period.

However, Cytotec is hard to get, as pharmacies are not allowed to sell it over the counter. Ethnographer Leo Diego tells the story of Lily, who was a high school student in Roxas, a small town on the island of Palawan, the Philippines. Lily had a boyfriend and became pregnant, which led her to consult friends who had experienced an abortion. On their advice, she first took a concoction of *malunggay* roots for one week, but this did not work. She then tried drinking a mix of the energy drink Cobra and Coke for two weeks, which she stopped because she suffered from stomach aches, nausea, and dizziness. Feeling that they were too young to have a family on their own, she and her boyfriend decided to consult a traditional midwife (*hilot*), who massaged her belly and sold her Cytotec, which she was to insert in her vagina. This hybrid procedure eventually resulted in an abortion, which left Lily feeling very weak. After weeks of stress and pain caused by the massages and the abortion itself, she wanted to forget about the incident. Lily broke up with her boyfriend and found it hard to keep the incident secret from her family. She also had to pay her debt of US $60 to the *hilot*, which was a lot of money for a high school student.

Co-creating Youth-Sensitive Sexual Health Products

The contraceptive pill came on the market in the 1960s, building on the research of pre-war reproductive biologists who discovered that naturally occurring estrogens and progestins could be used to prevent conception. Clinical researchers designed the contraceptive pill such that it would be taken on a daily basis, while also allowing women to have their monthly period. In the past decades, following the aims of the ICPD to provide reproductive choice, many new forms of administering contraceptives (hormonal vaginal rings, injections, implants, and pills) have come on the market, along with emergency contraceptives and abortion pills. However, despite global commitments to the sexual health of youth, these technologies fail to meet the sexual health aspirations of young people at our field sites. For example, while young women were happy with using emergency contraceptives as a mode of fertility regulation, it was only made available to them as the Postpill, or Plan B. Why not as Plan A, for women who occasionally have sex? And why does comprehensive sex education not address the needs of transgender women who want to grow breasts?

Educators and reproductive scientists, if they are serious about promoting sexual health, should attend to young people's diverse gender-bending aspirations and to their many desires for sexual hygiene, disease protection, performance, and pleasure. They should also attend to the realities of young people's sexual lives, which call for post-coital contraceptive options. Family planners could consider providing emergency contraception through youth-friendly services, specifically for girls who have sex irregularly. This would acknowledge their reluctance to swallow a contraceptive pill every day. Reproductive health programs could advise *waria* how to safely use contraceptive hormones to grow breasts, and point them to the pros and cons of contraceptive pills vis-a-vis alternatives such as having breast implants. Educational strategies could be used to teach young men to talk with their lovers about their sexual desires, which may increase their sexual confidence. Young men need to know that wet tissues will not prevent the transmission of HIV, and students should be informed that taking contraceptives before and after sex is not an effective way to prevent pregnancy. Young women who face an unwanted pregnancy in settings where they have difficulty accessing contraceptives need to know how misoprostol can be used effectively and safely, and where they can order these pills without paying exorbitant fees to local abortionists. Taken together, this means that educators and designers of reproductive health technologies need to acknowledge the embodied ways that young people express their sexuality and learn from their collaborative chemical experiments (Hardon et al. 2019). They could invite young people to join in the co-production of better chemicals for sex. The learning objectives of comprehensive sex education, highlighted in the introduction, and, more specifically, attention to sexual pleasure, gender diversity, and the relational dimensions of sexuality fit well with young people's concerns and practices.

Such educational approaches could be further strengthened if they were built into peer knowledge sharing, if they worked with grassroots organizations trying out sexual health technologies, and if they provided medical information tailored to the chemical sexualities of youth.

In Conclusion

This chapter provides further insight into how youth make chemicals efficacious in response to their everyday concerns. In the introduction to this book, we characterized chemicals as "informed materials" that are rendered efficacious in laboratories, therapeutic settings, and everyday lives. While family planners and sexual health advocates seek to educate youth on unambiguous benefits and harms, our researchers found that young people used many chemicals off-label—that is, not in line with medical guidance—to achieve their sexual needs and desires. This was the case for the use of contraceptive hormones to feminize bodies and grow breasts, the use of emergency contraceptives as a primary contraceptive method, and the use of Viagra by young men to enhance the duration of their erections. Our informants tinkered with dosages and indications to achieve beneficial effects, while also monitoring their bodies for adverse effects. They shared experiences with each other and gave new users advice. These appropriations are also a kind of collaborative experiment, rearticulating chemical efficacies, and informing chemicals in new ways.

How does the informing of chemicals through such collaborative experimentation differ from that of scientific medical experiments, referred to as randomized controlled trials (RCTs), that are designed to generate knowledge about chemical efficacies? We asked ourselves this and answered it as follows (see also Hardon and Idrus 2014). First, RCTs measure the effects of specific chemicals on individual bodies, with the "double-blind" method ensuring that both the users of the products and those administering them do not know whether the active ingredient or an inert substance is ingested (Goldstein 2012). Collaborative youth-led experiments also evaluate the effects of chemicals, but through self-observation, rather than with a control group.

A second difference is that RCTs define specific outcomes prior to an experiment. In collaborative experimentation, in contrast, young people try out chemicals and observe what happens based on information that they receive from peers. They find out through their experiments what chemicals can do, such as the development of hard tissue and a base for breasts in the case of contraceptive steroids, or feeling confident when dating in the case of Viagra. These "endpoints" emerge out of the sharing of experiential knowledge on what specific drugs can do to alter sexual experiences and gendered ways of being in the world.

Third, youth-led experiments differ from RCTs in how they investigate adverse effects. Prior to a trial, clinical researchers define the kinds of adverse effects that may emerge, and then during the trial they measure these in standardized ways. They do so because scientific evidence on safety and efficacy needs to be submitted to regulatory agencies, which then weigh a drug's benefits and risks. This means that unexpected side effects that emerge during a trial are not likely to be examined. In contrast, our researchers found that youth experimenters observed broadly what the effects of a chemical were on their bodies, and then tinkered with dosages or substituted a chemical to reduce unwanted effects.

A fourth difference between RCTs and youth-led collaborative experiments with drugs pertains to how drugs are administered. Drugs in laboratory experiments are tested in isolation and in fixed dosages to allow for the standardized measurement of effects. Youths, in contrast, "tried out" different dosages and forms of administration, mixing substances with drinks, foods, and other drugs in their quest for better, stronger, or faster effects.

Finally, RCTs assume a universal body (Goldstein 2012; Adams 2016). If substance A is proven to be effective in population B, it is assumed to work identically in population C as well. In contrast, in assessing the effects of substances on their bodies, youth start from the assumption that chemicals need to be attuned to their bodies. We saw how they did so using relational notions of compatibility, such as *cocok* (in Indonesia) and *hiyang* (in the Philippines). A drug is cocok or hiyang if there is a "fit" between the drug and the person taking the drug. This notion that a drug may have different effects aligns with a new trend called "personalized medicine." But, this approach still has no place in standard clinical experiments on new drugs, which are generally funded by pharmaceutical companies. Pharmaceutical companies would rather base testing on the premise of universal bodies, as too much diversity would limit the market for specific drugs (Epstein 2003).

While RCTs are designed to "fix" the evidence of a substance's safety and efficacy, and thus inform chemicals for specific medical indications, youth appropriate products that they buy in pharmacies and rearticulate efficacies for their everyday sexual needs. They develop their own experiential and relational understandings of what chemicals do—trying out substances, mixing them with food and drinks, experimenting with dosage and administration, and sharing what they learn with peers—using these collaborative experiments in their quests for a good life (Hardon and Idrus 2014). Sexual health policymakers could learn from such experiments, as they reveal young people's sexual health desires and needs. Young people, we suggest, should become collaborators in future research on sexual and reproductive health technologies, making sure they fit with their everyday realities and sexual desires (Hardon et al. 2019).

ChemicalYouth Ethnographers

Diana Pakasi is a researcher at the Center for Gender and Sexuality Studies, University of Indonesia. Under the ChemicalYouth project, her PhD research looked at the practices of penis and sexual enhancement in order to understand evolving masculinities in West Papua. Based on the project, she published a book chapter titled "Virility Medicines and Changing Sexualities in Precarious Transformations in West Papua" in the Sage Handbook of Global Sexualities (Fig. 4.5).

Fig. 4.5 Diana Pakasi

Rosalijn Both is a researcher at Rutgers, an international center of expertise on sexual and reproductive health and rights in the Netherlands. Her PhD research focused on young people's use of sexual and reproductive health technologies (e.g., emergency contraceptives & sildenafil citrate) in Addis Ababa, Ethiopia. Rosalijn has also worked on livelihood and HIV-related research and intervention designs in Ethiopia, Kenya, Zimbabwe, and Zambia (Fig. 4.6).

Fig. 4.6 Rosalijn Both

Romain Amaro was a researcher for the ChemicalYouth project and contributed to the project with an ethnography on young gay men engaging in risky sexual and substances use practices. This study reflected his interests in sociology of health, gender, sexuality, and mental health. He is currently a doctoral candidate at the University of Paris (Fig. 4.7).

Fig. 4.7 Romain Amaro

Floralice Basco Rengel-Josol was a researcher for the ChemicalYouth project and conducted fieldwork on gender identities and chemical use among young students in the Philippines.

Notes

1. Heteronormative is a term used to refer to identities, relationships and structures reinforce hegemonic notions of masculinity and femininity. Non-heteronormativity, in contrast, refers to forms of gender and sexuality that

question and transcend this normative order, and leave "open the possibility that the dynamics at play may be a matter of gender, sex, sexuality or yet other categories" (Alexeyeff and Besnier 2014, p. 2).

2. Viagra, now sold as a treatment for erectile dysfunction, has an interesting chemical history. Its pharmaceutical content (sildenafil) was originally developed and tested by Pfizer for the treatment of high blood pressure and chest pain due to heart disease. In clinical trials, researchers discovered that the drug was more effective at inducing erections than treating heart conditions; male trial subjects didn't want to stop using the pharmaceutical because of this secondary efficacy. This led to new trials in which the endpoint was erectile dysfunction, an indication for which it is registered in most countries in the world (Holt 2009).
3. Expanding on this broad definition of sexual health, the World Health Organization now defines sexuality in a way that encompasses sex, gender identities and roles, sexual orientation, eroticism, pleasure, intimacy, and reproduction. It recognizes that sexuality is experienced and expressed in "thoughts, fantasies, desires, beliefs, attitudes, values, behaviours, practices, roles and relationships" (World Health Organization 2006).
4. A term used to refer to injecting drugs in recreational settings.

References

Adams, V. (2016). *Metrics: What counts in global health*. Durham, NC: Duke University Press.

Alexeyeff, K., & Besnier, N. (2014). Gender on the edge: Identities, politics and transformations. In N. Besnier & K. Alexeyeff (Eds.), *Gender on the edge: Transgender, gay and other Pacific Islanders* (pp. 1–30). Honolulu: University of Hawai'i Press.

Amaro, R. (2016). Taking chances for love? Reflections on love, risk, and harm reduction in a gay slamming subculture. *Contemporary Drug Problems, 43*(3), 216–227. https://doi.org/10.1177/0091450916658295.

Ayden Store. (2017). *Super magic man tissue original tisu tahan lama*. Ayden Store. https://www.lelong.com.my/super-magic-man-tissue-original-tisu-tahan-lama-aydenstore-197098962-2018-10-Sale-P.htm. Accessed December 10, 2019.

Beers, S. J. (2001). *Jami: The ancient Indonesian art of herbal healing*. East Jakarta: Periplus Editors.

Boellstorff, T. (2007). Queer studies in the house of anthropology. *Annual Review of Anthropology, 36*(1), 17–35. https://doi.org/10.1146/annurev.anthro.36.081406.094421.

Both, R. (2015). Emergency contraceptive use in Addis Ababa, Ethiopia: Challenging common assumptions about young people's contraceptive practices. *Reproductive Health Matters, 23*(45), 58–67. https://doi.org/10.1016/j.rhm.2015.06.005.

Both, R. (2017). *Sex, tension, and pills: Young people's use of contemporary reproductive and sexual health technologies in Addis Ababa, Ethiopia* (Doctoral dissertation). Anthropology department, Amsterdam: University of Amsterdam. https://pure.uva.nl/ws/files/9794196/Thesis_complete_.pdf.

Butler, J. (1993). *Bodies that matter: On discursive limits of 'sex'*. Oxfordshire: Routledge.

Correa, S., & Reichmann, R. (1994). *Population and reproductive rights: Feminist perpsectives from the South*. New York: Zed Books.

Darroch, J. E., Woog, V., Bankole, A., Ashford, L. S., & Points, K. (2016). *Costs and benefits of meeting the contraceptive needs of adolescents*. London: Guttmancher Institute.

Eager, W. (2017). *Global population policy: From population control to reproductive rights*. Farnham UK: Ashgate.

Epstein, S. (2003). Inclusion, diversity, and biomedical knowledge making: The multiple politics of representation. In N. Oudshoorn & T. Pinch (Eds.), *How users matter: The co-construction of users and technologies* (pp. 173–193). Cambridge: Massachusetts Institute of Technology Press.

Famaloan, F. R., & Reyes, S. D. (2018). Puke and puhunan. In A. Hardon, M. Tan, & E. Taqueban (Eds.), *Making bodies work: Young people's everyday body management in urban Mindanao* (pp. 77–95). Quezon City: University of the Philippines. https://pure.uva.nl/ws/files/47815299/Making_bodies_work.pdf.

Fournier, S. (2010). Usages de psycho-actifs, roles sexuels et genre en contexte festif gay (Paris/Toulouse, 2007). *Clio: Femmes Genre, Histoire, 31*, 169–184. https://doi.org/10.4000/clio.9648.

Gaissad, L. (2013). La demence ou la depense? Le circuit festif gay entre consommation et consumation. *Ethnologie Francaise, 43*(3), 409–416.

Goldstein, D. M. (2012). Experimentalite: Pharmaceutical insights into anthropology's epistemologically fractured self. In S. Levine (Ed.), *Medicine and the politics of knowledge* (pp. 118–151). Cape Town, South Africa: Human Science Research Council.

Handajani, S. (2008). *Western inscriptions on Indonesian bodies: Representations of adolescents in Indonesian female teen magazines.* Intersections. http://intersections.anu.edu.au/issue18/handajani.htm. Accessed on November 11, 2019.

Hardon, A. (1997). Women's views and experiences of hormonal contraceptives: What we know and what we need to find out. In *Beyond acceptability: Users' perspectives on contraception* (pp. 68–77). http://dare.uva.nl/search?identifier=ba104698-1caf-4dbe-bf87-c0e2cecf3e42.

Hardon, A., & Idrus, N. I. (2014). On coba and cocok: Youth-led drug-experimentation in eastern Indonesia. *Anthropology & Medicine, 21*(2), 217–229. https://doi.org/10.1080/13648470.2014.927417.

Hardon, A., & Idrus, N. I. (2015). Magic power: Changing gender dynamics and sex-enhancement practices among youth in Makassar Indonesia. *Anthropology & Medicine, 22*(1), 49–63. https://doi.org/10.1080/13648470.2015.1010114.

Hardon, A., Vernooij, E., Bongololo-Mbera, G., Cherutich, P., Desclaux, A., Kyaddondo, D., et al. (2012). Women's views on consent, counseling and confidentiality in PMTCT: A mixed-methods study in four African countries. *BioMed Central Public Health, 12*(1), 26. https://doi.org/10.1186/1471-2458-12-26.

Hardon, A., Pell, C., Taqueban, E., & Narasimhan, M. (2019). Sexual and reproductive self care among women and girls: Insights from ethnographic studies. *British Medical Journal.* https://doi.org/10.1136/bmj.l1333.

Hegarty, B. (2018). Under the lights, onto the stage. *Transgender Studies Quarterly, 5*(3), 355–377. https://doi.org/10.1215/23289252-6900738.

Heinonen, P. (2011). *Youth gangs and street children: Culture, nurture and masculinity in Ethiopia.* New York: Berghahn Books.

Holt, M. (2009). 'Just take Viagra': Erectile insurance, prophylactic certainty and deficit correction in gay men's accounts of sexuopharmaceutical use. *Sexualities, 12*(6), 746–764. https://doi.org/10.1177/1363460709346112.

Idrus, N. I. (2018). *Gender relations in an Indonesian society: Bugis practices of sexuality and marriage.* Leiden, NL: Brill.

Jackson, P. A. (2009). Global queering and global queer theory: Thai [trans]genders and [homo]sexualities in world history. *Autrepart, 49*(1). https://doi.org/10.3917/autr.049.0015.

Josol, F. B. R. (2017). Pampapogi/pampaganda: Achieving desired gender identities. In A. Hardon & M. Tan (Eds.), *Modernizing Frontier: Chemical transformations of young people's minds and bodies in Puerto Princesa.* (pp. 89–129). Quezon City: University of the Philippines. https://pure.uva.nl/ws/files/47815299/Making_bodies_work.pdf.

Kotta, S., Ansari, S., & Ali, J. (2013). Exploring scientifically proven herbal aphrodisiacs. *Pharmacognosy Reviews, 7*(13), 1–10. https://doi.org/10.4103/0973-7847.112832.

Mains, D. (2013). Friends and money: Balancing affection and reciprocity among young men in urban Ethiopia. *American Ethnologist, 40*(2), 225–346.

Pakasi, D. (2018). *Doing chemical sexualities, becoming a jago: Masculinities, personhood, and precarity in West Papua* (Doctoral dissertation). Anthropology Department, University of Amsterdam, Amsterdam. https://pure.uva.nl/ws/files/28324208/Thesis.pdf.

Preciado, P. B. (2013). *Testo junkie: Sex, drugs, and biopolitics in the pharmacopornographic era.* New York: The Feminist Press.

Sobo, E., Thompson, M., & Russel, A. (2000). Introduction: Contraception across cultures: Technologies, choices, constraints. In E. Sobo, M. Thompson, & A. Russel (Eds.), *Contraception across cultures: Technologies, choices, constraints* (pp. 3–26). Oxford, UK: Berghahn Books.

Sommer, M., Caruso, B. A., Sahin, M., Calderon, T., Cavill, S., Mahon, T., et al. (2016). A time for global action: Addressing girls' menstrual hygiene management needs in schools. *PLOS Medicine, 13*(2), e1001962. https://doi.org/10.1371/journal.pmed.1001962.

Sweeney, L.-A., Molloy, G. J., Byrne, M., Murphy, A. W., Morgan, K., Hughes, C. M., et al. (2015). A qualitative study of prescription contraception use: The perspectives of users, general practitioners and pharmacists. *PLoS ONE, 10*(12), e0144074. https://doi.org/10.1371/journal.pone.0144074.

Tadele, G. (2006). *Bleak prospects young men, sexuality and HIV/AIDS in an Ethiopian town.* Leiden: Leiden University.

UNESCO. (2018). *International technical guidance on sexuality education: An evidence-informed approach.* UNESCO digital library. https://unesdoc.unesco.org/ark:/48223/pf0000260770. Accessed on November 4, 2019.

United Nations (ICPD). (1994). *United Nations, programme of action (POA) adopted at the International Conference on Population and Development*. United Nations. https://www.unfpa.org/publications/international-conference-population-and-development-programme-action. Accessed on November 4, 2019.

van der Sijpt, E. (2012). "The vagina does not talk": Conception concealed or deliberately disclosed in eastern Cameroon. *Culture, Health and Sexuality, 14*(1). https://doi.org/10.1080/13691058.2011.634925.

van Eijk, M. (2014). Ideologies of self, suffering, and gender nonconformity at work in a US gender identity clinic. *Medical Anthropology: Cross Cultural*

Studies in Health and Illness, 33(6), 497–512. https://doi.org/10.1080/01459740.2014.896909.

Wood, K., & Jewkes, R. (2006). Blood blockages and scolding nurses: Barriers to adolescent contraceptive use in South Africa. *Reproductive Health Matters, 14*(27), 109–118. https://doi.org/10.1016/S0968-8080(06)27231-8.

World Health Organization. (2006). *Sexual and reproductive health: Defining sexual health.* World Health Organization. https://www.who.int/reproductivehealth/topics/sexual_health/sh_definitions/en/. Accessed November 4, 2019.

World Health Organization. (2020). *Maternal, newborn, child and adolescent health: HIV and youth.* World Health Organization. https://www.who.int/maternal_child_adolescent/topics/adolescence/hiv/en/. Accessed on November 4, 2019.

5

Skin-Lightening Practices and Chemicals

Young men and women, all dressed in white, take over the central plaza of a sprawling shopping mall in Metro Manila, and begin dancing energetically to upbeat music. When the song is over, they pick up large signs and together form advertisement for Lactacyd White Intimate, a new version of Lactacyd's vaginal wash. The next song begins, and the youth start to resume their sexy dance moves. More people stand around and watch, and when the dancing ends again, then banners are raised once more. Type "Lactacyd White Intimate Flash Mob" into YouTube's search bar, and you can see a number of videos of flash mobs done in and around Metro Manila (Fig. 5.1).

Why is Lactacyd promoting the whitening of vaginas? Our ethnographies on skin whitening across multiple urban sites in Indonesia and the Philippines show how whiteness is associated with confidence and cleanliness, ideas which Lactacyd mobilizes to promote its vaginal wash, as do other companies that sell personal care products. Content analysis of advertisements reveals that "good" skin is presented as young, smooth, pore-less, bright, and "white"; while "bad" skin is dark, dry, and rough (Li et al. 2008). In disseminating these ideas, companies

Fig. 5.1 Screenshot of the signs held up by the young flash mob dancers (*Source* Photo taken by Anita Hardon, January 10, 2019 from Lactacyd White Intimate Flash Mob video, Vengill Gutierrez 2012)

such as Lactacyd, Unilever, and L'Oréal perpetuate and reinforce prevailing notions of colorism (Glenn 2008), in which white skin signals, youthfulness, success, confidence, and beauty.

Historical analysis shows that the privileging of lighter skin in the Philippines and Indonesia reaches back to pre-colonial times. Abrera (2009) studied pre-colonial texts that describe how women who belonged to the chiefdoms were veiled since childhood and thus stayed lighter skinned; their light skin was a marker of their elite status, as they did not have to engage in agricultural labor under the scorching Filipino sun. American, Spanish, and Dutch colonizers reinforced such pre-existing hierarchies. Thompson (2013) writes about how American colonizers praised the light skin and beauty of elite women (who generally had some Spanish ancestors), assigning to them a level of civilization equal to the best of American and European society, while lower-class Filipinas were described as brown, ugly, and uncivilized. Reports of similar color coding are found in Indonesian historical sources. In her reading of the ninth-century Javanese adaptation of the epic Indian poem

Ramayana, Saraswati (2013) shows how light women were presented as desirable, likened to the whiteness and brightness of the moon, while evil characters were black-skinned. The epic poem also describes women using the pollen of pandanus palms as a whitening face powder; nowadays their descendants use Johnson's Baby Powder.

White skin privileging is not only done through the dissemination of ideas. It is also done in everyday interactions, in which darker skin is disvalued, leaving those with it feeling ashamed. In a fascinating analysis of skin-whitening among 46 Indonesian women from Jakarta and the rural town of Balikpapan, Saraswati (2013) discusses how the cultural preference for white skin is reflected in peer-to-peer interactions. One of her informants, Nina, who worked in a fitness clubs, said that her colleagues often commented, "Goodness, you have the darkest skin," which made her feel insecure in her job. Other informants told Saraswati (2013) similar stories, such as Ina, a 32-year-old, who said, "When I had to meet with many people and my skin was dark. I didn't feel confident," (p. 115) and Wati, a 30-year-old, who explained, "Because I was born dark-brown, I didn't have self-confidence. So I whiten my skin to be more confident" (p. 115). Saraswati concludes that women's use of facial lightening creams was driven by a profound desire to feel confident, and to avoid shame and embarrassment.

Colorism is perpetuated in everyday interactions between people and their skin-whitening products, making up what Markus and Conner (2013) refer to as the "culture cycle." Explaining how these daily and mundane interactions are shaped by economic, legal, and religious institutions as well as by underlying colorist ideas, the authors suggest that the cycle can be broken if we become aware of the messages in our everyday environment and the institutional regimes that shape our behavior. Such awareness can be the basis for "doing" race differently, which is not an easy thing to do, as it means intervening in complex systems of ideas and practices that link character and intellectual capacity to skin tone, and taking on cultural, representational, and institutional dynamics that perpetuate colorist dynamics (Moya and Markus 2010).

Investing in Whiteness

Our ethnographies show that having light skin takes on a specific value in interactions in the service sector, where lighter skin can attract clients and thus have economic value. Skin lightening made our interlocutors feel more confident in their interactions with their clients, and they believed that having lighter skin helped them compete for jobs. Indeed, having light skin does increase one's chance of getting a job in malls, given discriminatory institutional policies that add to the precariousness of youth not born with light skin. These ideas, interactions, and discriminatory work policies are not just harmful because they perpetuate a culture cycle (Markus and Conner 2013) that privileges having white skin and discriminates against people of color. They are also harmful because many of the skin-whitening products contain toxic chemicals, which can disfigure and can cause potentially life-threatening metabolic disturbances. Thus, this chapter examines the distinct nature of interpersonal dynamics in the service sector, institutional policies that perpetuate colorism, the chemical content of skin-whitening products, as well as the colorist scripts that companies use to market them. The chapter attends to the highly material work that service sector workers "*do*" in order to present the white skin that their employers expect them to embody. We also analyze relevant gender dynamics, showing how young men in the Philippines are competing with women for service sector jobs, which has led to their new use of skin whiteners. We end the chapter with a description of some of the arts initiatives organized by the ChemicalYouth project to both celebrate skin diversity and raise awareness of the cultural notions and institutional dynamics that perpetuate skin tone-based inequality.

Social scholars have emphasized the "immaterial" nature of labor in the service sector, in contrast to the material nature of manufacturing (Leidner 1999; Hardt and Negri 2000; Oksala 2016). Service sector workers manage affects and desires, and are trained to perform certain scripts to encourage customers to buy. Often cited as illustration is Hochschild's (1983) fascinating analysis of the "acting" done by flight attendants, who must put on a smile even when they don't feel like it. Such emotional labor, Hochschild argues, is alienating, because it demands that workers perform empathy that they do not feel. Farrugia (2018) draws attention to the particular relevance of youthfulness in the service sector, describing it as a "heterogeneous quality produced within forms of sociality that are enacted both within and outside of the formal labour relation, and that is infused with meaning and intensity through the process of immaterial labour" (p. 516). He argues that youthfulness in this context is produced as an "affective capacity for playful enjoyment, cutting edge taste-making, savvy consumption and desirable embodiment" (Farrugia 2018, p. 516).

While our ethnographies underscore the immaterial and affective work conducted by young people in the service sector, we found that they also did highly material work to achieve the "desirable embodiment" of having a fair skin. Our interlocutors bought a range of products to lighten their faces and bodies, in order to present the eternal youth promised by the products they sold (see also Chua 2000; Lan 2001 on this issue). Human resource agents select job applicants with light skin for service sector jobs, and also demand that their workers "retouch" their faces regularly while interacting with the public.

The investment in whitening skin by service sector workers can be understood economically, as a form of investment, which generates biocapital. When seeking to address the colorist notion involved in the skin-whitening practices of service sector workers, we need to attend to the economic logic at stake in this institutional setting.[1] But, our ethnographies show, achieving lightness is taxing, just as the flight attendants' acting is. Changing one's skin tone and texture is hard work that has to be repeated every day, and it comes with health risks. Our female informants used multiple products on a daily basis, applying them in layers: soap, then skin creams and lotions, then foundations and powders. Many of our interlocutors were unsure if the soaps, creams, and lotions really did lighten their skin, and they kept on switching brands to find one that worked better.

The accumulated biocapital, moreover, readily fades, however, as exposure to daylight leads to greater melanin and thus darker skin tones. Hence skin-lightening regimens need to be repeated over and over again. The more effective skin-lightening products, such as exfoliating products containing hydroquinone, and skin creams containing melanin-disabling mercury, also have severe long-term adverse effects, including skin cancer and disruptions to the production of melanin, evident as blackspots. Our interlocutors' investments in biocapital were many, exacerbating the already-precarious economic states of service sector workers. Further, as their skin deteriorated, their chances of having their contract renewed and attracting clients decreased, further increasing skin tone-based inequalities, rather than diminishing them.

Toxic Whiteness

The transnational companies that sell skin-whitening cosmetics have been criticized for degrading women with dark skin and thereby adding to racialized discrimination, as well as for including toxic chemicals in their products (Glenn 2008; Deacon 2011). In all the countries where ChemicalYouth conducted ethnographic research, governments rely on companies to police themselves. Food and drug authorities do not demand tests before a product enters the market. Rather, their safety is usually only regulated after there have been incidents.

Cosmetics contain thousands of chemicals, most of which have not been adequately tested, and though companies are expected to list contents on their labels, these often include general terms such as "fragrance." Commenting on consumer protection by the US Food and Drug Administration (FDA), David Michaels, professor at the George Washington University School of Public Health says in a recent documentary: "The FDA works very hard on drugs, on medical devices. Perhaps a little less well on food … Protecting people from dangerous materials in cosmetics is not even in the backseat, not even in the car" (quoted in Ellis 2019).

Dangerous and toxic incidents occur regularly. For example, after we had discussed a draft of this chapter, one of my colleagues sent me an article from the *Los Angeles Times* that reported that a women from Sacramento had been hospitalized after using a bottle of Pond's cream she had bought from a pharmacy from Mexico (Reyes-Velarde 2019). She had gone to the emergency room with symptoms of numbness in her hands and face, finding it difficult to speak. County administrators tested the product, and found that it had very high levels of mercury, and tests of her blood revealed that she had 2630 micrograms of mercury per liter in her blood. A spokeswoman from Pond's said they do not use mercury in their products.

Mercury is one of the toxic chemicals often used in skin-lightening products. Hydroquinone is another. Both chemicals are only allowed in amounts under specified thresholds in cosmetics in Indonesia and the Philippines, but our studies show that commonly used skin-lightening products contain high levels of these chemicals. The World Health Organization warns that mercury causes skin rashes and scarring, as well as increased risks for cancer, because it reduces the protective function of melanin (a body chemical that gives color to skin, hair, and eyes). It can also damage the nervous, immune, and renal systems; the nerve-tingling sensation felt by the woman in the *Los Angeles Times* story may have been caused by mercury poisoning. Studies have furthermore linked elevated mercury levels in the body to endocrine disruptions, infertility, and miscarriage. Moreover, the chemical is transformed by bacteria into organic forms that accumulate in living organisms, which can affect the safety of our food.

In response to all of these serious adverse effects, countries from around the world signed onto the 2013 Minamata Convention,[2] which bans the manufacture, import, and export of mercury-added skin-lightening cosmetics with a mercury content over 1 part per million, including soaps and creams. National governments are expected to adopt legislation to ensure implementation of this ban by 2020.

A survey by the Zero Mercury Working Group of the European Environmental Bureau (European Environmental Bureau 2018) found highly toxic levels of mercury in various products sampled in shops in Indonesia and the Philippines. For example, RDL Whitening Treatment Night cream, samples in Indonesia (and produced in the Philippines) was found to contain 5959 ppm, much higher than the 1 ppm threshold. And Goree Beauty Cream (manufactured in Pakistan), bought in a Philippines store, was found to have a mercury content of 10.576 ppm. The Ecological Waste Coalition of the Philippines (EcoWaste Coalition), an alliance of school, community, church, environmental, and health groups, has pushed the Philippines' Food and Drug Administration to take action to regulate the online sales of mercury-containing products, and has been working with local governments to ban such products from markets and beauty shops (EcoWaste Coalition 2011).

Hydroquinone is used as an exfoliant, which can also temporarily lighten the skin. Its adverse effects include irreversible patches of hyper- or hypopigmentation and skin cancer, and it is dangerous to use when pregnant (Ladizinski et al. 2011). The Philippines and Indonesia followed the United States in allowing cosmetics with hydroquinone to be on the market as long as the product contains less than 2% hydroquinone, a concentration that, according to our informants, still causes redness and irritation, and over time, paradoxically, can also cause skin darkening. Moreover, our interlocutors often used exfoliants with concentrations of hydroquinone above 2%, suggesting that the ban is not well implemented.

Marketing Whiteness

Today's sprawling cosmetics industry promotes skin-whitening products across Asia, and it is hard to find products in pharmacies that don't tout skin-whitening claims. Skin-whitening facial creams, scrubs, capsules, and vaginal washes are advertised online, through mass media, on billboards along busy traffic routes, and, as we saw above, through flash mobs in malls. In Indonesia, such advertisements depict young women with light-skinned faces; while in the Philippines advertising is directed at both young women and young men, targeting not only faces, but also arms, legs, and armpits (see Fig. 5.2).

The markets in the Philippines and Indonesia are saturated with all kinds of products, many made by the multinational companies Unilever, L'Oréal, and Shiseido, the three global market leaders. Unilever sells the Pond's line of products, which offers Indonesia consumers a choice of different kinds of white beauty: pinkish, spotless white, UV protected, and acne blemish lightening. Pond's provides a color-grading bar, which women are encouraged to use to measure their skin-lightening progress.

Fig. 5.2 Products sold in the Philippines: Glutamax, with the tagline *Kutis Mayaman* (Skin of the Rich) and Belo, which is marketed as an armpit whitener (*Source* Screenshots taken by Anita Hardon, November 2018, the Philippines)

The company is known for its strategic use of social media to promote its products. One campaign by Pond's calls on Indonesian women to do the "half-face challenge"—that is, apply ponds only to half of their face—and share the results on Instagram with the hashtag #Pondstagram (see Fig. 5.3).

In the Philippines, Pond's TV advertisements are directed toward working women and aired during primetime TV shows. One of the advertisements shows an attractive young professional, with light skin, coming home to her family, who says:

> I have to work hard and take care of my face if I want to succeed. So I use only the best. I use Pond's.... I worked hard to achieve my dream [her

Fig. 5.3 The range of Pond's products sold in Indonesia (*Source* Photos taken by Anita Hardon, January 2014, Indonesia)

husband gives her a kiss]. So, I love my life now, because Pond's loves my skin.[3]

Young people in Indonesia and the Philippines use skin-lightening products to increase their capacity to make a living, just as the above Pond's advertisement suggests they should do. Our collaborative fieldwork across sites revealed that skin lightening is an important pragmatic regime for youths who engage in precarious work in the service sector, where many of our informants belong to what Davis (2004) calls the "*outcast proletariat*," or the urban poor who are "structurally and biologically redundant to global accumulation" (Davis 2004, p 11).

Doing White in Retail Jobs

Often seen as docile and hardworking, millions of Filipinas have gone abroad to work and have become the human face of the Filipino diaspora. But there is also a significant internal diaspora of young women of various ethnicities who have moved from the rural hinterlands to boomtowns like Cagayan de Oro, a prosperous town on the southern Philippines island of Mindanao. Efenita Taqueban, as part of the ChemicalYouth project, conducted her dissertation fieldwork on skin-whitening practices among youth working in the retail sector in Cagayan do Oro.

City officials have sought to attract Filipino companies and multinational corporations, pointing to Cagayan de Oro's well-educated, friendly, hospitable, and cheap workforce. In recent decades, the growing presence of migrants from nearby municipalities and provinces, lured by the prospects of jobs and education, has transformed the urban landscape. The city is youthful and growing: around 600,000 people currently live there—five times its population of 40 years ago—and half of the population is younger than 25 years old (Philippines Statistics Authority 2013). Taqueban examined retail workers in malls, and observed "that having a 'pleasing personality'—code for a well-groomed face and body, preferably with light, smooth skin—was a requirement to be hired as a sales girl" (Taqueban 2018a, p. 1). Ellie, one of her interlocutors, told Taqueban how she spent her money on a bar of Kojic whitening soap, when she was applying to be a sales consultant:

> I wanted to look good… The girl selling Kojic was very pretty. Her skin was white and really smooth. I asked her what she was using and she told me she used Kojic. So, I bought the soap. But had to stop using it because it was very expensive. Also, I felt like it was burning my skin. It seems the girl selling the soap was just naturally white. (Taqueban 2018b, p. 39)

Joanna, a human resources manager at a local department store was adamant that she prefers to hire applicants who are light-skinned, explaining to Taqueban that sales girls with a pretty, fair face will sell products better.

Once on the job, human resource managers teach sales girls how to become presentable and pleasing. The use of beauty products becomes a crucial part of their everyday regimens. Felisa, another human resources manager, described how she explained to the girls why they should groom themselves well:

> So the client can see that you can take care of your face. You need to promote the product. They'd say you won't be able to sell your product if you don't put on make-up. Even if you're not very pretty, the make-up will help. Use concealers! When you go around, you won't see anyone working in the malls without make-up. Without make-up, you're not attractive. (Taqueban, 2018b, p. 39)

The retail stores in the malls also made use of a make up merit–demerit system. Not putting on make up could result in a demerit, and the girls risked a fine of 50 pesos (approximately US$1). Company guards inspected them when the girls arrived in the morning, ensuring that the girls were "presentable and ready" before allowing them inside the stores. Supervisors also conducted surprise visits to check the girls' appearance during the day.

Young women had a hard time financing these beauty demands on top of paying rent and buying food, which was more expensive in the city. Twenty-year-old Jana, who worked at a clothing store and used unregistered imitation products, explained:

> Budget is always an issue if you don't have enough for maintenance. Once you use the product you need to maintain it. People notice and appreciate how you look. If you don't maintain, they'll wonder, "How come you're darker now when you used to be fair?" (Taqueban 2018b, p. 42)

Earning only about US$100 per month, our interlocutors did what many young people do in the Philippines: buy whitening creams in small quantities, as sachets. "You economize your use, just a little bit every time. I can use one sachet for two days," explained Mel. In local neighborhood *sari-sari* stores, young people bought small packets of SkinWhite and Pond's (Taqueban 2018b, p. 43). A SkinWhite sachet cost 7 pesos (US$0.15), while the Pond's ones cost 24–30 pesos (US$0.50–0.60) (Figs. 5.4 and 5.5).

Young women working in the mall also bought what they referred to as "Class B" products at the local market, imported from China and other Asian countries, which the sales girls claimed were effective whiteners. These are the kind of informal stores where the Zero Mercury Working

Fig. 5.4 Sachets for sale at *sari-sari* store (*Source* Photos taken by Anita Hardon, October 2014, Cagayan de Oro)

Fig. 5.5 A popular Chinese-Filipino actress models a "power" whitening face cream.

Group found many creams containing high levels of mercury. Nora, one of the young saleswomen whom Taqueban interviewed, told her that even though "cosmetics made in China feel like they have alcohol and sting," she nevertheless continued to use them: "It's how you know it works" (Taqueban 2018b, p. 45). Such Class B products are likely to contain mercury.

On their days off, our interlocutors tended to just use Johnson's Baby Powder to feel clean and to lighten their faces. Alas, even simple powder can have adverse effects on health: in the United States and Canada, concern has arisen about the safety of this product, but these concerns have not yet reached the Philippines. In the United States, the Johnson and Johnson company lost a lawsuit filed by 22 women who claimed that this popular skin product causes ovarian cancer, because it is contaminated by asbestos, a mineral often appearing underground near talc (Rabin and Hsu 2018). The court agreed with the women and awarded them US$4.69 billion, one of the biggest personal injury payments ever.

Taqueban's study of skin-lightening practices in the retail sector suggests that the sales girls were under pressure to lighten their skin on daily basis, not only to get jobs but also to keep them. Disciplinary actions by the companies, including fines, motivated them to keep on using this type of product. But because of the costs involved, they bought cheap sachets and Class B products, thereby likely increasing their exposure to mercury. As a result, they risked not only deteriorating their skin but also negatively affecting their overall health. They managed such risks by evaluating the effects of skin-lightening products, and switching brands if they experienced negative effects. But some of the longer term risks, such as skin cancer or damage to renal, immune, or nervous systems, are not immediately apparent. While trying to make a living in this flourishing town, these young women's work may cause them to live more precarious lives.

Doing White in Karaoke Bars

Karaoke bars are common establishments in towns across Indonesia and the Philippines. They employ women, who keep the customers company if they offer the women a beer (referred to as a "ladies' drink"). The women are generally paid an amount for each offered drink. Where in the retail sector, managers demand that sales girls groom themselves well, in the karaoke bars, girls do so on their own to compete with peers for customers.

We conducted research on skin-whitening practices in karaoke bars in coastal towns that are local tourist destinations, in both Indonesia and the Philippines. In Indonesia I did fieldwork with Nurul Ilmi Idrus (see Hardon and Idrus 2015) in a beach destination town in South Sulawesi that we call Isidro,[4] which attracts young women from across the region in search of better livelihoods. Isidro is a popular destination for fun-seeking locals; its karaoke bars are located on a ridge in the woods, far from the town center, thus concealing the sale of alcohol which is illegal in the town. The bars cater to men of all ages who come to sing, smoke, drink, and relax with the attractive waitresses. While the bars do not openly provide sexual services (also illegal), the waitresses can make their own informal arrangements to augment their income. Our informants (all female) were employed by the bars, whose owners charged them for both lodging and their necessities, including their skin-lightening products.

Many of our interlocutors in Isidro had migrated from Bali, Papua, Kalimantan, and Toraja. They left behind their families, most of whom were very poor. Some had become pregnant as teenagers, and they had also left their children behind. Having experienced family breakups and economic hardship, many had sought out opportunities to improve their lives. All of them stressed that they wanted to have a steady income to save money for a better future.

Twenty-two-year-old Putri told us that her family couldn't afford to support her high school education, so she took a job at the bar. It was only once she was in Isidro that she realized that the waitresses working in the bar were also providing sexual services. Nevertheless, she did not initially see herself as a sex worker. Early on during her stay in Isidro, she met a man with whom she fell in love with and married. His parents, however, refused her as their daughter-in-law after learning that she was coming from Isidro, an area known for prostitution. Putri's husband then took her back to Isidro and returned to his hometown; she later found out that he was cheating on her and asked him for a divorce. Though she wanted to return to her own home, Putri was afraid that her parents wouldn't take her back. When we met, she had been working in Isidro for three years.

Rina was another of our interlocutors. A thin, outwardly cheerful, and talkative young woman of 20, she had graduated from junior high school but did not continue her education, as her father had died and her mother had no money to pay for her studies. Rina said she had been fooled by a friend who offered her a waitress job, and only when she arrived did she too realize that the women working at the bar were expected to also provide sexual services. She recalled feeling trapped, unable to leave because the bar's owner demanded that she pay back the money he had given her friend for recruiting Rina. She also ran up debts buying cosmetics and other products at the store owned by the bar-owner's wife (Fig. 5.6).

During fieldwork, we usually talked to the young women in the afternoons, after they had woken up—many of them worked late, especially if a client hired them for sexual services. When we held a group discussion on the commonly used skin products, our informants stressed that, above

Fig. 5.6 Workers in a karaoke bar with their "ladies' drinks" (*Source* Photo taken by Sari Damar Rati March 2014, Indonesia)

all, they desired soft and light-colored skin, and bright, shining faces free of pimples and black spots. This was not only to attract clients; having such well-groomed skin also, they said, increased their chances of finding a husband, a long-term goal held by everyone, including those who were single mothers. The karaoke bar workers recounted to us how they used skin-whitening soaps, powders, foundations, and facial creams on a daily basis. They preferred to use foundation when on the job, because it appears more natural; baby powder, as we found in the Philippines, was used when the girls did not work. When they had a day off, they also used a relatively aggressive exfoliating lotion called RDL Hydroquinone Tretinoin Babyface exfoliant.

Though freely available in stores and markets, RDL is not registered as a cosmetic in Indonesia, nor is it advertised on TV or the radio. Instead, information circulates through RDL Facebook. We heard from sources in Makassar that the products enter Indonesia through the port of Manado, which is very close to the Philippines island of Mindanao. Small trading vessels carry Philippine products to Indonesia, and then transport batik sarongs, clothes, and spices back. The women we interviewed asserted that RDL works by peeling the outer layer of skin; the treatment lasts for three consecutive days, and so they scheduled it on days off and when there were few customers. The wife of the bar owner sold our informants RDL for 15,000 rupiah (a little less than US$2), while their total earnings for bar work were usually about US$30. This was not enough to pay for their daily needs, and many like Rina had debt, which pushed them to go out with clients and earn some more money as sex workers (Table 5.1).

The declaration of contents that we found on the packages suggests that the products used in the karaoke bars of Isidro have a 4% hydroquinone concentration, making them illegal by Indonesian regulatory standards for cosmetics. Notice that this package of RDL does not declare mercury contents—a substance found by the Zero Mercury Working Group in the night cream version of RDL (a product that also did not declare its mercury content).

While our informants in the karaoke bars of Isidro complained that the exfoliating products felt *pedas* (hot) on their skin, they suggested this was a sign of their efficacy. When we opened a bottle of RDL, it smelled more like a strong chemical stain remover than a skin cream.

Table 5.1 RDL product information, copied from the package, October 2016

Brand	Manufacturer	Content	Product information
RDL hydroquinone tretinoin Babyface solution	RDL Pharmaceutical Laboratory, Davao, Philippines	Each ml contains 40 mcg hydroquinone and 20 mcg tretinoin	• Anti-acne/Keratolytic depigmenting agent • For topical treatment of acne vulgaris and pathological hyperpigmentation • Use once or twice a day • Warning: should not be used for longer than 2 months; do not apply to broken skin; do not use to treat more than 10% of body surface; should not be used by pregnant women • Precaution: avoid excessive exposure to sunlight

Most women nevertheless endured weekly treatments. In our focus group with the bar workers in Isidro, Neni admitted: "It feels so hot, it makes me cry." After applying the exfoliating liquid, the young women sat in front of a fan to cool their faces. Only two young women we spoke with refrained from using skin-peeling products, stating that they were bad for their skin and that the products were not *cocok* (suitable) for them. They cultivated an oriental identity, which they said some Korean businessmen found attractive (Hardon and Idrus 2015).

Skin lightening was also a key chemical practice for our interlocutors in the karaoke bars in Puerto Princesa, a rapidly growing tourist destination on the island of Palawan, the Philippines. Unlike in Isidro, the bars are legal in this city, and the municipal health department checks the workers regularly to make sure they don't have sexually transmitted diseases or HIV. The bars are along the main roads in the town, welcoming the many Filipino tourists who visit this town annually, and downtown near the tourist market. Every year in November business is good, because American soldiers visit Puerto Princesa after completing military practice with their Filipino peers.

Alvie Bergado Timbancaya and I visited two karaoke bars regularly: one relatively expensive club, which also caters to foreigners, and one lower-end bar with mainly local Filipino clients (see Bergado Timbancaya 2017). We went early in the evening, when the young women were hanging around and waiting for clients, and talked with them about their life trajectories, family, income, and investments in beauty. We bought them ladies' drinks, which meant that they could join us and talk, and we watched them parade around on the bar's catwalk and do pole-dancing to entertain their clients.

At the low-end bar, the young women earned money when a customer bought them a drink (70 Philippines pesos per glass of beer, or about US$1.40), just as their peers in Isidro did. They sang and drank with their customers, and they told us that fair-skinned young women get picked first by clients, something we also observed firsthand.

Kaye, 22 years old at the time, had been working at the low-end bar for more than eight months. She did not finish high school because she got pregnant when she was a teenager. When we met her, she had two sons, still too young for school, who stayed with her parents in a village in Puerto Princesa. Kaye visited them twice a week. She started working in the karaoke bars after her husband died in a traffic accident. She initially applied to be a waitress, but realized she could earn more for her family by working in karaoke bars. On average she earned 140 pesos a night, and more (around 500 pesos) if a customer hired her for a few hours and paid a fee to her manager. Kaye regularly used Silka Papaya soap, which she said was *hiyang* with her skin, to lighten her complexion. She also used Yoko Pearl Cream twice a day to lighten and moisturize her skin after washing it with Silka. Kaye explained that her skin is sensitive, so she carefully tried out products and used only those that didn't irritate her skin. Her coworker Mhay, a 20-year-old, used products that were less gentle, including Maxi-Peel body scrub (which contains hydroquinone 2%, just at the threshold level, hence not banned) on her body when she took a bath, twice a day. After bathing she used Pond's whitening facial scrub on her face, and then Eskinol lightening toner to remove cosmetic residue from the night before, followed by Pond's whitening facial cream. Pond's is a relatively expensive brand.

The Filipino company Splash promotes hydroquinone-containing Maxi-Peel as follows on its Facebook site:

> Launched in 2001, Maxi-Peel is the leader in the exfoliants category, with its complete range of skin care products that aim to help women achieve fairer, smoother, and beautifully renewed skin. What makes Maxi-Peel work? Over the years, its breakthrough and unique formulation of Tretinoin and Hydroquinone, which is used to treat and prevent mild to severe pimples, was able to build its credibility and loyalty with its consumers due to its effectiveness. Only Maxi-Peel provides potent exfoliation technology that removes blemishes, smoothens and lightens in just two weeks. (Maxi-Peel Skin Care 2020)

Ella, another interlocutor who was 23 years old when we met, worked in the high-end bar, where she could earn a slightly better income than in the lower-end one. Ella was born in Laguna, on the island of Luzon, and had been recruited in her home village by an agent who brought her to Puerto Princesa to work in the karaoke bar. She was single and did not have children. She lived above the bar, and received 50 pesos per day as food allowance from her manager. She explained to us that she earned 100 pesos for every ladies drink, and could earn more—as much as 1500 pesos—if a customer took her out. In total, customers paid the bar 3500 pesos to hire a young woman for a few hours, of which 2000 was given to the manager as a fee.

Like Mhay and Kaye, Ella aspired to have fairer skin and considered girls with lighter skin more beautiful, but she had trouble achieving it because her skin was quite dark. She was grateful to learn that some foreigners, including Europeans and Koreans, were attracted to her "oriental" looks. Still, she tried to become more attractive by making her breasts bigger with hormonal pills, but stopped doing this because she couldn't afford to take the pills every day. Instead, she invested in rebonding her hair, whenever she had a client who took her out. Rebonding made her hair silky and noticeable when she walked the pretend catwalk in the club. The bar invited Ella and the young women to do so a couple of times per evening, to allow clients to select which women they wanted to offer a drink and/or take out.

Mercury, hydroquinone, and Johnson's Baby Powder (possibly contaminated by asbestos) were some of the chemicals contained in the cheap products used regularly by hospitality workers in our field sites in the Philippines and Indonesia. They used these products to have lighter skin in order to attract clients, but this was a double-edged sword: if their skin deteriorated due to these products, they were likely to lose their jobs. The painful reality as that they were unaware of the risks, and when skin damage occurred it was too late.

Keeping Up with the Times

The Philippines has witnessed a feminization of its labor force, along with an expanding service sector (Pingol 2001). Young women in the Philippines are generally better educated than men and they are more likely to be employed in the booming service sector. Young men who grow up to be providers for their families often have adjusted their aspirations (Eder 2006). If they wanted to compete with women for service sector jobs, having whiter skin could increase their chances of being selected. It could also be an advantage in dating, as lighter skin was associated with wealth and upward mobility.

Changing representations of masculinity in popular youth culture have also affected male skin-lightening practices. Non-heteronormative men are popular presenters and actors on Filipino TV shows and series, and South Korean TV dramas show androgynous men portraying feminine beauty and tenderness. These cultural representations have paved the way for men to care more about their skin and appearance (Lasco and Hardon 2019). According to industry reports, skin-lightening products for men have achieved "robust penetration" (Global Industry Analysis 2018). The advertisements below reflect the changing times (Fig. 5.7).

Glutamax is heavily advertised on billboards and in the mass media for its whitening effects, and glutathione, its key ingredient, is registered in the Philippines as a food supplement. It is an antioxidant that plays a role in a range of cellular processes in humans. It can convert melanin to

Fig. 5.7 Advertisements of whitening products for Filipino men. Note how GlutaMAX targets both gay men and apparently heterosexual sportsmen, while Pond's Men appeals to men who aspire to join the middle class (*Source* Photo taken from Lasco and Hardon [2019])

a lighter color, which is how it changes skin tones. Toward the end of our fieldwork in 2018 we noticed new clinics offering glutathione injections and drips. The Philippines Food and Drug Authority (PFDA) was alerted about this new trend and issued a statement in 2019 to the general public, stating that there had been no published clinical trials to evaluate the use of injectable glutathione for skin lightening, and that the PFDA had therefore not approved any injectable product for this indication. The statement also warned that side effects from injectable glutathione for skin lightening include toxic effects on the liver, kidneys, and nervous system; and that glutathione affects the production of melanin, which raises concerns about the long-term risk of skin cancer (PFDA 2019).

Advertising strategies for skin-whitening creams and washes feed into and reinforce these new aspirations among young men to lighten their skin. They present the use of skin whiteners as "solutions to gender and class-based 'status problems'" (Atkinson 2007, p. 170). The ad for Belo Men Whitening Body Bar—"10% lighter, 100% more social: a little whitening makes a big difference"—for example, feeds into worries about finding a job and promises its users upward social mobility (Lasco and Hardon 2019), see Fig. 5.8.

Very popular, as well, were masculine facial washes, which promise deep cleaning, acne control, and "active whitening." These facial washes are sold in black sachets, in small neighborhood stores, making them accessible to men with little money. Capsules and injections containing glutathione are more upmarket forms of whitening. The advertisements and packages of skin-whitening products for men both reflect and reinforce prevailing gender identities and skin ideals, while also indexing that light skin is associated with good jobs (Lasco and Hardon 2019). We noticed that in Manila, the male students from high-income households

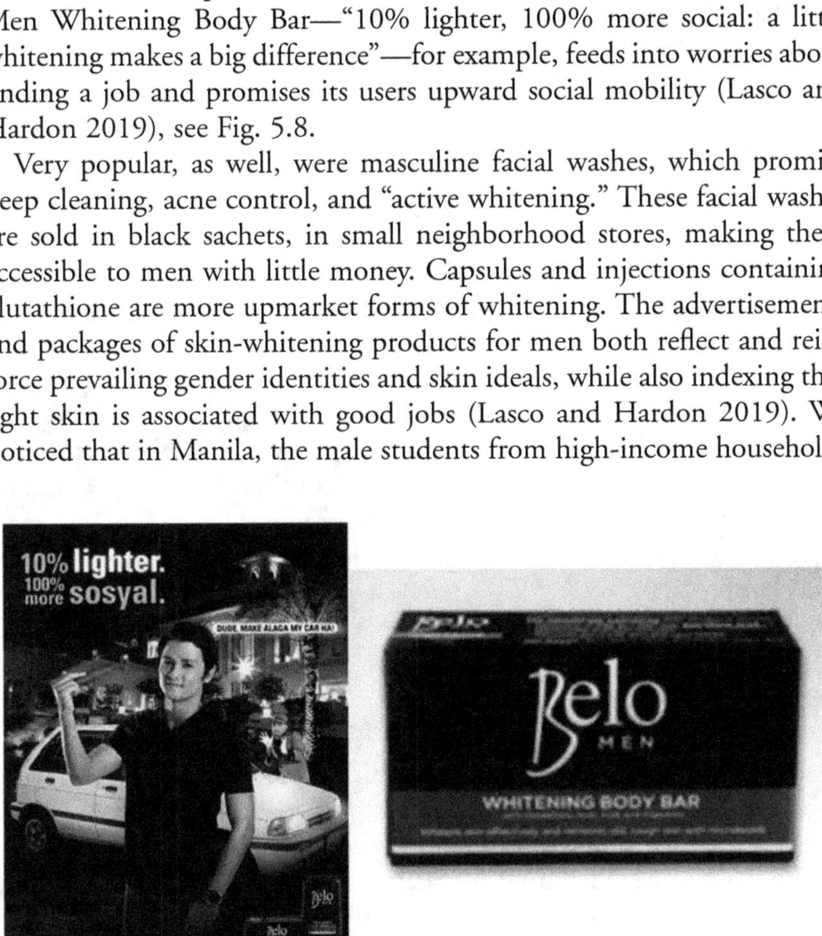

Fig. 5.8 "10% lighter and 100% more social," with Belo Men Whitening Body Bar (*Source* Photo by Gideon Lasco, September 2018, the Philippines)

did not see a need to lighten their skin. They expected to find a job easily or knew they could rely on their families, but those with a poorer starting position in life were reluctantly experimenting with ways to lighten their skin.

Take, for example, this exchange between Karl, a 17-year-old high school student, and Gideon Lasco, who conducted ethnographic research in Quezon City:

> *Karl*: Some jobs won't accept you if you are dark-skinned.
> *Gideon*: What kind of jobs?
> *Karl*: Many—they just don't accept dark-skinned applicants.
> *Gideon*: So, you know anyone who wasn't accepted because he was dark?
> *Karl*: Well, they wouldn't say that they rejected you because of the color of your skin, they just won't contact you again, and they will prefer the others. They will just tell you that the position has been taken and they will call you back [if they still want you] (Lasco and Hardon 2019, pp. 9–10).

Cyrus, a 19-year-old living in university housing, told us about his peers: "They do [skin-lightening practices] very late at night, around 1 to 2 AM, when no one's watching." He continued: "In the common shower room, I see all kinds of whitening products like Kojic Acid soap, papaya soaps, glutathione creams, even lotions and face-masks" (Lasco and Hardon 2019, p. 1).

Celebrating Skin Diversity

To counter the culture cycle through which the notion that having white skin equals intelligence, beauty, and wealth is perpetuated, we sought out ways to celebrate skin diversity. We noted counter-discourses emerging in popular culture, including magazines that showed celebrities seeking to darker skin by tanning and showing off their bikini lines. And they are present in the lyrics of a Filipina American rapper named Ruby Ibarra, who migrated to the United States with her family when she was still a child in 1991. Her lyrics reflect on her mixed identity, experiences, and struggles, and tells stories of racial discrimination and colorism, as well as her pride in being a woman. For her album *Us*, Ibarra gathered a group of female artists, who were proud of their roots, and declared their unique heritage as they transitioned through life-stages and lived in different places (Salanga 2018). In the title song, Ibarra calls on her Filipino peers to resist hegemony: "Island woman rise, *walang makakatigil* [nothing can stop you]. Brown, brown woman, rise, *alamin ang yung ugat* [know your roots]."

To contribute to this emerging trend, the youth ethnographers worked with art students and resident artists at the University of the Philippines to produce a set of multimedia translations. One of these translations was the *Kataw(h)an* exhibit, the name of which combines the words for "body" (*katawan*) and "stories" (*katawhan*), and which was intended to celebrate body narratives and skin tone diversity in the Philippines (UP Diliman Information Office 2018). At the entrance to the exhibit was a gallery called "Subconscious Substance." It had shelves of popular skin products (as in a small grocery shop), which, instead of showing their brands, featured the back of the products, showing their long lists of chemical contents. Visitors to the exhibit recognized their brands from the shape and color or the containers, but were drawn to inspect the chemical lists, which many had never previously scrutinized (Fig. 5.9).

The gallery was explained in a panel with the following text that was written by the team of arts student which designed the gallery:

> From the visible areas of the body to its hidden parts, we consume all substances to enhance our appearance, improve our health and ultimately feel good about ourselves. We apply, rub, spray and even ingest these chemicals in order to maintain what we believe is a good sense of hygiene and to satisfy the criteria of our concept of the ideal body. We consume most of the products that we patronize due to the influence of peers and the testimonies of people who have undergone the process of maintaining their look and their lives. We place our faith the in the products with carefully phrased taglines, sometimes even disregarding the chemicals that we put on our hair, face, genitals, skin and even let flow in our blood-stream. This gallery is a collection of the products used by actual people who believe in these products' providence in realizing and preserving their notions of beauty. (UP Diliman Information Office 2018)

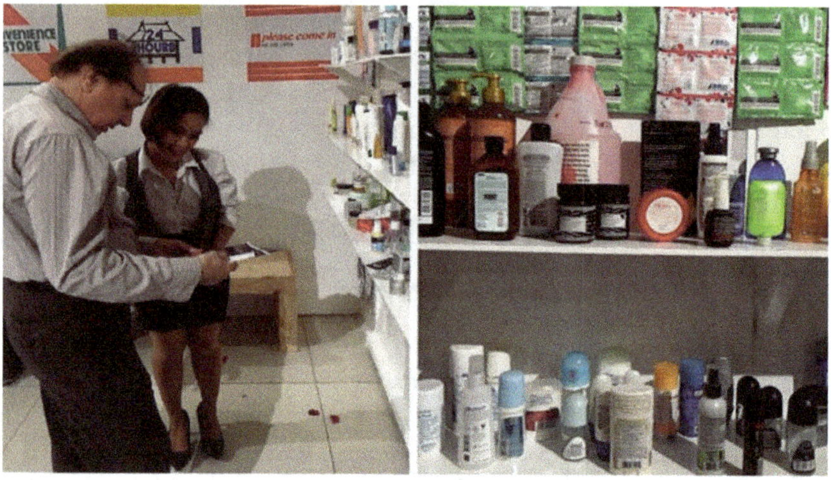

Fig. 5.9 Picture of one of the panels in the *Kata(h)wan* exhibit, where a makeshift pharmacy presented skin-whitening products with their lists of chemical contents facing customers, rather than the brand names (*Source* Photos by Anita Hardon, January 2018, the Philippines)

Another visual arts project, which also culminated in an exhibit at the University of the Philippines, was designed to celebrate Filipino heritage and cultural diversity. The multidisciplinary project became a collaboration among geneticists, social scientists, and artists, who together explored what it is to be Filipino in the contemporary Philippines. An animated video in the Stasis and Mobility exhibit, designed by Christian Paolo Bautista, told the story of early Austronesians whose seafaring technology brought them to and from the archipelago as they moved throughout the Pacific, centering the Philippines as an important hub in exchange of goods and knowledge (Fig. 5.10).

The exhibit included an installation by visual artist Aidan Blaise Zamora, entitled the "*Citizen's Gallery*" which used several hundred found or directly sourced family photos from University of the Philippines students. The photos were strategically hung to represent the shape of a sailing ship (mirroring the sailboat in the image below), yet viewed up close, distinctive facial features of people and families illustrated the diversity of a nation whose citizens have mixed ancestry.

Fig. 5.10 Peopling of the Philippines, reproduced with permission from Stasis and Mobility exhibit "*Nasa Dugo Natin 'Yan*?!" (Tiatco 2018)

The contemporary migratory flows of people through the Philippines has added several sociocultural identifying markers to the story of the archipelago's peopling: "mestiza, mestisaje and peninsulares during the Spanish colonial era; Amerasian, amboy, and tisoy during the American colonial period; and the current waves of Fil-Am, Fil-European, Kopinoy, and Japinoy" (Fig. 5.11).

Fig. 5.11 Citizens Gallery, photo installation from Stasis and Mobility exhibit (*Source* Photos taken by Andie Thompson, October 2018, the Philippines)

Finally, we worked with young filmmakers to produce two mini-documentaries (*Fair and Flawless* and *Natural Lang*) that examined skin-whitening practices in Manila, and contrasted these with the embrace of brown skin in a surfing community in the south of the Philippines. *Natural Lang* shows female surfers, who did not lighten their skin, because doing so would make surfing impossible: they need melanin to protect them from the sun. ChemicalYouth presented their point of view—as women who are proud to be brown—in a 15-minute documentary accessible on Vimeo (Op den Kamp and Sanchez 2014) (Fig. 5.12).

Fig. 5.12 Proud to be brown: Surfer women in Siargao Island, Philippines (*Source* Screenshot by Anita Hardon January, 2018 from *Natural Lang* [mini-documentary] by Op den Kamp and Sanchez [2014])

In Conclusion

This chapter examined the interpersonal dynamics and institutional policies that perpetuate colorism in the service sector, attending to the highly material work undertaken by service sector workers in order to "do" the white skin that their employers expect of them. Gender shapes these practices, as we saw with the young men in the Philippines who are competing with women for service sector jobs, which has led them to embrace skin whiteners just as their female peers do. Having light skin takes on a specific value in interactions in the service sector, where lighter skin can attract clients and thus have economic value. We show how having light skin does increase one's chance of getting a job in malls in the Philippines; this form of institutional colorism contributes to the precariousness of youth people who are not born with light skin. But the discriminatory work policies, and the selling and marketing of skin-whitening products by personal care companies are not just harmful because they perpetuate a culture cycle (Markus and Conner 2013) that privileges having white skin: they are also harmful because many skin-whitening products contain toxic chemicals, which can disfigure those who use them.

The production of the multimedia exhibits and mini-documentary created experimental spaces in which to resist hegemonic notions that equate white skin with intelligence, beauty, and wealth; in the process, values attached to skin colors are re-imagined. But the impact of these cultural expressions is limited in countries with retail markets that are saturated with skin-whitening creams, scrubs, and soaps, and media landscapes that amplify the idea that fair skin is better. To counter the culture cycle that perpetuates white privilege, we believe that personal care companies should stop producing and marketing skin-whitening creams, scrubs, soaps, and washes; governments should regulate the colorist advertising of such products; and occupational health policies should impose sanctions against colorist hiring and human resource strategies. Perhaps a global treaty, similar to the one adopted for tobacco, is needed. The harms caused by skin-whitening products are symbolic and social, as well as economic and biomedical. They channel youths' scarce resources away from basic needs to unnecessary cosmetic practices that require multiple products and applications. They also cause harm because they reinforce colorism, which disadvantages youth with darker skin. Moreover, they push young people into using products that can cause harm, further increasing inequalities.

While finalizing this chapter for publication amid the June 2020 global protests against racial injustice, I was sent a press release in which Unilever (the manufacturer of Pond's skin-lightening cream mentioned in this chapter) announced that it will remove the words "fair/fairness," "white/whitening," and "light/lightening" from its products, packaging, and communications. Sunny Jain, president of Beauty & Personal Care, says this change is being made because the company is "fully committed to having a global portfolio of skin care brands that is inclusive and cares for all skin tones" (Unilever 2020, p. 1). Activists, however, insist that rebranding products are just a start. Much more is needed to address the mental and emotional damage done by colorism (Berger 2020).

ChemicalYouth Ethnographers

Efenita (nickname Mai) Taqueban is an Assistant Professor in Social Anthropology at the University of the Philippines. She teaches social anthropology, with interests in gender, global political economy, and social suffering. Her master's thesis drew from the stories of induced abortion by mothers from an urban poor community in Manila. She received her Ph.D. from the University of Amsterdam, where she studied young women and their cosmetic and skin-whitening practices in a swiftly urbanizing southern Philippine boomtown. She also serves as a legal advocate (Fig. 5.13).

Fig. 5.13 Efenita Taqueban

Gideon Lasco is a physician and medical anthropologist. He obtained his Ph.D. from the University of Amsterdam as a member of the ChemicalYouth project and his M.D. from the University of the Philippines, where he currently teaches anthropology. His research includes the chemical practices of young people, the meanings of human height, the politics of health care, and the lived realities of the Philippine "drug war." A Palanca-winning essayist, he maintains a weekly column in the *Philippine Daily Inquirer*, where he writes about health, culture, and society (Fig. 5.14).

Fig. 5.14 Gideon Lasco

Alvie Bergado Timbancaya was a researcher for the ChemicalYouth project at the Palawan Studies Center at Palawan State University and conducted fieldwork on gender identities and chemical use among sex workers and service sector workers in the Philippines.

Notes

1. Biocapital has been used in anthropological literature to describe how value is generated through the insertion of biological materials, such as stem cells and patented genes, into capitalist modes of production. For example

Rajan (2006) and Franklin (2003) argue that biocapital is accumulated by powerful actors in the global economy, including biochemical industries and bioresearch labs.

2. The Minamata Convention is an international treaty designed to prevent emissions of mercury into the environment, and to prevent people from suffering its toxic effects. This convention was approved by delegates representing close to 140 countries in October 2013 and entered into force in 2017. It is named after the Japanese city Minamata, which experienced a devastating incident of mercury poisoning.
3. The text of this advertisement was transcribed from a TV advertisement. The video of the advertisement is included in the mini-documentary *Natural Lang* (see Op den Kamp and Sanchez 2014). The advertisement was also aired in July 2009 in a NPR podcast "Skin whitening a global practice" https://www.npr.org/templates/story/story.php?storyId=106419771.
4. This is a fictitious name, to protect our informants who were engaged in activities that were illegal according to local Islamic laws.

References

Abrera, M. B. (2009). Seclusion and veiling of women: A historical and cultural approach. *Philippine Social Sciences Review, 60*(1), 34–56.

Atkinson, M. (2007). Playing with fire: Masculinity, health, and sports supplements. *Sociology of Sport Journal, 24*(2), 165–186. https://doi.org/10.1123/ssj.24.2.165.

Bergado Timbancaya, A. (2017). The use of chemical products by market vendors in Puerto Princesa, Palawan. In A. Hardon & M. L. Tan (Eds.), *Modernizing Frontier: Chemical transformations of young people's minds and bodies in Puerto Princesa* (pp. 81–88). Quezon City: University of the Philippines Diliman. https://pure.uva.nl/ws/files/47815148/Modernizing_Frontiers.pdf.

Berger, M. (2020). After protests, a Unilever skin cream popular in India will no longer promote a 'Fair & Lovely' look. *Washington Post*. https://www.washingtonpost.com/world/2020/06/25/after-protests-unilever-skin-cream-popular-india-will-no-longer-promote-fair-lovely-look/. Accessed June 25, 2020.

Chua, B.-H. (2000). Where got Japanese influence in Singapore! In J. Ben-Ari & E. Clammer (Eds.), *Japan in Singapore: Cultural Occurrences and cultural flows* (pp. 133–149). Surrey: Curzon Press.

Davis, M. (2004). The urbanization of empire: Megacities and the laws of chaos. *Social Text, 22*(4), 9–15. https://doi.org/10.1215/01642472-22-4_81-9.

Deacon, G. (2011). *There's lead in your lipstick: Toxins in our everyday body care and how to avoid them.* Toronto: Penguin Canada.

EcoWaste Coalition. (2011). *EcoWaste coalition finds mercury in skin whitening products, pushes crack down on dangerous cosmetics.* EcoWaste Coalition. http://www.ecowastecoalition.org/ecowaste-coalition-finds-mercury-in/. Accessed January 20, 2020.

Eder, J. F. (2006). Gender relations and household economic planning in the rural Philippines. *Journal of Southeast Asian Studies, 37*(3), 397–413. https://doi.org/10.1017/S0022463406000701.

Ellis, P. (dir.). (2019). *Toxic beauty.* Canada: Kew Media.

European Environmental Bureau. (2018). *Zero mercury working group: Mercury-added skin-lightening creams: Available, inexpensive and toxic.* European Environmental Bureau. https://eeb.org/library/mercury-added-skin-lightening-creams-available-inexpensive-and-toxic/. Accessed on January 20, 2020.

Farrugia, D. (2018). Youthfulness and immaterial labour in the new economy. *The Sociological Review, 66*(3), 511–526. https://doi.org/10.1177/0038026117731657.

Franklin, S. (2003). Ethical biocapital: New strategies of cell culture. In S. Franklin & M. Lock (Eds.), *Remaking life and death: Toward an anthropology of the biosciences* (pp. 97–128). Santa Fe, NM: School for Advanced Research Press.

Glenn, E. N. (2008). Yearning for lightness: Transnational circuits in the marketing and consumption of skin lighteners. *Gender and Society, 22*(3), 281–302. https://doi.org/10.1177/0891243208316089.

Global Industry Analysis. (2018). *Skin lighteners. Market analysis: Trends and forecasts.* Global Industry Analysis. https://www.strategyr.com/MCP-6140.asp. Accessed on January 3, 2020.

Hardon, A., & Idrus, I. (2015). Chemicals, biocapital and the everyday lives of sex workers and waitresses in South Sulawesi. In L. R. Bennett & S. G. Davies (Eds.), *Sex and sexualities in contemporary Indonesia: Sexual politics, health, diversity and representations* (pp. 129–147). Oxfordshire: Routledge UK.

Hardt, M., & Negri, A. (2000). *Empire*. Cambridge, MA: Harvard University Press.

Hochschild, A. R. (1983). *The managed heart commercialization of human feeling*. Berkeley: University of California Press.

Ladizinski, B., Mistry, N., & Kundu, R. V. (2011). Widespread use of toxic skin lightening compounds: Medical and psychosocial aspects. *Dermatologic Clinics, 29*(1), 111–123. https://doi.org/10.1016/j.det.2010.08.010.

Lan, P. (2001). The body as a contested terrain for labor control: Cosmetics retailers in department stores and direct selling. In R. Baldoz, C. Koeber, & P. Kraft (Eds.), *The critical study of work: Labor, technology, and global production* (pp. 83–105). Philadelphia: Temple University Press.

Lasco, G., & Hardon, A. P. (2019). Keeping up with the times: Skin-lightening practices among young men in the Philippines. *Culture, Health and Sexuality*, 1–16. https://doi.org/10.1080/13691058.2019.1671495.

Leidner, R. (1999). Emotional labor in service work. *The ANNALS of the American Academy of Political and Social Science, 561*(1), 81–95. https://doi.org/10.1177/000271629956100106.

Li, E. P. H., Min, H. J., Belk, R. W., Kimura, J., & Bahl, S. (2008). Skin lightening and beauty in four Asian cultures. *Advances in Consumer Research, 35*(January), 444–449.

Markus, H., & Conner, A. (2013). *Clash! 8 cultural conflicts that make us who we are*. New York: Penguin Books.

Maxi-Peel Skin Care. (2020). *Maxi-peel skin care advertisement*. Facebook. https://www.facebook.com/MaxiPeelSkinCare. Accessed on January 3, 2020.

Moya, P., & Markus, H. (2010). Doing race: An introduction. In P. Moya & H. Markus (Eds.), *Doing Race: 21 essays for the twenty-first century* (pp. 1–102). New York: Norton.

National Public Radio podcast. (2009). *Skin whitening a global pratice.* National Public Radio. https://www.npr.org/templates/story/story.php?storyId=106419771&t=1589894655575. Accessed on May 19, 2020.

Oksala, J. (2016). Affective labor and feminist politics. *Signs, 41*(2), 281–303. https://doi.org/10.1086/682920.

Op den Kamp, J., & Sanchez, G. (2014). *A look at skin-whitening: Natural Lang*. The Philippines. https://vimeo.com/110724981.

Philippines Food and Drug Administration. (2019). *PFDA Advisory 2019-182. Unsafe use of Glutathione as skin lightening agent*. Philippines Food and Drug Administration. https://www.fda.gov.ph/?s=glutathione+injection. Accessed on May 19, 2020.

Philippines Statistics Authority. (2013). *The Philippine Statistical Act of 2013*. Philippines Statistics Authority. https://psa.gov.ph/content/philippine-statistical-act-2013. Accessed on January 3, 2020.

Pingol, A. (2001). *Remaking masculinities*. Diliman, Quezon City: University of the Philippines Press.

Rabin, R., & Hsu, T. (2018). Johnson & Johnson feared baby powder's possible asbestos link for years. *New York Times*. https://www.nytimes.com/2018/12/14/business/baby-powder-asbestos-johnson-johnson.html. Accessed on January 3, 2020.

Reyes-Velarde, A. (2019). Woman hospitalized with mercury poisoning after using face cream from Mexico. *Los Angeles Times*. https://www.latimes.com/california/story/2019-09-13/woman-hospitalized-with-mercury-poisoning-after-using-face-cream-from-mexico. Accessed January 3, 2020.

Salanga, G. (2018). *Ruby ibarra: The battlecry of the modern Filipina warrior*. Vesti Conversations. https://www.vesticonversations.com/all/2018/8/8/ruby-ibarra-the-battlecry-of-the-modern-filipina-warrior. Accessed on January 8, 2020.

Saraswati, L. A. (2013). *Seeing beauty, sensing race in transnational Indonesia*. Honolulu: University of Hawai'i Press.

Sunder Rajan, K. (2006). *Biocapital: The constitution of postgenomic life*. Durham, NC: Duke University Press.

Taqueban, E. (2018a). *Armed with red lipstick*. Fieldsights, Cultural Anthropology. https://culanth.org/fieldsights/armed-with-red-lipstick.

Taqueban, E. (2018b). *Lipstick tales: Beauty and precarity in a southern Philippine boomtown* (Doctoral dissertation, Universiteit van Amsterdam, Anthropology department, Amsterdam). https://dare.uva.nl/search?identifier=d21c374b-f1f5-459d-a883-5c3e62330a99.

The Daily Posh. (2014). *SkinWhite launches the #betterme campaign*. The Daily Posh. https://www.thedailyposh.net/2014/12/skinwhite-launches-betterme-campaign.html. Accessed on January 8, 2020.

Thompson, L. (2013). Aesthetics and empire: The sense of feminine beauty in the making of the US imperial archipelago. *Culture & History Digital Journal, 2*(2), e027. https://doi.org/10.3989/chdj.2013.027.

Unilever. (2020). *Unilever evolves skin care portfolio to embarce a more inclusive visoin of beauty*. Uniever. https://www.unilever.com/news/press-releases/2020/unilever-evolves-skin-care-portfolio-to-embrace-a-more-inclusive-vision-of-beauty.html?utm_source=UT&utm_medium=Social&utm_campaign=AlwaysOn. Accessed on 26 June 2020.

UP Diliman Information Office. (2018). *Kat(h)awan: UP Diliman celebrates the Filipino body*. UP Diliman Information Office. https://upd.edu.ph/kathawan-up-diliman-celebrates-the-filipino-body/. Accessed January 3, 2020.

Vengill Gutierrez. (2012). *Lactacyd white intimate flash mob @food court festival mall Alanbang*. YouTube. https://www.youtube.com/watch?v=7t0G7lmcyIk. Accessed on January 3, 2020.

6

Chemicals and Night Workers

We have so many ethnographic stories to tell about how young people use chemicals for energy, so many, that I have had a hard time developing a structure for this chapter. Having just moved back from to the Netherlands from the United States because of the coronavirus pandemic, I'm also still a bit jetlagged. I need a coffee. Thinking this, I'm reminded of a conversation I had with one of the youth ethnographers, Daan Kamps, a student and DJ in the Amsterdam nightlife scene, which he studied for the ChemicalYouth project. A few years ago, we were having lunch to discuss his interviews and observations, and I had just returned from a fieldwork visit to the Philippines. "I need a coffee," I told him. I'm jetlagged. Having just completed a course on chronobiology to educate himself on the circadian rhythms of humans, he lectured me on the health risks of jetlag: it can impair cognition, concentration, and motor coordination as well as cause metabolic disorders, such as obesity and high blood pressure (Roenneberg 2012). I should walk outside in the sun, he tells me. Real sunlight helps.

Nightwork—meaning all jobs that are executed during nighttime—increased as cities became connected to electricity in the early twentieth century, and as economies became more connected globally through the internet. In the current "gig economy"—dominated by those jobs in which people are paid by the task, rather than receiving a fixed salary—work never stops. Part of this "performance" has to do with adapting to the different temporal demands of the labor market—in other words, the management of sleep and wakefulness. As Crary (2013, p. 17) notes, our modern economies "[undermine] distinction between day and night, between light and dark, and between action and repose ... the planet becomes re-imagined as a non-stop work site or an always open shopping mall of infinite choices, tasks, selections, and digression."

But working at night is not necessarily good for us. Melatonin, the hormone involved in the regulation of our biological clock, is released when we are exposed to daylight. Our bodies follow circadian rhythms of approximately 24-hour cycles, and as Kamps warned me, these rhythms have an impact on our mental and metabolic health (Roenneberg et al. 2003).

Humans have a long history using chemicals to tinker with our circadian rhythms, with caffeine being the most ubiquitous substance used to stay awake, one that is accepted globally as beneficial despite its addictive properties. Historians trace the use of coffee back to the fifth century, in the Sufi monasteries of Mocha, now known as Yemen (Weinberg and Bealer 2001). Caffeine stimulates the central nervous system by blocking the action of adenosine (which causes drowsiness) on its receptors. The popular food writer Pollan (2020), in a recent analysis of caffeine, suggests that without this substance the industrial revolution wouldn't have happened. Studies in sports medicine attest to caffeine's positive effects in adults, including increased endurance and strength, improved reaction time, and delayed fatigue (Graham 2001; Sökmen et al. 2008). Adverse effects of caffeine, if taken in high amounts, include disturbed sleep, increased blood pressure, and physical addiction. Caffeine is considered safe to ingest up to about 150 mg per day (or two cups of coffee).

In addition to caffeine, those working at night often resort to cocaine and amphetamines for stamina and to stay awake. The use of cocaine for endurance goes back to the Incas in Peru who for thousands of years have chewed coca leaves for this purpose. The alkaloid cocaine, derived from the plant, was only isolated in the mid-nineteenth century. Amphetamines were discovered shortly thereafter by chemists. In *On Speed* Rasmussen (2008) traces the history of this category of drugs, showing how early twentieth-century pharmacies in the United States sold invigorating tonics containing cocaine and nasal decongestants containing amphetamines. Its first major use was during World War II, when soldiers used it to boost their performance and alertness, and to suppress appetite (see also Braswell 2005; Rawson et al. 2006). In Japan, it was given to soldiers before they performed their "kamikaze" suicide bombing missions; in England, 73 million amphetamine tablets were made available to pilots so they would not fall asleep (Braswell 2005). Three years after the war, in 1948, the Japanese Ministry of Health prohibited the production of both tablet and powder form of methamphetamine. Similar moves were made in the United States but, interestingly, the medical establishment continued to defend its legal status and deny its addictive potential. It was only when its use grew further, and more evidence about its addictive potential came to light, that the United States finally passed the 1974 Drug Control Act (Rawson et al. 2006).

Nowadays cocaine is an illegal drug. Amphetamines are sold legally as prescription tablets for ADHD, while methamphetamine is an illegal drug, sold on the street as "crystal" and "ice," and consumed in many different ways: ingested pills, snorted powder, injected liquid, or smoked (Rawson et al. 2006). Like caffeine, cocaine and methamphetamines increase alertness, strength, and coordination, while also increasing blood pressure and stimulating the heart rate (Koob et al. 2004). Both drugs cause pupils to dilate, allowing more light in, which activates our daytime metabolism (Paul et al. 2009). The pharmacological actions of cocaine and methamphetamine differ: cocaine works fast and is quickly removed from the body, while methamphetamines have a much longer duration of action, making it harder to sleep after using them and increasing the risk of addiction. Cocaine prolongs dopamine action in nerve cells, by blocking dopamine reabsorption, while methamphetamines work by both blocking dopamine re-uptake and increasing its release, leading to higher concentrations of the neurotransmitter in cells, which can be toxic. Long-term adverse effects of methamphetamines include insomnia, confusion, memory loss, and psychiatric conditions such as psychosis (National Institute on Drug Abuse 2019).

Social scientists have pointed to the widespread use of caffeine-containing "energy drinks" and the off-label use of drugs indicated for attention deficit hyperactive disorder (ADHD), such as Ritalin and dexamphetamine, by students trying to increase their focus and attention when studying, and to stay up late when partying. But these studies generally focus on student populations. In this chapter, we present ethnographic insights on the use of various stimulants to stay awake and fight fatigue by workers in the nighttime leisure economy, the bartenders, DJs, sound technicians, photographers, and event organizers who must perform professionally during the night. We contrast the 24/7 chemical practices in Brooklyn and Amsterdam, two leisure industry sites in the global North, with the 24/7 chemical practices of low-income service sector and manual workers in our field sites in the global South: Puerto Princesa and Cagayan de Oro (the Philippines), and Makassar (Indonesia). Here the substances are not only used to stay awake, but also to endure heavy physical labor. We find that practices differ depending on the availability, marketing, and policing of the various legal and illegal stimulants, and that risks are shaped by the structure of everyday life, the rhythms of stimulant use, and workplace policies. We also show how—across the sites—users moderate intake in order to avoid adverse effects, including their negative influence on the quality of sleep, and how they mitigate such effects by using other substances, such as cannabis or alcohol, to calm down.

Staying Awake in the Leisure Industry

In Brooklyn and Amsterdam our youth ethnographers conducted focused research on the nighttime leisure industry, with Tait Mandler studying DIY queer parties in Brooklyn and Daan Kamps studying popular clubs in Amsterdam. In these field sites, event managers organize the artists, barkeepers provide drinks, DJs create music, and sound technicians fine tune it. Mandler and Kamps found that the workers in these entertainment spaces balanced their engagement in the party and staying fit for work. All moderated their alcohol intake and they took stimulants to stay alert till the end of the night. Mandler (2016) observes that work in these sites is an inherently contradictory activity. When working, they have to appear to be enjoying themselves; leisure activities themselves become work. Cocaine helps workers be productive and enjoy themselves in their nighttime jobs.

Our interlocutors in these two cities presented themselves as experienced moderators of circadian rhythms. They had developed personal strategies of stimulant use, aimed at generating the right amount of alertness, while also enabling pleasure at work. They scheduled their use around work and other responsibilities, monitored their dosage to ensure moderation, and took breaks from using when necessary. But all attested to the heavy toll that nightwork has on their bodies, especially if they combine nightwork with daytime jobs, or coursework, both of which require rapid transitions from night wakefulness to daytime alertness.

In Brooklyn, Mandler (2016, 2018) found that the most common chemicals used to stay awake during the night shift were energy drinks, cocaine, and the ADHD drug Adderall. Cocaine helped his interlocutors stay alert during shifts, while also engaging in the party, which was a challenge. Jett, a bartender, said that after working in a bar for around six months, he realized that everyone around him was sniffing cocaine all the time. Jett preferred energy drinks because they were free to employees in the establishment (which was sponsored by an energy drink manufacturer). Mandler (2018) also found that many night workers combined day and nighttime jobs. Joshua, a drag queen and visual artist, described how they (Joshua's preferred pronoun) managed working 20 hours in two days with only a few hours of sleep:

> That morning I go to work all day, so I'll have a coffee there. I get home around 6:30 pm or 7 pm. … [I] get to the club around 10:30 pm … and drink a big non-alcoholic drink to bookend the night with. Like

> seltzer and a fruit juice ... Then right around midnight I start drinking ... something like vodka with a fruit mixer. Throughout the night I'll probably have two and half of those. Maybe someone had coke and I've done a bump [small snort] or two. Around 3 am or 3:30 am I'll have left the club ... I'll sleep for three and half or four hours before I have to get up and go to work where I'll drink a little coffee. (Mandler 2018, p. 263)

Alice produced underground queer events in warehouses that usually started around 11 pm and continued well past 4 am. She also worked for a nightlife magazine and was active on social media, which has made her a popular party host. Alice explained that she did not really enjoy the nightlife culture and was mainly interested in her own friends. However, her job was to promote events as if they were going to make for the best night ever. She didn't drink much at these parties, but made sure to hold a drink; this made her feel as if she was engaged in the party, and dissuaded people from asking why she was not drinking. If she consumed alcohol, she said, she could not produce the parties well, and she would be tired before they were over. Cocaine, in contrast, helped her be more assertive, "but sometimes this also [led] her to stand on the stage at the end of a party and watch the crowd dance to the final songs in awe" (Mandler 2018, p. 2).

For Cassandra, and many other nightlife workers, the use of cocaine was not the event of the night. They moderated use, spacing and sharing it, as Dan explains:

> I take smaller bumps, I try not to do a whole line. I space it out throughout the night. Also sharing kind of helps. If I'm going to do some and I have someone else to do it with, it sort of tricks me. (Mandler 2016, p. 269)

Val explained that he preferred cocaine because it:

> doesn't really affect my ability to judge ... so that's sort of the stimulant choice. I don't like coffee; it wrecks my stomach. I hate things like Adderall, they're too strong. Cocaine is light and it can keep me awake and after I get home I'll fall asleep maybe an hour later. (Mandler 2016, p. 263)

Moderating their substance use was a common goal among these nightlife workers. They monitored the chemical use of their friends, specifically checking if it negatively affected their ability to function on the job or socially; and used the same criteria to evaluate their own chemical practice. Some limited themselves to a few drinks or bumps. Even so, at times, they felt that they had gone too far, at which point they took a break from using a specific drug, or even all chemicals (Mandler 2016).

Kamps interviewed 24 people who work in Amsterdam clubs. He recorded systematically which stimulants they used to stay alert and awake at work. Out of the 24 participants, 23 drank energy drinks and/or Coca Cola, 16 consumed amphetamines (including ADHD drugs), and 15 used cocaine. As was the case in Brooklyn, the workers he spoke with asserted that they had developed personal strategies to stay awake and alert on the job. Many smoked cigarettes and drank alcohol; the two go well together, they said. Alcohol helped them feel more engaged with and connected to the clients at the clubs. But they felt compelled to moderate their alcohol consumption so as not to become too drunk to work.

Event organizers and venue programmers are responsible for the overall success of the party. They pick up the DJs, manage the guest list, decorate the venue, and are present for the sound check. They feel responsible for getting the dance floor filled and creating the euphoric ambience. Maarten, a venue manager used cocaine to stay alert and be sociable when preparing for events and to tune in with the atmosphere of the party. Meike, an event organizer and hostess, said she often worked long, 10-hour shifts, till 8 am the next morning. Besides taking smoking breaks, she often drank Club Mate, which she combined with vodka. Club Mate is an energy drink with 50 mg caffeine per 250 ml and low sugar content (less sugar than Red Bull). Nadine, too, who worked as a barkeeper, used cocaine for energy, alertness, and confidence.

DJs need to keep the crowd going through the night. Sander, a well-known DJ, talked about using ADHD drugs to keep up the vibe. His girlfriend had been diagnosed with ADHD and prescribed dexamphetamine. Before he left for work in the evening, Sander usually took two 20 mg tablets of dexamphetamine, and then took another dose if he felt tired during the night. Sander said that dextroamphetamine worked well: it kept him alert, without anyone noticing that he had taken drugs. The DJs interviewed by Kamps all attested to the highly desirable effects of amphetamines. The substances create very energetic states of being that contribute to the party atmosphere. The sound technician makes sure the music reaches the audience as well as possible. "Being alert and focused—paying continuous attention to sound levels, depth, clarity, and space—is of utmost importance, and the longer the event lasts, the greater the challenge," explained one sound tech (Kamps and Hymans forthcoming, 2020, p. 10). Another said that he used Red Bull in the early hours of the morning (around 3 am), when he became unable to hear certain frequencies.

Kamps also talked with night workers about what they did to catch some sleep after work, especially after using amphetamines (the effects can last for around 8–12 hours, see Keogh 2010). His informants told him that, to ensure sleep, they stopped taking amphetamines around 2–3 am and smoked some cannabis once they got home. Others used melatonin to reset their biological clocks. But other factors also could keep them awake. If a performance or event went particularly well, the excitement could still be palpable after returning home. For the event organizers, whether money was made or lost greatly affected their state of being; returning home, they often sat on the couch, contemplating, with images of the evening going through their heads, what went well and what went wrong. These emotions, together with the rhythm of their internal body clocks and the chemical stimulants still coursing through their bodies, made it hard to fall asleep, even if they actually felt tired. Andy explained that one could be exhausted yet unable to fall asleep:

> You might lay in bed at seven in the morning, be half asleep for three hours and then be fully awake again around eleven." He would then get out of bed. Bart described the same phenomenon: "Your body is fully awake but your brain is lagging behind." (Kamps and Hymans forthcoming, 2020, p. 11)

Our fieldwork in leisure sites in Amsterdam and Brooklyn showed that these nightlife workers were cautious users of stimulants, striving to meet the various demands of their nighttime work. Many used cocaine, which has as an advantage that its effect fades fast, allowing the workers to sleep when they get home. But amphetamines, in the form of ADHD drugs or speed, were also used often, and these made sleeping harder. In addition, several workers managed their stamina with energy drinks, which generally contain around 50 mg of caffeine per 250 ml (similar to a cup of coffee).

While moderating their stimulant use, and complementing it with other substances such as cannabis and melatonin to sleep, many of the interlocutors admitted to feeling burned out over time, which they attributed not only to their substance use but also simply to the lack of daylight in their lives.

Long Working Hours in Physically Demanding Work

In the Philippines and Indonesia our focused ethnographies examined how young people used stimulants to have energy and strength enough to conduct physically challenging work, laboring long hours as porters, construction workers, and security guards. The use of amphetamines as fuel for labor in Asia has been observed by Sherman and colleagues (2008), who describe how methamphetamines—called *yaba* (crazy drugs) in its pill form in Thailand, and *shabu* in its powder form (also known as crystal meth) in Indonesia and the Philippines—entered the market in the 1990s to enhance performance in physically demanding roles. A young construction worker in Thailand reports:

> I felt I could work more and earn more as well... When we delivered cement powder, we got 400 baht for one trailer... If we didn't take *yaba* we would be able to deliver only one or two trailers. But when we took *yaba* we became diligent. (Sherman et al. 2008, p. 42)

Participating in the ChemicalYouth project, Lasco examined the use of *shabu* among unemployed young men hustling for work in a Philippines harbor city. They worked as *tambays* (stand-by) porters in the harbor, vendors to the bus passengers that frequent the port, and occasionally at night as sex workers. Their work comprised of long hours hanging around till boats and buses arrived. Some of them combined working as a porter with selling freshly roasted peanuts and drinks to bus passengers. Lasco learned that their work as street vendors also, ocassionally, involved stealing mobile phones from travelers, joining in "car-napping operations," and engaging in sex work.

Lasco described how his informants killed time while "standing by" by smoking cigarettes, as many as 10–20 cigarettes a day. *Shabu*, they asserted, provided them with confidence and stamina, and reduced their inhibitions, allowing them to engage in a multitude of services. One told Lasco (2014), "We are not educated and we have nothing. Where will we get the confidence to talk to others, if not from *shabu*?" (p. 785). Young men were initiated into *shabu* inhaling by their *barkada*, which is both a social and economic group consisting of peers. The cost of one small sachet of *shabu*, which can be used by three people, is 500 pesos (US $12.5); the paraphernalia, consisting of three bits of aluminum foil and a lighter to heat the substance, was also shared. Everyone in a *barkada* uses *shabu*, which expresses loyalty, thereby forging social bonding in the group. "Scoring" sessions take place in ordinary port houses called "*pwesto*" (from the Spanish "*puesto*," or place). The owner of the *pwesto* collects 20 pesos from the users, in exchange for providing them with the security of being in a private home where the substance can be used away from the gaze of the police. The young men said that, after an immediate euphoria, they experience a sustained effect of being "*kalmado*" (calm) and "*ganado*" (enthusiastic). They said that using *shabu* boosted their skills, abilities, and industriousness. Like Kamps's informants in Amsterdam, they treated any insomnia caused by their *shabu* use with cannabis and Red Horse beer, which they routinely used to fall asleep. Several evenings a week, the *barkadas* gathered at night to drink alcohol together (*inuman*); this was leisure time. The costs for these evenings

Table 6.1 Weekly drug expenses vs. weekly income of seven drug users (in Philippines pesos; 50 pesos equals US $1) (Lasco 2013, p. 81)

Weekly expenses	1	2	3	4	5	6	7
Shabu	1400	1400	1400	1000	1400	600	800
Cannabis	140	140	100	100	40	60	60
Cigarettes	262	262	175	175	175	175	150
Alcohol	280	280	200	280	280	280	200
Total	2082	2082	1875	1555	1455	1090	1210
Weekly income	1050	1050	1400	1400	1050	1050	1050

were shared by the whole *barkada*, unless someone was celebrating his birthday, in which case, the celebrant was expected to foot the bill. In the *inuman*, Red Horse often gave way to harder alcohol, such as a brandy called "Empi Light" (Emperador Light, 30% alcohol).

Alerted to the precariousness of his interlocutors' lives, Lasco (2013) calculated how much they spent using multiple substances, as well as how much they earned from various sources. The results are presented in the Table 6.1. His findings reveal that the substances cost more than what was actually earned; the shortfall was met by occasionally doing sex work (earning around 500 pesos for oral sex services provided to gay men, and more if anal sex is done), or stealing and selling a mobile phone.

Lasco writes that, while most of his informants used *shabu*, there were also a few young men who resisted doing so. One of them explained that users often lost the ability to distinguish between using in order to work, and working in order to use (Lasco 2013). The users asserted that the greatest danger in using *shabu* was its illegality, speaking of weekly raids, youths getting jailed, and worries about their safety. They nevertheless perceived the benefits to outweigh the costs. In publishing this case study, Lasco decided to not publish the name of the city where he did fieldwork, and we followed his example in this book, worrying that Philippine drug authorities might crack down on the young men working in the harbor. Little did Lasco know that just a year later Rodrigo Duterte would be elected president, and that he would declare a war on *shabu*, giving local police officers the green light to shoot any drug user without due process.

Another focused ethnography in the Philippines was conducted by Leo Diego, who examined stimulant use among 21 security guards in Puerto Princesa, Palawan (Diego 2017). Providing security is the most common job for young men in the Philippines, and security guards are an omnipresent feature of contemporary Philippine society, seen everywhere, in schools, malls, banks, and other big establishments where people frequent. Diego observed that being alert during their long shifts was a key challenge for these workers, and that they relied on energy drinks as the main substance they use to help stay awake.

The majority of the participants entered the security industry because of their lack of college degrees; most of them were high school graduates. They worked at pawnshops, banks, department stores, hotels, and schools. Work circumstances differed at these sites. The pawnshops demanded a high level of security, as money was exchanged there and had to be protected. Security guards in pawnshops were bound to follow a no-sitting policy while on duty. Thus, alertness was crucial: as guards, they had to check the body language of customers, distribute forms to be filled out, and make sure that no trouble transpired. Banks also hired security guards for the same reason—money matters. Working in a bank was full of tension, especially for guards who drove armored vans. With their lives at stake, guards had to pay utmost attention to every movement in their surroundings. On the university campus, the work of security guards was very different. With its almost 20,000 students, Palawan State University was the largest tertiary educational institution in the province, and security guards were needed to check that students entering the premises had proper identification: no ID, no entry.

In general, the work of security guards is undervalued in the Philippines, with some seeing it as a job for lazy people. Many people believe that security guards just stand there, not thinking, all day at their posts. For example, Roland, a security guard who worked at a bank, always heard that being a security guard was a job for a bystander, because guards not only just stand and walk at their posts, but can also sleep if no one is watching. Roland explained that, because of this misperception, some people from his neighborhood said that when you applied for a security job, it must be your last choice. But Ric, a security guard at a mall, defended his work: guards must be conscious of everything that is happening in their vicinity at all times. They must constantly be reading the body language and facial expressions of the people around them. Their minds must always be aware of what is to be done in case of unexpected trouble. They must be observant at all times. The greatest challenge reported by security guards was maintaining their alertness and fighting off sleep. This challenge had to do with the long and irregular working hours assigned to security guards. Three guards often shared a single post; each of them had to have a shift of eight consecutive hours, and their work schedules could change with little or no notice.

Despite the stress involved, being a security guard was not a well-paid job. Most security guards in Puerto Princesa earned the minimum wage of US \$5 per day, or approximately US \$140 per month. Many paid rent to a boarding house, which in Puerto Princesa cost at least US \$30–60 a month, excluding water and electricity. Most guards commuted to work (spending US \$0.40 daily for fare) and bought their lunch (US \$1). Most of our interlocutors also supported families and other dependents, and struggled in the face of the rising costs of basic necessities, such as rice, fish, and gasoline. Many fell into debt, and lived in a perpetual struggle to pay their bills and promissory notes. The precarious economic situation of most security guards meant that they depended on keeping their jobs, and any absence from work meant that they lost pay. Furthermore, many feared being caught sleeping on the job, which could result in an instant dismissal. Many security guards thus resorted to chemical stimulants, which they called "*pampa*-alert," their term for something that can be used to foster alertness.

Generally, "to be alert" meant being aware of anything in the vicinity. Troubles and crimes could come along at any time. In this manner, the guards' lives were at risk, as they were expected to protect people and the establishment for which they are responsible. Most security guards were men, and most were on duty at night. Some security agencies told us that female guards were not permitted to work the night shift, because, they said, female guards were not on par with male guards in terms of alertness and self-defense. But still, female guards were often found at the entrances of department stores and malls, to name a few.

Fourteen of the security guards interviewed by Diego drank instant coffee to keep themselves awake (Nescafe 3-in-1, Great Taste, and Kopiko Brown are popular; all contain large amounts of sugar), and 12 of them also drank energy drinks during their shifts, see Table 6.2.

Table 6.2 Kinds of stimulants used by security guards in Puerto Princesa (N = 16)

Name	Post	Sex	Energy Drink	Cigarette	Coffee
Joker	Bank	Male	Cobra energy drink during night duty	Fortune White cigarettes, 1 pack per week	Nescafe 3-in-1 coffee
Jerry	Bank	Male	Cobra on duty	Nonsmoker	Great Taste coffee (no side effects)
Mantal	Bank	Male	Cobra almost every day	Nonsmoker	Great Taste (no side effects)
Roland	Bank	Male	Not using energy drinks	2 packs per day	Nescafe 3-in-1
Ric	Department store	Male	Cobra, Sting, Red Bull, Extra Joss every week	2 packs of Fortune every other day	Kopiko Brown coffee every day
Bryan	Department store	Male	Cobra during the day	Nonsmoker	Nescafe 3-in-1, thrice a day
Netz	Department store	Female	Cobra during the day	2 cigarettes per day	Great Taste twice a day
Ged	Hotel	Male	Not using energy drinks	Nonsmoker	Kopiko Brown twice a day
Charm	University	Female	Cobra during night duty	Nonsmoker	Creamy latte-flavored coffee twice a day
Ems	University	Female	Cobra during day shift	Nonsmoker	San Miguel coffee twice a day
Salad	University	Female	Cobra during night duty	2 cigarettes per day	Great Taste twice a day
Ann	University	Female	Cobra during the day	Nonsmoker	Great Taste every morning
Jacky	Mall	Female	Not using energy drinks	Nonsmoker	Kopiko Brown every morning
Vicky	Mall	Female	Not using energy drinks	Half-pack a day	Great Taste every morning before duty
Allan	Pawnshop	Male	Cobra every other night	Winston, 3 cigarettes a day	Great Taste

(continued)

Table 6.2 (continued)

Name	Post	Sex	Energy Drink	Cigarette	Coffee
Mag'z	Pawnshop	Male	Cobra every night duty	Nonsmoker	Not drinking coffee

Table 6.2 shows the popularity of the Cobra energy drink, which was used by 12 of the 16 informants. Five of the Cobra drinkers specified that they used the energy drink during night shifts. It also shows that half the informants did not smoke cigarettes; the reason for this is the strict anti-smoking policy in Puerto Princesa, where smoking is only allowed in designated areas.

A 350 ml bottle of Cobra costs US $0.40 and contains 134 mg caffeine (the same amount as two cups of coffee; this is about double the content of the energy drinks sold in Amsterdam). It also contains B vitamins, ginseng, and sugar. Cobra is the market leader in the energy drinks segment of the beverages market in the Philippines, accounting for 74% of sales (Euromonitor International 2020). The brand's bottles are sold in *sari-sari* stores (informal neighborhood shops) and the brand is heavily advertised on TV and through Twitter, Facebook, and YouTube. Everyone in the Philippines knows Cobra's slogans: "*May Laban Ka*" (you're up against it) and "*Tunay na Lakas*" (full of strength). Its popularity is attributed to the fact that it is promoted by the award-winning Filipino actor Coco Martin (the attractive muscular guy on the left in below advertisement) (Fig. 6.1).

See Fig. 6.2, for an image of a typical neighborhood outlet for Cobra; notice how Cobra is placed prominently in the store along with Coca Cola, Sprite, and Fortune cigarettes.

Despite the popularity of this energy drink, users' experiences are mixed. Bryan, a 25-year-old security guard at a department store, told us that sometimes when he uses Cobra he felt wide awake, but there were also times when he couldn't help falling asleep. Charm, a female guard at a university, said that Cobra caused her to suffer a urinary tract infection. When she stopped using Cobra, she just walked around her post in order to avoid feeling sleepy while on duty.

Fig. 6.1 Screenshot of Cobra advertisement (*Source* Photo taken by Anita Hardon, 2019, the Netherlands)

Fig. 6.2 *Sari-sari* store selling bottles of Cobra (yellow liquid toward the front of the window) (*Source* Photo taken by Anita Hardon, March 2014, the Philippines)

Only a few of the security guards admitted to using *shabu* to stay alert during the night shift, perhaps because Puerto Princesa has a zero tolerance policy for drug use. One of the guards, Joker, told us of how he used *shabu* when he needed to serve as a shift reliever, meaning he had to be at his post almost 22 hours in a row. He also shared that there was a popular drug called Fly High that could also be used to stay alert and was also effective in increasing stamina during sexual intercourse. He said that this drug was a combination of methamphetamine, Viagra, and ecstasy, and could be bought for around US $30–60 per tablet. When asked about the effect of the drug, Joker responded, “For three to four days you will not feel hungry, your being awake is continuous, your awareness will be active, you are unstoppable, and you have more stamina for sex” (Diego 2017, p. 75).

For our final case study, we turn to the use of stimulants by two categories of low-income workers: porters and construction workers in Makassar, Indonesia. This research was carried out by Amalia Anwar (2017) in infrastructure development locations (such as housing and offices) that employed construction workers and in the seaport with dockworkers. The manual laborers involved in this study were 30 construction workers (15 men and 15 women) and 20 dockworkers (all men), aged between 17 and 24 years (Fig. 6.3).

Energy drinks, which are classified as “health drinks” in Indonesia, were the most commonly used stimulants in these fieldwork sites. Kuku Bima and Extra Joss are popular local brands, sold in sachets (US

Fig. 6.3 Dock workers buying an energy drink from a local vendor—break time (*Source* Photos taken by Sari Damar Ratri, October 2015, Indonesia)

$0.06/sachet) in groceries and informal stalls, and mixed with water by vendors (as illustrated in Fig. 6.2). Advertisements for such drinks in various print and electronic media are plentiful and varied, with provocative slogans such as "*lelaki pemberani*" (brave man), "*jiwa laki bukan pengecut*" (men's souls not cowardly), and "Extra Joss, perfect goal" (aired during the world football championships) that stimulate men to buy and consume them. The sachets are also marketed by sales promotion girls, see Fig. 6.4.

The ad for KukuBima Ener-G drink features Ade Rai, an athlete and artist, and shows a picture of his muscular body, evoking strength and vitality, accompanied by a picture of ginseng, which is known for its virility enhancement effects.

The slogans of such ads promote not only masculinity—for example, with slogans like these: (This is the King, Brave Man, Energy of the Brave, Stamina Plus Courage, For Men Trusted Men, Men's Souls are not Cowards); and strength (Restores Tired Stamina, Stamina for the

Fig. 6.4 Left: sales promotion girl selling a box of six sachets of Extra Joss for 5000 Rupiah (US $0.36) in the port of Makassar; across her breasts is printed the slogan *Laki minum* (male drink) (*Source* Photo taken by Anita Hardon, May 2014, Indonesia; right, screenshot of an advertisement for Extra Joss from the website Shopee with the slogan "Stamina plus *nyali*" [stamina plus courage] Shopee [2020].

Country, Fresh, Full of Energy, Real Energy)—but also competition (The Essence of Football, Secret of the Champions, Premier Energy Drink in the World).

Although advertising plays an important role in promoting the use of energy drinks, workers generally learned about energy drinks from their coworkers who first consumed them. Table 6.3 lists the contents of the energy drinks that were popular among manual laborers we spoke with. Note how all three of the popular brands contain 50 mg of caffeine per sachet along with ginseng, different kinds of vitamin B, flavors, and sweeteners (honey and/or sugar). The main difference is taste.

Limited rest periods and the heavy workload made it difficult for manual laborers to take a lunch break, so consuming energy drinks became a substitute for lunch. Surti (24-year-old construction worker), for example, felt full and energetic after consuming KukuBima Ener-G, even when she had not eaten. Ulla, a 24-year-old dockworker, admitted to frequently consuming KukuBima Ener-G (grape flavor) while resting in order to restore her stamina before her next shift. Ella and her coworkers would regularly consume such energy drinks in large volumes, often mixing five or six sachets with a jug of cold water.

Energy drinks were used not only to work during the day but also for overtime shifts. Foremen regularly asked workers to work 12 hours a day and to continue working over the weekend to get the job done. Ariana, a 23-year-old construction worker, said she drank energy drinks (Extra Joss Active) only when working overtime, after a 12-hour shift. For some of our interlocutors, energy drinks were panaceas, used to overcome body aches, increase appetite, and improve sleep quality.

The construction workers preferred KukuBima Ener-G. Their foreman bought the sachets for them, and deducted these costs from their salary. Ratih, a 20-year-old, explained:

> In the workplace, they buy it for us, usually bought in the morning, and also the afternoon, the foreman notes it. Usually we make one box of grape flavored KukuBima Ener-G mixed with milk, mixed with water in a jug, and we drink it together. (Anwar 2017, p. 196)

Table 6.3 Nutritional information on packages of popular energy drinks

No.	Name	Manufacturer	Contents	Benefits
1.	KukuBima Ener-G	PT. Sido Muncul	300 mg ginseng powder, royal jelly 30 mg, honey 100 mg, taurine 1000 mg, caffeine (1,3,7 trimethylxanthine) 50 mg, vit. B3 20 mg, vit. B6 5 mg, vit. B12 5 mcg, flavor, Brilliant Blue CL 42090	Restores stamina, body metabolism and refreshes body
2.	Extra Joss Active	PT. Bintang Toedjoe	Taurine 1000 mg, 350 mg ginseng powder, vit. B2 3 mg, vit. B3 16 mg, vit. B5 5 mg, vit. B6 1.5 mg, vit. B8, 10 mg, vit. B9 100 mcg, vit. B12 1 mcg, royal jelly 2 mg, 1,3,7 trimethylxanthine (caffeine) 50 mg	Helps maintain stamina and refreshes body
3.	Kratingdaeng	PT. Asia Health Energy Beverages under license from TC. Pharmaceutical Industries, Co., Ltd.	Taurine 1000 mg, caffeine 50 mg, inositol 50 mg, niacinamide 20 mg, pyridoxine HCL (vit. B6) 5 mg, dexpanthenol (Pro-vitamin B5) 5 mg, cyanocobalamine (vit. B12) 5 mcg, sugar (25 grams of pure sugar), Ponceau flavoring	Supplement drink. Helps refresh body during hard work or exercise

Energy drinks were consumed not only for work but also for fun. After receiving their wages, the construction and dock workers would gather and hang out with friends, staying up late watching movies together while eating junk foods and drinking energy drinks. Energy drinks were mixed with milk or with cheap alcohol. Our interlocutors explained that the alcoholic mixes made them sleep well, relieved body aches, and strengthened them for work the next day.

The widespread use of energy drinks for both work and recreation in our field sites in Makassar meant that the workers had a relatively high intake of caffeine. We wondered: did our interlocutors care about the dangers of consuming energy drinks? Sari, a 24-year-old construction worker, claimed she did not know about the high level of caffeine, and was surprised that energy drinks were considered harmful in excess. Ruslan, a 24-year-old dockworker, said that he had tried to consume a M-150, but experienced heart palpitations. Although Extra Joss Active did not have a negative effect on his body, he preferred KukuBima Ener-G because of its grape flavor, which he found delicious. Asril, a 20-year-old construction worker, moved from one energy drink brand to another. While he found Extra Joss Active tasty, he, like Ruslan, preferred KukuBima Ener-G because of its grape taste; for him, Kratingdaeng was not an option because it caused a variety of negative effects: heartburn, dizziness, stomach ulcers, and nausea. Kamaruddin, a 20-year-old dockworker, also chose KukuBima Ener-G rather than Extra Joss Active, because Extra Joss Active caused a burning sensation in his throat every time he consumed it.

Among those concerned about the side effects of regularly consuming energy drinks, some had reduced their energy drink consumption, and some were looking for alternatives to overcome tiredness. Jamal, a 20-year-old construction worker, had limited his consumption of energy drinks, replacing them with other cold drinks that contain lots of sugar (like Teh Gelas) or water. Others quit consuming energy drinks cold turkey. Muhlis, a 24-year-old dockworker, for example, stopped consuming all energy drinks because he often experienced stomach pain and heat in his throat. He tried to prevent these adverse effects by consuming plain soda water mixed with milk and Pilkita—an analgesic drug sold as a "strength drug"—because he believed that the mixture could relieve his pain. Ulla, a 24-year-old dockworker, had replaced energy drinks with a mixture of soda water and raw chicken eggs.

In Conclusion

Scholars of youth have described how young people use stimulants—mostly ADHD drugs—to work long hours to keep up with academic requirements, a practice that is considered problematic because it is an "off-label" use and because it may create academic advantage in allowing users to unfairly enhance their performance (Coveney et al. 2011; DeSantis and Hane 2010; Garnier et al. 2010; McCabe et al. 2006). However, young people's use of other stimulants like energy drinks to increase productivity has received much less scholarly attention. This is remarkable given the high sales of energy drinks across the globe, as well as the health risks associated with their frequent consumption.

One of the rare studies that examines the use of energy drinks by youth found that nearly one in five students of a secondary school in Ontario consumed energy drinks to be alert (Reid et al. 2015). Another web-based study conducted across campuses in the United States found that almost half of the 667 respondents had used energy drinks. This study reported that energy drink use was associated with poor sleep and tiredness the next day (Patrick et al. 2018), an observation also made in a study of energy drinks by US soldiers in Afghanistan (CDC 2010). Researchers at the Center for Food Policy and Obesity at Yale University (Pomeranz et al. 2013) view the increasing use of energy drinks by youth in the United States as a public health hazard, because the high levels of caffeine in the drinks can lead to caffeine overdose. In addition, they warn that these products contain both high levels of sodium and novel ingredients, such as taurine, guarana, and ginseng, the combined effects of which have been understudied. Finally, they point to the heavy advertising of these products to youth through digital media, Facebook, and sports events and brands.

Our approach of examining situated chemical practices allowed our youth ethnographers to observe both the use of stimulants and the use of chemicals to address sleep problems. Across our sites in Amsterdam,

Brooklyn, Puerto Princesa, and Makassar, we found that patterns of stimulant use differed. The porters in the Philippines earned money not only by carrying wares from buses to boats and back. They also earned money by selling goods and sex. For this interactional labor, they valued the confidence enhancement that amphetamines offer. The security guards whom we interviewed in Puerto Princesa sought products to keep them awake during their night shifts. For them, energy drinks did the trick. But they earned very little money, and energy drinks took a substantial part of their limited income, which forced them to moderate their use. In Indonesia, energy drinks are very cheap, and people used them as a panacea, not only to have stamina at work but also for virility and for bodily aches, and they valued the flavor that energy drinks brought to mixed alcoholic drinks. But the consumption of the caffeine in these drinks can lead to adverse effects, such as heart palpitations and nausea. Several of our interlocutors were trying to quit using energy drinks for these reasons. In Amsterdam, our ethnographic research found that nightlife workers also used amphetamines to stay alert, but they could easily get ahold of ADHD drugs for this purpose. Moreover, in both Brooklyn and Amsterdam night workers often used cocaine, which is much more expensive than crystal meth, to enhance their work performance. Both ADHD drugs and cocaine have less potential for addiction and less severe adverse effects than crystal meth (NIDA 2019). In both cities, users moderated their intake to manage sleep patterns, though the tiredness reported among students in the United States and soldiers in Afghanistan is a common feature of the ChemicalYouth narratives of our interlocutors.

Harm reduction programs, designed to mitigate drug harms, fail to recognize the health risks, including tiredness and sleep problems, related to the widespread use of energy drinks and other legal stimulants by youth (Hardon and Hymans 2016). Instead, such programs focus on risks of recreational drugs such as heroin, cannabis, and cigarettes and their potential for addiction (see also Chapter 9). However, since stimulant use for work and school is arguably a bigger problem than recreational use, as it takes place every working/school day and not only occasionally during free time, it is surprising that this area has been overlooked. This everydayness of use adds to the health risks.

Our field studies suggest that, to address these health risks, student and occupational health programs are needed to not only inform youth of the risks of using stimulants frequently but also to address the study demands and work conditions that give rise to the need for these drugs in the first place. Academic cultures place high demands on students, normalizing night work. Participating in stress-inducing academic cultures, working the night shift as security guards and club staff, and putting in long hours doing heavy labor on construction sites and in harbors—all of these fuel demands for energy drinks and amphetamines to stay alert, to have the stamina, and to feel the physical strength needed for the job.

The tiredness and sleep problems experienced by our interlocutors need to be remedied by better work conditions, as pointed out by Costa (2010) and Wolf-Meyer (2011), who recommend that shift schedules should be designed to reduce stress and adverse effects on health, and to minimize circadian disruption, sleep deficits, and fatigue. Sufficient time for recuperation after night shifts is needed, as is decent compensation for heavy and irregular work. Workers engaged in hard, physical labor could be offered time to rest and provided with nutritious meals, rather than energy drinks, to fuel their bodies and give them time to recover. Our study of young workers' situated chemical practices suggest that the widespread use of stimulants threatens to disrupt their circadian regimes even further, causing potentially severe metabolic disorders, especially when they use such products on a daily basis because they cannot afford to take a rest.

ChemicalYouth Ethnographers

Daan Kamps graduated from the Research Master's program in Social Sciences at the University of Amsterdam. His current research interests lie in urban nightlife work, chronobiology, and drug use, which he studied as a researcher for the ChemicalYouth project. For more than five years, he has been active within the Amsterdam club circuit as a DJ and event organizer, which provided him the opportunity to become familiar with the field (Fig. 6.5).

Fig. 6.5 Daan Kamps

Tait Mandler carried out research in Brooklyn, New York, on the lives of workers in queer nightlife spaces. Their research explored the ways that workers use chemicals to get their jobs done and how they care for themselves and others (Fig. 6.6).

Fig. 6.6 Tait Mandler

Gideon Lasco is a physician and medical anthropologist. He obtained his Ph.D. from the University of Amsterdam and his M.D. from the University of the Philippines, where he currently teaches anthropology. His research examines the chemical practices of young people, the meanings of human height, the politics of health care, and the lived realities of the Philippine "drug war." A Palanca-winning essayist, he maintains a weekly column in the *Philippine Daily Inquirer*, where he writes about health, culture, and society (Fig. 6.7).

Fig. 6.7 Gideon Lasco

Leo Diego was a researcher for the ChemicalYouth project at the Palawan Studies Center at Palawan State University and conducted fieldwork on security guards' chemical practices in the Philippines.

Ahsani Amalia Anwar was a researcher for the ChemicalYouth project at the Palawan Studies Center at Palawan State University and conducted fieldwork on the social lives of energy drinks among physical laborers in Indonesia.

References

Anwar, A. A. (2017). Bekerja versus bersenang-senang. Social lives minuman berenergi pada pekerja fisik di Makassar. In N. I. Idrus & P. M. Kutanegara (Eds.), *Bukan Narkoba Bis Berbahaya: Produk Kimia, Aspirasi dan Kehidupan Remaja* (pp. 183–217). Yogyakarta: Pustaka Penajar.

Braswell, S. R. (2005). *American meth: A history of the methamphetamine epidemic in America.* New York: iUniverse.

Centers for Disease Control and Prevention (CDC). (2010). Energy drink consumption and its association with sleep problems among U.S. service members on a combat deployment. *Morbidity and Mortality Weekly Report, 61*(44), 895–898.

Costa, G. (2010). Shift work and health: Current problems and preventive actions. *Safety and Health at Work, 1*(2), 112–123. https://doi.org/10.5491/SHAW.2010.1.2.112.

Coveney, C., Gabe, J., & Williams, S. (2011). The sociology of cognitive enhancement: Medicalisation and beyond. *Health Sociology Review, 20*(4), 381–393.

Crary, J. (2013). *24/7: Late capitalism and the ends of sleep.* New York: Verso Book.

DeSantis, A. D., & Hane, A. C. (2010). Adderall is definitely not a drug: Justifications for the illegal use of ADHD stimulants. *Substance Use and Misuse, 45,* 31–46.

Diego, A. L. (2017). Pampa-alert: Security guards' use of chemicals. In A. Hardon & M. Tan (Eds.), *Modernizing frontier: Chemical transformations of young people's minds and bodies in Puerto Princesa* (pp. 57–81). Quezon City: University of the Philippines Diliman. https://pure.uva.nl/ws/files/47815148/Modernizing_Frontiers.pdf.

Euromonitor International. (2020). *Passport: Energy drinks in Indonesia—context.* Euromonitor International. https://www.euromonitor.com/energy-drinks-in-indonesia/report. Accessed on March 1, 2020.

Garnier, L., Arria, A. M., Caldeira, K. M., Vincent, K. B., O'Grady, K. E., & Wish, D. E. (2010). Sharing and selling of prescription medications in a college student sample. *Journal for Clinical Psychiatry, 71*(3), 262–269.

Graham, T. E. (2001). Caffeine and exercise metabolism, endurance and performance. *Sports Medicine, 31*(11), 785–807. https://doi.org/10.2165/00007256-200131110-00002.

Hardon, A., & Hymans, T. D. (2016). Guest editors' introduction: Harm reduction from below. *Contemporary Drug Problems, 43*(3), 191–198. https://doi.org/10.1177/0091450916663247.

Kamps, D., & Hymans, D. (forthcoming, 2020). *The downside of uppers: Chronobiology, stimulant use, and working in the nighttime leisure economy.*

Keogh, J. (2010). *Pharmacology*. New York: McGraw Hill Book Companny.

Koob, G. F., Ahmed, S. H., Boutrel, B., Chen, S. A., Kenny, P. J., Markou, A., et al. (2004). Neurobiological mechanisms in the transition from drug use to drug dependence. *Neuroscience and Biobehavioral Reviews, 27*(8), 739–749. https://doi.org/10.1016/j.neubiorev.2003.11.007.

Lasco, G. (2013). *Tamang tama: Drug use in the everyday lives of male urban poor youth in a Philippine port community* (Master's thesis). University of the Philippines.

Lasco, G. (2014). Pampagilas: Methamphetamine in the everyday economic lives of underclass male youths in a Philippine port. *International Journal of Drug Policy, 25*(4), 783–788. https://doi.org/10.1016/j.drugpo.2014.06.011.

Mandler, T. (2016). Producing pleasure, minimizing harm. *Contemporary Drug Problems, 43*(3), 258–276. https://doi.org/10.1177/0091450916651185.

Mandler, T. (2018). Producing pleasure: Emotional labor and substance use in Brooklyn's queer nightlife. *Society for Cultural Anthropology.*

McCabe, S. E., Teter, C. J., & Boyd, C. J. (2006). Medical use, illicit use, and diversion of abusable prescription drugs. *Journal of American College Health, 54*(5), 269–278.

National Institute on Drug Abuse (NIDA). (2019). *Methamphetamine.* National Institute on Drug Abuse. https://www.drugabuse.gov/drugs-abuse/methamphetamine. Accessed on March 4, 2020.

Patrick, M. E., Griffin, J., Huntley, E. D., & Maggs, J. L. (2018). Energy drinks and binge drinking predict college students' sleep quantity, quality, and tiredness. *Behavioral Sleep Medicine, 16*(1), 92–105. https://doi.org/10.1080/15402002.2016.1173554.

Paul, K. N., Saafir, T. B., & Tosini, G. (2009). The role of retinal photoreceptors in the regulation of circadian rhythms. *Reviews in Endocrine and Metabolic Disorders, 10*(4), 271–278. https://doi.org/10.1007/s11154-009-9120-x.

Pollan, M. (2020). *Caffeine: How caffeine created the modern world*. New York: Audible Originals.

Pomeranz, J. L., Munsell, C. R., & Harris, J. L. (2013). Energy Drinks: An emerging public health hazard for youth. *Journal of Public Health Policy, 34*(2), 254–271.

Rasmussen, N. (2008). *On speed: The many lives of amphetamine*. New York: New York University Press.

Rawson, R. A., McCann, M. J., Flammino, F., Shoptaw, S., Miotto, K., Reiber, C., et al. (2006). A comparison of contingency management and cognitive-behavioral approaches for stimulant-dependent individuals. *Addiction, 101*(2), 267–274. https://doi.org/10.1111/j.1360-0443.2006.01312.x.

Reid, J. L., Hammond, D., McCrory, J., Dubin, A., & Leatherdale, S. T. (2015). Use of caffeinated energy drinks among secondary school students in Ontario: Prevalence and correlates of using energy drinks and mixing with alcohol. *Canadian Journal of Public Health / Revue Canadienne De Santé Publique, 106*(3), 101–108. www.jstor.org/stable/canajpublheal.106.3.e101.

Roenneberg, T. (2012). *Internal time*. Cambridge: Harvard University Press.

Roenneberg, T., Wirz-Justice, A., & Merrow, M. (2003). Life between clocks: Daily temporal patterns of human chronotypes. *Journal of Biological Rhythms, 18*(1), 80–90.

Sherman, S. G., German, D., Sirirojn, B., Thompson, N., Aramrattana, A., & Celentano, D. D. (2008). Initiation of methamphetamine use among young Thai drug users: A qualitative study. *Journal of Adolescent Health, 42*(1), 36–42. https://doi.org/10.1016/j.jadohealth.2007.07.002.

Shopee. (2020). *Extra joss energy drink 10 boxes per package*. Shopee. https://shopee.com.my/Extra-joss-energy-drink-10-boxes-per-package-i.110261307.1937551005. Accessed on March 4, 2020.

Sökmen, B., Armstrong, L. E., Kraemer, W. J., Casa, D. J., Dias, J. C., Judelson, D. A., et al. (2008). Caffeine use in sports: Considerations for the athlete. *Journal of Strength and Conditioning Research, 22*(3), 978–986. https://doi.org/10.1519/JSC.0b013e3181660cec.

Weinberg, B., & Bealer, B. (2001). *The world of caffeine: The science and culture of the world's most popular drug*. Oxfordshire, UK: Routledge.

Wolf-Meyer, M. (2011). Natural hegemonies sleep and the rhythms of american capitalism. *Current Anthropology, 52*(6), 876–895. https://doi.org/10.1086/662550.

7

Youth and Supplement Use

HI THERE,

We don't have to tell you that exercising, nutrition and relaxing are the key elements to feel comfortable in your own skin. Nutrition becomes even more important if you have specific goals for yourself. A couple of years ago it came to our attention that there were no healthy products on the market which supported woman with a healthy lifestyle. Lots of protein products contain unnatural additives, taste terrible and looked as if they were designed for Arny (Arnold Schwarzenegger) himself! Not something that we – and lots of woman with us – were happy about. Thats [*sic*] why we launched FITSHE in 2015.

Lots of women believe that consuming protein will lead to unwanted muscle mass development or weight gain. Luckily, you know better nowadays! It is imperative to feed your body what it needs! And it is with protein that you support your body in the after-effects of your training. If you lead a busy and active life, protein becomes essential. Additionally, protein is extremely satiating. If you give your body what it needs, you will notice it will ask much less of you.

This is the text that we found on the "about" section of the website of Caroline Glasbergen (FITSHE 2018), one of the fitness enthusiasts we interviewed in the Netherlands. She didn't just consume fitness products: she also created and sold a new protein product, FITSHE, which the website describes as follows:

> Your life is full enough as it is:
> – Your career
> – Social events
> – Family
> – Constantly developing yourself
> – And finding the time to exercise regularly, on top of everything!
>
> We demand a lot from our bodies and expect to always be able to rely on it. But have you ever taken the time to contemplate what you give your body back?

After an image of a greenish substance, looking like a protein shake, the text reads, "PUSH PLAY," under which it declares:

> We are convinced that an active lifestyle does not mean to limit yourself. In other words, while we truly believe stepping outside of your comfort zone and challenging yourself is crucial for your personal growth, we think being kind to yourself and blow of [*sic*] some steam every once in a while is as important to become the best version of yourself. So do both: push AND play.

In their ethnography of food science, Errington et al. (2013) report on a meeting with a young British professional named Deborah Maxwell, a similarly entrepreneurial peer of Glasbergen's. Maxwell had developed Big Shotz, an "attractively packaged supplement-loaded fruit smoothie" (Errington et al. 2013, p. 108) which she designed for daily use. She told the anthropologists that in developing Big Shotz (GroceryTrader 2008), she targeted the young and healthy:

> college graduates, in their twenties, generally fit, employed, on the run, and essentially responsible just for themselves. Such people likely eat a croissant for breakfast, a pizza or kebab for lunch, and then go out with

> friends for wine and a meal in the evening. They know that they are failing, and they never or only rarely have an optimal, perfect day. They can easily afford the daily cost of 1.50 £ for the convenience of Big Shotz, grabbed on the way to work. (Errington et al. 2013, pp. 110–111)

Maxwell had big ambitions for her concept, envisioning multiple types of Big Shotz, including Sport Shotz, Sleep Shotz, and Sex Shotz (Errington et al. 2013).

Glasbergen and Maxwell had developed supplements that consumers could use as tools to keep up with the hard work of living up to their aspirations and surviving in the urban environments in which they lived. Indeed, the demands of service sector labor, the strain of night work, the excitement of weekend raves, growing concerns about environmental toxins, and the endless circulation of images of lean and muscular bodies all fuel the demand for these types of products.

Supplementing dates back to the early twentieth century, when chemists learned they could isolate vitamins from organic materials and medical researchers started experimenting with vitamins to treat nutritional deficiencies, such as scurvy, a disease that was first noted on trade ships in the seventeenth century. Sailors spent months on boats, without fresh fruit and vegetables, which caused anemia, bleeding, and often death (Kodicek and Young 1969). After World War II, the emerging food industry incorporated vitamins into staple foods such as margarine, milk, and flour, no longer to treat deficiencies, but to boost the health of entire populations. As engineered food production evolved, manufacturers started adding vitamins to their products to boost their health value. Today, breakfast cereals that are oversaturated with sugar are advertised as being a good source of vitamin D, and reconstituted orange juice is touted as a source of vitamin C.

But supplements have only become a mass global commodity in the past 30 or so years, the period in which our interlocutors grew up. Price (2016) writes that a key factor in the growth of the supplements industry was the regulatory success of US Senator Hatch (Republican from the state of Utah), who designed the 1994 Dietary Supplement and Health Education Act, which eased the regulation of supplements.[1] Under this act, all supplements are assumed to be safe, unless the US Food and

Drug Administration detects evidence of harm, which usually means after many consumers have been exposed to the product. This lax regulation led to a more than tenfold increase in the number of supplements on the market in the United States, from 4000 in 1994 to 55,000 in 2012 (Cohen 2016).

But before this regulation came into effect, the new subdiscipline of nutritional science called "functional foods" was founded in the 1970s and 80s (Eussen et al. 2011), to examine the health benefits of manufactured foods and food supplements. The evidence that is produced within this discipline is used by manufacturers to inform their products with health claims. Apart from protein shakes that promise to "give something back" to our bodies, we can buy probiotic yoghurt to improve gut health, Omega 3s to have smooth skin and healthy veins, and magnesium for better sleep. While popular culture has embraced these opportunities for enhancement, some scholars are more critical. Among them, Scrinis (2013) raises concerns about the trend, which he characterizes as thus: "Food corporations have colonized the nutriscape, flooding the food supply with nutritionally engineered products and marketing claims and accentuating the nutritional anxieties and nutritional needs of consumers" (p. 8).

Public health experts do not advise the regular consumption of vitamins and supplements for lack of evidence on their health effects, pointing out that some studies even suggest that such effects may be negative, including increased rates of heart disease and cancer among people who take vitamins (Offit 2013). For example, researchers from the University of Copenhagen reviewed 14 randomized trials involving 17,000 healthy volunteers who were using vitamins A, C, and E to prevent intestinal cancer. The researchers concluded that the trials did not provide evidence that the vitamins protect against intestinal cancer; on the contrary, they seemed to increase overall mortality: death rates were 6% higher in the group taking vitamins (Lonn 2005).

Some medical researchers, moreover, share concerns about the unknown health risks of elevated amounts of specific functional ingredients in diets and the possibility of interactions with medicines. In pharmacies, possible drug interactions are checked for, but pharmacists usually do not know all the supplements their clients are taking (Eussen et al. 2011). There are also regular reports of food supplements being mixed with synthetic drugs to enhance their efficacy (Rocha et al. 2016).

Given the possible harms of supplements, it is surprising that drug regulatory authorities do not require medical evidence of their safety before allowing the products on the market. In the European Union, the United States, Indonesia, and the Philippines, supplements are legally considered to be food items, which means that they cannot be marketed for the treatment of disease. But, by claiming they promote gut health, better sleep, and muscle development, manufacturers can circumvent this limitation.

Having grown up in the supplements era, our interlocutors had been socialized into taking vitamins. Their mothers likely gave them multivitamins to augment their meals, and taking supplements had become part of their habitus (Bourdieu 1992), defined as the system of predispositions, which include perceptions about the need for as well as acts of consuming these commodities. Living in urban environments, our interlocutors were anxious about the combined effects of pollution, stress, and the lack of nutrients in their fast food diets of noodles, burgers, and pizzas. They used vitamins and supplements as protective shields to ward off negative environmental influences and lifestyles, and as insurance for future health. Supplements and vitamins were one part of their general health practices, alongside exercise, sleep, and good food. The fact that vitamins and food supplements appear to be natural made them even more attractive to our interlocutors. What harm could a food supplement have? Surely, they reasoned, there's nothing wrong with adding some nutrients to your daily routine.

The focused ethnographies presented in this chapter show how our interlocutors embraced vitamins and foods supplements to stay healthy and to confront the challenges of their busy lives. And it makes clear that, as the vignette at the beginning of this chapter suggests, young people also participated in selling and making of such products. What do young people hope to achieve when turning to supplements and vitamin-fortified products? And what can we learn about their lives by examining their supplementing practices? The chapter illustrates how in "doing" chemicals, young people are more than just consumers. Also involved in the selling and creating of supplements, they are co-producers of an urban way of being in the world in which supplementing has become a normal part of everyday life.

In this chapter, we zoom in on several of our fieldwork sites where we observed supplementing. We start in Puerto Princesa, the Philippines, where Gideon Lasco observed mothers giving their sons a popular multivitamin to help them grow. These vitamins were also used by young people who felt that, in a culture that idolizes height, they could still grow taller. In the same town, we found young professionals using expensive multivitamins for stamina, while also distributing them through multilevel marketing.

We then shift our attention to the use of supplements in fitness clubs. Amanda Kalangit studied supplementing among young women in Manado, Indonesia, who worked out in gyms to achieve the ideal lean and muscular body. Then, we examine the marketing of supplements in the Netherlands, including a product called FITSHE, marketed to women. In the conclusion we consider the core questions of this chapter: Why were young people seduced into using supplements, and why did they make and distribute them? What do these engagements with supplements tell us about what is at stake in their lives?

Hight Is Might

Enter any pharmacy in the Philippines and you will appreciate the popularity of Cherifer, a multivitamin that figures prominently on the shelves, usually placed behind or close to the cashier. Cherifer is offered in various forms: syrups for children and tablets for teenagers. Jane, a 24-year-old pharmacy assistant, explained to us that Cherifer was usually bought when salaries were paid out.

Lasco (2017), one of our ethnographers, reports:

> Vitamins are seen as a potent way of making children grow taller. In particular, "growth supplements" like Cherifer, with their promise of "reaching your growth potential" and "tangkad-sagad" (height to the

> fullest) have captured the imagination of parents and children alike. (p. 71)

Lasco, a community health physician, became aware of the importance of vitamins in child-rearing when he observed that most of the questions he received in his practice revolved around them. Mothers didn't ask questions about food, but they did ask advice on Cherifer.

In one of Puerto Princesa's pharmacies, Lasco met Ellen, who regularly bought Cherifer for her children. Costing US $0.43 per tablet, she pays US $13 for Cherifer tablets for her 19-year-old son, and US $9 for the bottles of Cherifer syrup for her younger son. When Lasco presented his calculations to Ellen, she justified it as an "investment" and repeated the advertising slogan of Star Margarine from her own youth: "*Iba na ang matangkad*" (it's really different if you are tall). She explained that she and her husband's short stature was a liability to her sons, and that they might have a hard time finding a job, as many come with height requirements (Lasco 2017).

Being tall is not a trivial aspiration in the Philippines. Job advertisements often list height requirements, including those for military service. The Navy and the Coast Guard both demand a height of 5' (152 cm); hotels and restaurants often require men to be at least 5'7" (170 cm) tall and women to be at least 5'3" (160 cm). Surprisingly, height requirements also exist for caregiving and pharmacy assistant jobs.

The following job advertisement for a food attendant is typical:

> High school or college graduate
> With or without experience
> With pleasing personality, neat looking, and well-groomed
> Must be of good moral character, hardworking, fast
> Good communication skills
> Willing to learn and be trained
> Must have basic knowledge in banqueting or in food functions service
> Male or female, 18-26 years old
> At least 5'3" (female), 5'7" (male)[2]

Such requirements can be traced to American colonization, in the first half of the twentieth century, when standards of height were introduced (see Table 7.1).

Note how height (along with English-language skills for prison guards) was related to salary. The taller you were the more you could earn. Candidates who were 5'2" (157 cm) could earn $180–240 annually, while candidates who were 5'6" (168 cm) tall or more could earn up to $900, which is substantially more.

The manufacturer claims that Cherifer helps children grow taller due to what it calls the "Chlorella Growth Factor." This efficacy is backed up by highly seductive advertising campaigns, including young boys playing basketball, and banners that claim "Height is might" (see Fig. 7.1). Cherifer is endorsed by Kobe Paras, a popular Filipino basketball player, who plays in the team of Cathedral High School in Los Angeles. His mother, a former actress, is an American citizen, so he is too.

Table 7.1 Salaries and physical requirements of selected civil service positions

Position	Salary per annum	Height and weight requirement
First class patrolman	900 USD	5 feet 8 inches (173 cm), 145 lbs. (66 kg)
Third class patrolman	300 USD	5 feet 4 inches (163 cm), 110 lbs. (50 kg)
First class fireman	900 USD	5 feet 4 inches (163 cm), 125 lbs. (57 kg)
Second class fireman	240 USD	5 feet 2 inches (157 cm), 125 lbs. (57 kg)
First class engineer, fire service	1200 USD	5 feet 4 inches (163 cm), 125 lbs. (57 kg)
Second class engineer, fire service	240 USD	5 feet 4 inches (163 cm), 110 lbs. (50 kg)
Prison guard, first class (English speaking)	900 USD	5 feet 6 inches (168 cm), 110 lbs. (50 kg)
Prison guard, second class (non-English speaking)	180–240 USD	5 feet 2 inches (157 cm), 110 lbs. (50 kg)

Source Philippines Bureau of Civil Service (1906, p. 49), reproduced from Lasco (2017, p. 44)

Fig. 7.1 Cherifer is endorsed by basketball players (*Source* Photo taken by Gideon Lasco, July 2017, the Philippines)

The advertisement in Fig. 7.1 shows Paras's father, himself a basketball legend of the 1990s, with his hand above his son's head, showing his "potential" to viewers. Television commercials of Paras and his father use the slogan "*Tangkad sagad*" (as tall as can be), implying that with Cherifer, one's genetic potential can be achieved. On Katipunan Avenue, the road to three of Manila's biggest universities, a very large image of Paras appears on a billboard along with the words "Take your potential to new heights." A clarification in much smaller print reads: "Achievable with adequate sleep, proper diet, and avoidance of drinking and smoking" (Lasco 2017).

In Puerto Princesa, a teacher at the local State University told Lasco that her seven-year-old demanded that she buys Cherifer for him, after seeing a TV commercial. One of our colleagues from the University of the Philippines in Manila had the same experience. His son, who was quite short for his age, wanted to try Cherifer, despite his father's explanation that it was not likely to work. When we spoke with high school students in Puerto Princesa, Lizette (19, 4'9") recalled buying and drinking Cherifer with classmates who considered also themselves too short. During our research in Puerto Princesa, we found that the need for supplementing was reinforced by the city health programs. Four times a year, community health workers went house to house to offer families vitamin A and iron supplementation. A pediatrician with whom we consulted on the issue said that there really was no evidence that the supplements were effective increasing the height of children:

> I tell [the parents], maybe that's really the limit of [the child's] height… Genes also set a limit, that's why we compute the mid-parental height. If that's really the height, we cannot do anything. (Lasco 2017, p. 77)

Some of our interlocutors recognized the limits of Cherifer. One mother (47 years old, with three children) in Puerto Princesa told Lasco: "Whatever their height is, that's really how tall they will be. One of my sons took Cherifer, but the one who didn't take it is even taller than him" (Lasco 2017, p. 76). A high school student, when asked if Cherifer is effective, responded: "I think it's effective because I grew tall." But when probed about the effects on her peers, she replied, "Maybe for some it's effective, but not for others. I really can't tell for sure" (Lasco 2017, p. 76).

Metabolic Potentials

Given the prominence of vitamins in their childhood, it is not surprising that supplementing was a theme in our discussions with young adults in Puerto Princesa. One of our research assistants, Jaime, took one capsule of a supplement called C24/7 every day, which cost him about 10% of his monthly earnings. At the time of our research, Jaime was a lecturer at the local university, and taught many classes to pay for his younger siblings' school fees. He needed energy, he said, and C24/7 helped him feel healthy, and prevented hangovers (Hardon et al. 2019).

C24/7 is a food supplement produced by Nature's Way in Wisconsin, United States. Its promotional materials suggest that the capsules contain 14 "super" green foods, 12 whole fruit juice blends, 12 whole vegetable juice blends, and 12 mushrooms, along with 19 different vitamins and minerals. They are advertised as a "new breakthrough," with "manufacturing allowing all the ingredients to deliver the highest level of anti-oxidants" (see Fig. 7.2).[3]

Oxidation is a metabolic pathway that takes place at the cellular level, where mitochondria convert food to energy. Oxidation generates free radicals, and manufacturers such as Nature's Way warn that these can cause damage to DNA and cell membranes, thereby potentially causing cancer and premature/accelerated aging. Food supplements often advertise their "antioxidant" properties, but critics point out that the human

Fig. 7.2 Promotional material for C24/7, obtained from its distributors in Puerto Princesa (*Source* Photo taken by Anita Hardon, January 2018, the Philippines)

body is perfectly capable of making antioxidants, and that vegetables and fruits are packed with them. Put plainly, we don't need supplements to have healthy cells (Price 2016). Still, the promotional claims have wide appeal.

To get C24/7 at a discount, Jaime became a member of the Alliance in Motion (AIM) Global, a Philippine company which distributes C24/7 through multilevel marketing. In fact, the product was not available in ordinary pharmacies but was sold by distributors who were encouraged to reach out to new clients and recruit new members for the company. Distributors were encouraged to share their own experiences with the products to increase sales, and to tailor C24/7 to prevailing metabolic concerns, selecting from a long list of declared "benefits" of the supplements (see the list on the right-hand side of the image in Fig. 7.2, which includes: promotes longevity, prevents cancer from any origin, controls blood sugar, enhances sexual vitality, and reduces fatigue).

Jaime entered the multilevel marketing scheme because he needed the stamina promised by the capsules. Other young people were attracted to the scheme because it provided them an opportunity to make a living. Buying a membership came with an initial stock of C24/7 at discounted price, which they sold in order to earn back their investment. They attended training seminars at AIM Global headquarters to learn how best to sell the products. "Be your product" is an important principle of AIM Global's sales strategy. "The best drug pusher is a drug user," said one of the trainers. Trainers encouraged the distributors to use their own experiences to persuade others to use C24/7, and invited distributors onto the stage to provide testimonials. Twenty-eight-year-old security guard Jess, for example, told the audience how he had been married for eight years and he and his wife had not yet conceived when a friend told them about C24/7. His wife became pregnant shortly after she began to take the supplement (Hardon et al. 2019).

We observed AIM Global trainers talking a lot about prevailing health problems. They pointed to the rise of chronic diseases and cancer, and referred to the high costs of treating these diseases. Their statements suggested a state of emergency: "There are many more diseases now than ever before!" "There was no cancer in the past, but there are now all kinds of cancer!" "We are all prone to illness, and our diets cannot protect us" (Hardon et al. 2019, p. 435).

Before and after pictures, shown at the training sessions, depicted patients experiencing amazing recoveries from cancer and other illnesses after taking C24/7. They were offered as a kind of proof, to convince the distributors of the supplement's potential. In an article on this high-stakes strategy, we wrote: "The trainers ask, 'How much is chemotherapy? How much is kidney dialysis per session? Will you be able to pay for it?'" (Hardon et al. 2019, p. 435).

The strategy also invokes powerful health authorities. For example, the products' packaging includes the logo of the US Food and Drug Authority (FDA). Trainers, in the seminars, referred to the World Health Organization's advice to consume five portions of vegetables and fruits each day, and then asked: "Who among us has the money to buy six different vegetables and fruits every day?" This seems a strange message in Puerto Princesa, where so many people still eat vegetables and fruits from their very own backyards (Hardon et al. 2019). The trainers' messages resonate, however, with Filipinos' anxieties about whether they are getting enough nutrients. Surveys conducted in Metro Manila by researchers of the Philippines Food and Nutrition Research Institute found that in 2008, 69% of respondents strongly agreed with the statement that the nutrients supplied by food needed to be supplemented, while ten years earlier, in 1998, this percentage was only 42% (Cruz et al. 2011). In a 2016 Euromonitor International report, industry analysts note a staggering growth—10%—in sales of supplements (reaching an annual value of US $137 million). They relate this growth to the promising health claims made by supplement manufacturers, suggesting also that consumers turn to these products for their "value for money" (Euromonitor International 2016).

Taking advantage of the strong family ties in the Philippines, the young distributors we spoke with were encouraged to profile their extended family members to identify their health concerns, and then to tailor their "pitch" to their needs, even though they generally had little to no medical background.

Our fieldwork suggests that becoming a C24/7 distributor is a risky investment, especially for youth who have few resources to begin with. Our interlocutors ran into trouble when clients blamed them for adverse health events, which added to the intensity and stress of their work as distributors. Over time, many of them quit selling C24/7 because their expectation of earning additional income was not met, and because the multilevel marketing labor was very time consuming and complex. When they stopped selling C24/7, they couldn't afford it anymore, and they turned instead to vitamin C-containing products (Enervon C, Fern C, and the generic ascorbic acid) and multivitamins such as Revicon and Centrum to keep up with their demanding lifestyles.

Building Bodies

Supplements were also very popular in sports, a domain where there has been concern about unfair competition and the health risks related to the use of illegal steroids by athletes to boost their performance. Social scientists have studied the increased use of supplements in gyms, where young men try to achieve desirable masculine bodies that are "lean, muscular, powerful, free from blemish yet rugged, and sexually attractive" (Atkinson 2007, p. 172). Atkinson, who studied this practice among young Canadian men, quotes a 21-year-old man named Cliff, who uses several kinds of proteins (not illegal steroids):

> I take what I take because I wasn't born with the right gifts… I'm not trying to get jacked [muscular], but I want to look strong and be strong, right. Dieting and hard work gets you [only] so far, and then you need an edge to make gains… That's what it's about to me, self-improvement and progress. I spend tons of money on supplements, but it's worth it… I want people to like me for how I look. (Atkinson 2007, pp. 172–173)

Atkinson relates the increased use of supplements by young men to prevailing crises in masculinity, specifically that men are threatened by women's entrance into the labor market and by changing gender power relations. Another one of Atkinson's informants, Brad, a 25-year-old, argues:

> I don't want to have a girlfriend with bigger muscles than me. Women today are much smarter and fitter and in control, and guys have to step it up [get bigger] … that's nature; it's the law of the jungle. Guys should be bigger, even if we have to work together and share just about every other social role in the world. (Atkinson 2007, p. 177)

Latham and colleagues (2019) have analyzed these self-transformation practices as part of "make-over culture," emphasizing that it's not the outcome that matters, but, "making visible the labor of working on the self" (p. 155). Their informants take supplements to "see the results" of working out in gyms.

Two focused ethnographies in the ChemicalYouth project examined how young women also work out in gyms, seeking to make visible the results of their labor in the form of lean and muscular bodies. Images of such bodies increasingly appear on posters and on TV, and are shared among fitness enthusiasts online. We begin in Manado, Indonesia, where Amanda Kalangit did fieldwork in a gym catering to young professionals. Gyms used to be only for the elites in Indonesia, but nowadays they also cater to young people who form the emerging middle class. Kalangit conducted participant observations and interviews with ten fitness enthusiasts who held a variety of professional positions: government workers, bank staff, sales promoters, sexy dancers, and police officers. They frequented Zumba and combat classes, and engaged in weight lifting and cardio workouts. They wanted to radiate many things through their bodies—bravery, confidence, and attractiveness—in a rapidly changing urban job market and dating scene. Our interlocutors said that an ideal body is balanced, as explained by Rose, a 24-year-old: "Not thin, not fat, just right, proportional, in proportion to the height, body weight also according to height. Must be healthy, with long hair" (Kalangit 2015, p. 8).

Among these professional women, vitamins and supplements were part of a broader strategy to achieve beauty and health. They balanced eating, sleeping, working, and exercising, attending to both the inside and outside of their bodies. They educated themselves on the nutritional content of food and chose foods that are easily absorbed by the body.

Indicators of a well-balanced body, they explained, are shiny hair, radiant skin, and moist lips. To achieve these, they invested in a range of hair products (shampoo, conditioner, hair masques); skin lotions such as Ever E, Natur E, Nivea, and Victoria's Secret; as well as facial washes, sun screens, and lipsticks. To achieve health "from the inside" they drank lots of water, and used a variety of traditional and modern products, including tamarind concoctions, vitamin C (Ester C and C-1000), vitamin E (Ever E), glutamine, fish oil, vitamin B complex, and Herbalife supplements, all products that promised to give them stamina and prevent them from becoming sick. They blamed ill-health on irregular eating patterns, a lack of fruits and vegetables, not exercising, and not sleeping well.

Nutrition was key, according to our interlocutors; eating well meant consuming fruits, vegetables, eggs, fish, whole grain breads, and other foods with high nutrition on a daily basis. They substituted bad foods with good ones, replacing whole milk with yoghurt, which was considered to be healthier and lower in fat, and snacking on products with a high nutritional content such as Fitbar. Water was also considered to be of utmost importance. Our interlocutors all referred to the need for a 5–10 minute (bottled) "water break" during their gym practice. The following quotes give a sense of the importance of water:

> As for the drink, it has to be plain water, whether the weather's hot or cold. Especially during gym, during the break I have to drink water. (Wilma, 21)

> As early as I wake up, I drink water first because it is most important to neutralize. Because when we sleep our bodies release ions as well, we sweat a lot too, well, we're weak too, so we have to replace it with mineral water. Especially when we do heavy activities. (Asy, 26)

> Water break is the best! Drink until satisfied and also because Aqua is available free here, and also to replace ions and energy that we have spent through sweat. Now to replace the liquid in large quantities, we have

> to drink enough mineral water too. So that the energy in our body is maintained. (Evelyn, 23) (Kalangit 2015, p. 17)

Key is also taking time for the body to "rest," especially when they have eaten food which is "excessive" or "rich tasting," such as chocolate, *coto* (a local soup), pork, and fast food. The importance of good eating when frequenting the gym was explained by 23-year-old Evelyn, a bank employee:

> The most important menu is that of breakfast because it is to start the day and therefore must be nutrient-rich, when you choose your breakfast. Breakfast is indeed lighter in the portion, but it must be really healthy. The point is that there should be nutrients in it, because that is the most important thing, especially because I do gym activities, so I need everything to be extra healthy. I used to not have breakfast, and if I [did] so I would have an upset stomach. Since I [began] using the gym equipment, I have to have breakfast, because if not, I will definitely be limp all day long, and cannot go to gym after work. (Kalangit 2015, p. 11)

What stands out in the accounts of these female health enthusiasts is the balancing of healthy foods and supplements, and the combination of achieving health by consuming substances orally and by applying them on the skin, hair, nails, and lips. In doing so, our informants aimed to achieve total body health, which stood in contrast to the muscle-building make-overs of male gym-goers in Canada and Australia.

Fitshe

The final ethnography presented in this chapter is by Lisanne Claessens,[4] a youth ethnographer who delved deeper into the make-over culture of young professional women in Amsterdam, showing how they not only consume health-related products but also, like their peers in Puerto Princesa, engage in marketing and designing such products. Unlike those in Puerto Princesa, the youth in Amsterdam didn't have access to vegetables and fruits in their backyards. Our ethnographies found supplementing to be very popular, as indicated by this post by Heather Williams (2013), on the blog "All Women's Talk":

> I'm a huge fan of green superfood powders and honestly, I find it to be a hobby to try new ones out. Most people who have never used a green superfoods powder just don't understand the point. I get that; I used to be one of them. Until I started using some pretty amazing green superfood powders, I was of course healthy, but did have lower energy levels overall. I implemented certain green superfood powders into my diet after a friend recommended that I try some. I was learning to love smoothies for the first time in my life, so I thought I would give those oddly smelling, green powders a try. Even though some of them smelled weird, I got creative at flavoring my smoothies to get around the taste after I experienced how great they made me feel. Not all green superfood powders out there are as good as others. Check out my favorites that haven't only changed my smoothies, but also my energy, digestion and immunity. None of these powders have any sugar, gluten, dairy, GMOs and most are organic and 100% raw.

In the past decade, the phenomenon of "superfoods" entered the Dutch public arena, and it has shaken up public discussions of health and wellness. Despite the relatively short time frame in which this concept has emerged, it has gained immense popularity, especially among young, highly educated people. There is no official understanding of what a superfood is exactly, but it is generally used to describe "raw," unprocessed, and often times "ancient" products that are said to have extremely high doses of nutrients. Food and health blogs, such as the one cited above, are popping up all over the internet, becoming widely used and trusted sources of information. Such sources champion user experience as a kind of evidence, instead of advising people to seek out the expert knowledge of scientific researchers and medical doctors.

Paying close attention to various health practices and the consumption of (super)foods, chemicals, supplements, and vitamins, Claessen's project analyzed how young people decided what their bodies needed in Amsterdam, where her interlocutors experienced urban life as a negative factor that needed to be balanced through health-focused practices.

Claessen argues that the sense of being in control over one's health correlates directly with the feeling of being in control over one's life. City life, according to her interlocutors, was demanding, and it required one to be knowledgeable of one's body in order to perform well. It was therefore not only important to make *good* choices, but to make good choices for *you*.

Claessen examined the use of superfoods and supplements by becoming a salesperson at the Vitaminstore, a growing Dutch company with 26 branches across the Netherlands and five in Amsterdam alone. The Vitaminstore sells its own brand of vitamins and supplements, categorized into three groups, each marked with its own color: health (green), sports (blue), and beauty (pink), see Fig. 7.3. In the store where Claessen worked, customers could also order fresh juices, choosing from more than 40 mixes of fruit, vegetables, herbs, yoghurt, coconut cream, and superfoods. Working behind the juice bar required no additional training, but employees were provided with a textbook that listed all of

Fig. 7.3 Vitaminstore products: Huid Haar Nagel (Skin Hair Nail) on the left, and Super Magnesium, on the right (*Source* Photos by Lisanne Claessens, February 2015, the Netherlands)

the superfoods and powders that customers could choose to "boost" their juices.

Working behind the juice bar enabled Claessen to communicate with customers, asking and answering questions. She sometimes referred customers to knowledgeable colleagues and listened in on their conversations. It was an environment where workers and clients exchanged experiences of things that they have tried out and shared stories of success and failure. In these face-to-face interactions, boundaries between food and medicine, and sickness and health, were blurred, and in many ways were similar to what went on in the multilevel marketing of C24/7 that we described above.

Claessen's mentor at the Vitaminstore, Sara, was trained as a professional dietician, but she developed an aversion to her discipline. While she enjoyed learning about metabolism, organs, physiology, and chemistry, she became dissatisfied with how the body was approached, that is, as an engine whose fuel intake needs to be moderated. What bothered her most was that a training in dietetics left her helpless in meeting what people seemed to need from her.

Sara got her degree as weight consultant but did not establish her own practice until she had completed several courses of orthomolecular healing and a few years of work at a Vitaminstore, learning about vitamins and supplements. She changed her "personal brand" to "Sara, Health Coach and More." With this new title, she was able to expand her target group along with expanding her expertise in guiding people in the labor of self-improvement. Sara's appearance, she said, reflected on the product she sold, becoming like an advertisement that displayed her ability to transform others:

> If I take nutritional advice from someone who doesn't look healthy, then that's not really credible. Even though that person might be perfectly able to explain to me what is good for me, and at the same time doing his own thing. It should be possible, theoretically. But to me is doesn't feel right. (Claessens 2018, p. 13)

You have to "practice what you preach," she asserted. Her blog post on magnesium reflects how she integrated her own experience into her advice:

> I don't focus much on supplements because I prefer to get my nutrients from whole foods, but for the past few months I have been hearing a lot about the mineral magnesium and how it is an antidote for stress. I'm not particularly more stressed than usual, but I've always struggled with anxiety before bed so I thought I would look into this "relaxation mineral." While researching, I was surprised to find so many benefits of magnesium and what it can do to the body. I've been adding more magnesium rich foods into my diet and started taking a supplement a month ago and I can already feel a difference. (Larsen 2014)

Sara recognized that not everyone can afford to dedicate large amounts of time and resources to self-care in the way she did. Instead, she emphasized, she worked for her clients, testing products and lifestyle regimes on herself. In doing so, she argued, she spared her clients the time-consuming practice of figuring out what would work for them.

At the Vitaminstore Claessens met Caroline Glasbergen, as she was pitching FITSHE to Sara, calling it "a brand for women leading an active lifestyle." Sara, Caroline declared, was the ultimate FITSHE woman: "I never dreamed to meet someone like her. Beautiful, smart, successful and truly an expert in her field." Caroline had developed this product for young professionals with demanding social lives, many of which may have a family to maintain and a career to pursue. FITSHE, she explained, is the first Dutch after-work-out protein powder on the market targeting women.

FITSHE, Caroline pointed out, is for women who do intense workout sessions. Her product is designed for women who "go the extra mile," who "juggle eighteen balls at once," while maintaining a "fit" body. A graduate in business administration, Caroline started her career in the marketing department of Bacardi, where she learned the technique of experiential branding; from there, she moved on to Unilever. After that, when she started a new job at a small, innovative company in Amsterdam with mostly women her age, she found women who shared her intention to have a healthy lifestyle. In an interview with Claessens she recalled:

> We worked a lot, eighty hours a week at least. And everybody was focused on healthy living. We worked in the city center so there was an organic health store where we would buy lunch. We always had healthy snacks at the office. And we exercised with a personal trainer twice a week, all of us together. (Claessens 2017, p. 12)

Besides these communal work-out sessions, she exercised with her boyfriend twice a week; her body grew leaner, and her muscles started to become more pronounced and visible, but she was increasingly tired. Caroline said that her personal trainer introduced her to shakes and explained to her how proteins aid the recovery of her muscles. Being raised, like Sara, in the era of calorie counting, the logic of proteins opened up new understandings of metabolism. "So, there are carbs, fats and proteins, those are the macronutrients and the foundation of your diet. Then there are micronutrients, minerals and vitamins… But proteins are difficult to get enough of. So, I started taking the powder (Claessens 2017, p. 12)."

Caroline designed her own brand of protein powder a year later, specifically marketed for the female body. She explained, "I was sufficiently knowledgeable about healthy eating to realize that there's a lot of crap in those shakes. Additives and such, to improve taste, texture… I wanted a product to fit my needs" (Claessens 2017, p. 14). She identified her needs as feminine, stressing that it is important for women to have products which are free of "crap," because their endocrine systems are more sensitive than that of men. What followed was a year of intense research, during which she dedicated all her resources to her enterprise, while engaging her social network as "ambassadors" to promote her brand. Caroline sells her product online in order to maintain control over the distribution process.

Caroline advocates a balanced lifestyle, including exercise and the use of FITSHE, along with "letting go." On her website she declares:

> Since I started working on FITSHE about a year ago, it's a question I hear a lot: "You don't eat this, right?" People ask me this at parties for instance, when handing me the platter of bitterballen (deep fried meatballs) to pass to the next person. Then I surprise them by helping myself to one these greasy, but oh so tasty deep-fried morsels. And you should see their astonished faces when I drink a glass (or two) of wine. Apparently being a female health entrepreneur means never snacking, drinking or even dreaming of such unhealthy pursuits. I disagree. (FITSHE 2018)

The Seduction of Supplements

This chapter, along with others in this book, reveals that our interlocutors viewed their bodies as vehicles for achieving their aspirations in life. Supplements seem to be a fuel to keep bodies going. Across our field sites we observed, perhaps unsurprisingly, the popularity of vitamins C and E. Vitamin C is the cheapest and most accessible product, commonly used to prevent colds and coughs and to generate stamina; vitamin E was sought to achieve radiant skin and shiny hair. In addition, we observed a growing trend of consuming protein bars and shakes, especially by young men and women who frequented gyms, to increase muscle mass and shape lean bodies. However, a closer look reveals that such "making over" has less to do with giving into circulating body ideals and more with a pride in the labor that goes into working out and wanting to make results visible.

Supplements come with divergent health and wellness claims, which tend to be unregulated and can be tailored to specific needs. In Puerto Princesa, distributors worked to link a single product to divergent health needs; the product's multiplicity of health and wellness claims made such tailoring possible. In Amsterdam, we observed how the Vitaminstore chain sold a multiplicity of products, linking diverse vegetable and fruit blends to more than 40 additional products, again tailoring the blends to the health needs of the clients. In both cases young people did the work of linking products to client needs, expanding the market for these products. Our interlocutors also consumed the supplements they sold, and some also designed them, as a way of becoming a convincing salesperson an increasingly competitive, polluted, and precarious urban landscape.

Hard Work

The ChemicalYouth team in Puerto Princesa was concerned about the hard work done by young people who sell supplements through multilevel marketing. We decided to make a documentary to take a closer look, following how Leo (a high school teacher and one of our youth ethnographers) augmented his income by selling First Vita Plus, a food supplement that was competing for clients with AIM Global at the time. The resulting film, *Sweet Medicine* (Op den Kamp and Pulanco 2017), shows Leo going door to door in his hometown to find customers, often without much luck. His young wife is not happy with the time lost to this low income-generating activity and encourages him to help her sell popcorn instead. Part of the documentary process involved filming the manufacturing of the supplement and testing its nutritional content at a well-established food chemistry laboratory. The whole team, including Leo, was shocked to find out that First Vita Plus was actually not much more than a fruit-flavored drink containing lots of sugar, and that the product had much less vitamin content than promised on its label. After hearing about the sugar content, Leo decided to help his wife sell popcorn in their community.

The documentary was aired at universities in Manila and Puerto Princesa, and at various conferences in the Philippines and elsewhere, and was selected for Distribute 2020, a documentary film festival in Toronto. And it has been used in university classrooms all over the world. To have an even more profound impact, we aim for it to be included in the science and technology curriculum for senior high schools in the Philippines, which we view as an ideal space for social justice pedagogy (Greenberg 2017; Lasker and Simcox 2020). If incorporated into the curriculum, we hope that the documentary discourages youth from investing scarce resources in memberships to multilevel marketing companies. We also hope that they understand that being a distributor of food supplements in such schemes is hard work and unlikely to generate a satisfying return, and that one cannot trust the declared content of food supplements because companies are not held accountable for their marketing claims by governments.

In Conclusion

The efficacy of these products is ambiguous: how do we know if it was the supplement that gave us more energy, or made the common cold go away? One might ask: why linger on these questions? Especially when "better safe than sorry" seems to be the adage that drives supplement use. When I discuss the conclusions of this chapter with my daughter, she tells me to include the fact that she takes a multivitamin when she is tired and fears becoming sick. And, that she hasn't been ill in the past three years. The natural aura of supplements and vitamins adds to their appeal: they are just food. Surely they can't do any harm. This apparent "common sense" is not, however, supported by rigorous research, and the health claims that shape young people's use of supplements are not scrutinized by regulatory authorities, unless serious adverse effects emerge.

This chapter shows how health enthusiasts monitored the effects of the supplements that they took more intensively. The female fitness enthusiasts in Manado saw their bodies change, as did young women in Amsterdam who saw and felt their bodies change when they used various products. Diets, supplement regimens, and fitness schedules were adjusted in a total body project; sometimes these are shared online, creating more interest in the bodies displayed and the means through which to achieve them.

This chapter also highlighted how young people are not only consumers of supplements, they also help sell and make them. They do so in malls, drug stores and, increasingly, through multilevel marketing. They also do so in the juice bars that are popping up in cities all over the world, offering busy young people on the go blends of fruit and vegetable drinks, along with carefully selected supplements, catering to the changing health concerns of youth: immunity, stamina, beauty, stress relief. In the selling and creating of supplements, they are co-producers of an urban way of being in the world in which supplementing has become a normal part of everyday life. They co-create the efficacy of supplements as protective shields and body enhancers by giving testimonials based on their own experiences, which they share through social media and in face-to-face interactions. They are workers in the expanding service sectors of post-Fordist economies, in which young people's youthful performance and affective labor plays a key role (Farrugia 2018; Farrugia et al. 2018; McDowell 2009; see also Chapter 5 where we elaborate on how young people consume and sell skin whiteners in the service sector).

In the past, youth studies have focused on how young people acquire knowledge, skills, and competencies through formal education, which they then put to work in jobs for which they must compete with other youngsters. In such analyses, adulthood is located in this transition into work (Furlong 1992; Roberts 2007). However, in the service sector this shift from adolescence to adulthood is less defined. Young people often start to work before they have finished school, at times to pay for their tuition fees. And they acquire skills and competencies while on the job.

The nature of service sector work is also different from that in manual labor or white-collar jobs. In the interactive work of selling and marketing supplements, young people do both the affective labor of connecting with customers—sparking their interest in the products that the youth sell—and the embodied work of showing what the products can do. By "embodying" these products in their very youthful selves, they fuel an expectation that such supplements are efficacious.

When selling supplements and other chemicals, their work includes tailoring products to the metabolic needs of their customers. In Caroline's case, this was done by creating a new kind of protein that better fits women's bodies, which she then sells to her customers. In our case study on the multilevel marketing of C24/7 in Puerto Princesa, we referred to this combined affective and embodied nature of service sector work as "sociometabolic labor" (Hardon et al. 2019). Sociometabolic labor is omnipresent in malls, drugstores, pharmacies, juice bars, beauty salons, and gyms, all service sector spaces in which youth do the work of establishing, maintaining, and negotiating interpersonal relations with customers and embodying the efficacy of chemicals. Such work may involve creating and tailoring chemicals to build muscles, or mitigating bodily disturbances caused by toxic environments and precarious living conditions.

ChemicalYouth Ethnographers

Gideon Lasco is a physician and medical anthropologist. He obtained his Ph.D. from the University of Amsterdam and his M.D. from the University of the Philippines, where he currently teaches anthropology His research examines the chemical practices of young people, the meanings of human height, the politics of health care, and the lived realities of the Philippine "drug war." A Palanca-winning essayist, he maintains a weekly column in the *Philippine Daily Inquirer*, where he writes about health, culture, and society (Fig. 7.4).

Fig. 7.4 Gideon Lasco

Lisanne Claessens was a Ph.D. candidate with the ChemicalYouth project and conducted fieldwork with young people in Amsterdam while following them on their journeys to "super health." Her fields of interest include healthy lifestyles in urban settings and experience-based evidence (Fig. 7.5).

Fig. 7.5 Lisanne Claessens

Amanda Kalangit is a student from the Social Anthropology program of Universitas Sam Ratulangi. She did fieldwork in Manado for the ChemicalYouth project, which provided insights and quotes included in this chapter. She wrote her master's thesis on young women's body work.

Ian Anthony Davatos was a researcher of the Palawan Studies Center of Palawan State University for the ChemicalYouth project and conducted fieldwork on the chemical hygiene practices of tour guides in the Philippines.

Notes

1. Dietary Supplement Health and Education Act of 1994. Pub L No 103–417. 103rd Congress, 2nd session, S784 (U.S. Congress 2014).
2. This job advertisement is reproduced from Lasco (2017, p. 129).
3. These quotes are attributed to Dean Morris, master herbalist and director of technical affairs of Nature's Way. They are printed on promotional material of C24/7 collected in Puerto Princesa in 2015. See also video clip (Aim Global Product Testimonial 2018) for a 2020 statement on the supplement by Morris.
4. These and other quotes from discussion with Sara and Caroline are excerpts from fieldnotes, research reports, and unpublished writings by Lisanne Claessens, who was a Ph.D. student in the ChemicalYouth project (see biographical statement above).

References

Aim Global Product Testimony C24.7 Befits [*sic*]. (2018). *Where did C24/7 came* [*sic*] *from? Dr. Dean Morris of Nature's Way, USA*. Facebook. https://www.facebook.com/watch/?v=1879758465431073. Accessed on March 1, 2020.

Atkinson, M. (2007). Playing with fire: Masculinity, health, and sports supplements. *Sociology of Sport Journal, 24*(2), 165–186. https://doi.org/10.1123/ssj.24.2.165.

Bourdieu, P. (1992). *An invitation to reflexive sociology*. Chicago: University of Chicago Press.

Claessens, L. (2017). *Push and play* (Unpublished Research Report). Amsterdam: Anthropology Department, University of Amsterdam.

Claessens, L. (2018). *Making a living* (Unpublished Research Report). Amsterdam: Anthropology Department, University of Amsterdam.

Cohen, P. A. (2016). The supplement paradox negligible benefits, robust consumption. *Journal of the American Medical Association, 316*(14), 1453–1454. https://doi.org/10.1001/jama.2016.14252.

Cruz, A. J., Tanchoco, C. C., & Orense, C. L. (2011). Awareness, usage and perception of food supplements among adult residents in metro Manila.

Phillippine Journal of Internal Medicine, 49(1), 30–37. https://doi.org/10.3860/pjim.v49i1.2441.
Errington, F., Gewertz, D., & Fujikura, T. (2013). *The noodle narratives: The global rise of an industrial food into the twenty-first century*. Berkeley: University of California Press.
Euromonitor International. (2016). *Passport vitamins and dietary supplements in the Philippines*. Euromonitor International PDF report.
Eussen, S. R. B. M., Verhagen, H., Klungel, O. H., Garssen, J., Van Loveren, H., Van Kranen, H. J., et al. (2011). Functional foods and dietary supplements: Products at the interface between pharma and nutrition. *European Journal of Pharmacology, 668*(1), 2–9. https://doi.org/10.1016/j.ejphar.2011.07.008.
Farrugia, D. (2018). Youthfulness and immaterial labor in the new economy. *The Sociological Review, 66*(3). https://doi.org/10.1177/0038026117731657.
Farrugia, D., Threadgold, S., & Coffey, J. (2018). Youth subjectivities and affective labour in the service economy. *Journal of Youth Studies, 21*(3). https://doi.org/10.1080/13676261.2017.1366015.
FITSHE. (2018). *FITSHE: About*. FITSHE. https://www.fitshe.com/about/. Accessed on March 1, 2020.
Furlong, A. (1992). *Growing up in a classless society? School to work transitions.* Edinburgh: Edinburgh University Press.
Greenberg, D. (2017). Why science teachers should care about social justice. *iWonder: Rediscovering School Science, 1*(1), 70–73.
GroceryTrader. (2008). *The smallest next big thing in nutritional supplementation.* GroceryTrader. https://grocerytrader.co.uk/the-smallest-next-big-thing-in-nutritional-supplementation/. Accessed on March 1, 2020.
Hardon, A., Davatos, I., & Lasco, G. (2019). Be your product. *American Ethnologist, 46*(4), 429–443. https://doi.org/10.1111/amet.12830.
Kalangit, A. (2015). *"Tubuh butuh tubuh" Health practices and 'ideal bodies' among young women in Manado, North Sulawesi* (Master's thesis). Universitas Sam Ratulangi, North Sulawesi.
Kodicek, E., & Young, F. (1969). Captain Cook and scurvey. *The Royal Society Publishing, 24*(1), 43–63.
Larsen, S. (2014). *Benefits of magnesium.* Coach Sara. http://www.coachsara.com/shop.html. Accessed on April 20, 2020.
Lasker, G., & Simcox, N. (2020). Using feminist theory and social justice pedagogy to educate a new generation of precautionary principle chemists. *Catalyst, 6*(1), 1–13.

Lasco, G. (2017). *Height matters: The making, meanings and materialities of human stature in the Philippines* (Doctoral dissertation). Anthropology Department, University of Amsterdam, Amsterdam. https://pure.uva.nl/ws/files/12162788/Lasco_Thesis_complete.pdf.

Latham, J. R., Fraser, S., Fomiatti, R., Moore, D., Seear, K., & Aitken, C. (2019). Men's performance and image-enhancing drug use as self-transformation: Working out in makeover culture. *Australian Feminist Studies, 34*(100), 149–164. https://doi.org/10.1080/08164649.2019.1644952.

Lonn, E. (2005). Effects of long-term vitamin E supplementation on cardiovascular events and cancer: A randomized controlled trial. *Journal of the American Medical Association, 293*(11), 1338–1347. https://doi.org/10.1001/jama.293.11.1338.

McDowell, L. (2009). *Working bodies: Interactive service employment and workplace identities*. Chichester, UK: Blackwell.

Offit, P. (2013). *Do you believe in magic? Vitamins, supplements and all things natural- a look behind the curtains*. London: HarperCollins.

Op den Kamp, J., & Pulanco, R. (dirs.). (2017). *Sweet Medicine*. https://vimeo.com/234326045.

Philippines Bureau of Civil Service. (1906). *Manual of information relative to the Philippine civil service showing the positions, classified and unclassified, the methods governing examinations and certifications for appointment, the regulations for rating examination papers, specimen examination*. Philippines Bureau of Civil Service. https://quod.lib.umich.edu/cgi/t/text/text-idx?c=philamer;idno=ACF2655.1906.001. Accessed on April 30, 2020.

Price, C. (2016). *Vitamania: How vitamins revolutionized the way we think about food*. New York: Penguin Books.

Roberts, K. (2007). Youth transitions and generations: A response to Wyn and Woodman. *Journal of Youth Studies, 10*(2), 263–269. https://doi.org/10.1080/13676260701204360.

Rocha, T., Amaral, J. S., & Oliveira, M. (2016). Adulteration of dietary supplements by the illegal addition of synthetic drugs: A review. *Comprehensive Reviews in Food Science and Food Safety, 15*(1), 43–62. https://doi.org/10.1111/1541-4337.12173.

Scrinis, G. (2013). *Nutritionism: The science and politics of dietary advice*. New York: Columbia University Press.

U.S. Congress. (2014). *S.784—Dietary Supplement Health and Education Act of*

1994. U.S. Congress. https://www.congress.gov/bill/103rd-congress/senate-bill/784. Accessed on March 21, 2020.

Williams, H. (2013). *10 Creative smoothie recipes.* All Women's Talk. https://food.allwomenstalk.com/creative-smoothie-recipes/. Accessed on March 20, 2020.

8

Using Chemicals to Boost Creativity

> As you sit behind your desk, you may start to feel a little tingling sensation or a slight increase in awareness of things around you at the office, things that you didn't notice before. Words might appear brighter or sharper on the screen. And perhaps not so much changes around you but how you experience it changes quite a lot, you feel alive and quite present in your body. (Mishra 2020, p. 42)

This is an excerpt of an interview that Swasti Mishra (2020), one of the ChemicalYouth ethnographers, had with young professionals in Amsterdam who were self-experimenting with microdoses of lysergic acid, also known as LSD, and psilocybin, the active ingredient of "magic mushrooms." During the ChemicalYouth project, we observed that microdosing with psychedelics was emerging as a new trend among students and young professionals. Popular media such as *Forbes*, *Vice*, *Rolling Stone*, and *Marie Claire* published stories on this trend, with titles such as: "Micro-dosing: The Drug Habit Your Boss Is Gonna Love" (Dean 2017), "Interview With a Corporate Banker Who Microdosed His Way to the Top" (Fisher 2016), and "Can Very Small Doses of LSD Make You a Better Worker?" (Woods 2016).

O'Bryan Tear, a psychedelic researcher from the United Kingdom, defines microdosing as:

> taking a very small amount of LSD or magic mushrooms with the aim of boosting creativity, productivity or mood. So it does not give you a full recreational experience. It keeps you engaged and relatively sober, but it helps you work better and more productively". (BBC London News 2018)

Nina, one of Mishra's interlocutors, explains it as follows:

> It's not like taking a full dose....the tiny dose counteracts the "airy-fairy" psychedelic effect, and it lets you take advantage of the focus, the creative ways you can make new connections between different pieces of information, and even simply the good mood it puts you in. (Mishra 2018, p. 1)

In this chapter we explore this burgeoning practice of microdosing and three ways of gathering data to understand its effects: analyzing users' narratives, collaborating with users to aggregate user accounts, and organizing clinical experiments. In the first way, users' narratives show how they "do" microdosing, what they want to achieve by using these substances, and what they do to prevent or reduce harm. Mishra (2020), for example, examined the narratives of microdosers in Amsterdam, and followed their collaborative self-experiments over time. Some members of our team have also reviewed reports on microdosing in popular media and online, a form of "virtual ethnography" (see Krieg et al. 2017; Hupli et al. 2019). A second way of understanding the effects of microdosing is through the gathering of data that can aggregate users' experiences; such data has been generated through collaborations between researchers and users, and is reviewed here. Finally, a third way is through clinical trials that compare the effects of psychoactive substances with those of placebos. These studies use a "blinding" strategy, an administrative procedure that ensures that participants don't know if they are being given a psychoactive substance or pharmacologically inert one; in this way, researchers hope to unravel what the "real," that is material, effects of microdosing are.

In the conclusion, we reflect on the ways that the practical wisdom (Boothroyd and Lewis 2016) generated by young people in collaborative microdosing experiments is linked to larger scale surveys and trials that aim to generate scientific evidence on benefits and risks of microdosing. We outline the modes of "knowing" that these surveys and placebo-controlled studies produce, how they lead to re-articulations of chemicals efficacy and reflect on the ways it can be understood as regulation from below, a concept that we discussed in Chapter 2, and will further elaborate in Chapter 9, the concluding chapter.

A Brief History of Microdosing

People who engage in and study microdosing often mention Albert Hofmann, admired for his self-experiments with LSD. Hofmann was the first to synthesize the drug in 1938, when he worked for the pharmaceutical company Sandoz. He was exploring the alkaloids present in a fungus called ergot (used traditionally by midwives to induce labor). When synthesizing LSD he was interrupted in his work by "unusual sensations" due to ingesting a small amount accidently. He went home to lie down, reporting later that "in dreamlike state, with eyes closed. … I perceived an uninterrupted stream of fantastic pictures, extraordinary shapes with intense, kaleidoscopic play of colors" (as quoted in Pollan 2019, p. 22). In his 1979 memoir *LSD: My Problem Child*, Hofmann describes a series of self-experiments that followed and includes excerpts from his lab journals, such as this one from April 4, 1943:

> 4/4/43. 16.20: 0.5cc of ½ promil aqueous solution of diethylamide tartrate orally = 0.25 mg tartate. Taken diluted with about 10 cc water. Tasteless. 17.00: Beginning of dizziness, feeling of anxiety, visual distortions, symptoms of paralysis, desire to laugh: Supplement of 4/12: Home by bicycle. From ca. 18:00-20.00 most severe crisis. (Hofmann 1979, p. 48)

Reflecting back on that day, he then comments that:

> Here the notes in my laboratory journal cease. I was able to write the last words with great effort. … I had to struggle to speak intelligibly. I asked my laboratory assistant, who was informed of the self-experiment, to escort me home. We went by bicycle, no automobile being available because of wartime restrictions. (Hofmann 1979, p. 48)

Based on these self-experiments Hofmann (1979) concluded that LSD was a psychoactive substance with "extraordinary properties and potency" (p. 51). In 1947, Sandoz started marketing LSD (under the brand name Delysid) as a psychiatric drug.

James Fadiman was one of the first researchers to explore the effects of LSD on creativity, when he was still a graduate student at Stanford University in the 1960s. He designed an experiment to determine whether psychedelics could facilitate problem-solving of a technical nature. As Fadiman (2011) recalls:

> others had done work with artists—but we took on a different challenge. Could we use these materials and get people to work on highly technical problems. … We began this really gorgeous study with senior research scientists from a number of companies. We told them that we'd assist them in their most pressing technological problems, particularly if they were really stuck. (p. 233)

The experiments conducted by Fadiman and others in this first wave of psychedelic research gave users structured guidance during their "trips," including preparation in the form of "flight instructions." These helped users "set" how they would navigate their experiences during the trip; for example, the "setting" of being in a safe place, accompanied by trip "sitters" helped ensure users that they would be supported if they experienced anxiety, fear, or adverse physical effects. The Spring Grove Group, which conducted research to find out if LSD could help alcoholic patients overcome their addictions, established the following setting: LSD treatment was done in a comfortable room, with a sofa, carpet, flowers, and a good sound system. Music was played throughout the session, and the trial subject was given eyeshades, allowing the patient to retreat into their imagination. A therapist guided the experience and helped subjects feel cared for, encouraging them to go with the flow of the drug-induced effects (Oram 2014).

Fadiman's research into the creative potential of LSD stopped in 1966, when the US Food and Drug Administration (FDA) declared LSD a scheduled drug. One of the main reasons for this declaration was the alleged "misuse" of the drug for recreational purposes by young people in the Sixties' counterculture. Despite not being able to complete the study, Fadiman concluded that the scientists who had participated in the experiment were pleased with the results: the drug had in fact helped them solve technical problems. One scientist even won a major scientific award (Fadiman 2011).

Indeed, early on in the history of LSD, the substance came to be heralded for its aid stimulating technological breakthroughs. John Markoff, a co-fellow at the Center for Advanced Study in the Behavioral Sciences at Stanford University, where I have written much of this book, suggests that the use of LSD to promote creativity had far-reaching consequences, stimulating the innovations that emerged from Silicon Valley in the 1960s and 1970s (see Markoff 2005). Steve Jobs, a dropout from college who experimented with drugs and was part of the youth counterculture in the 1960s, told him that, "taking LSD was one of the two or three most important things he had done in his life" (Markoff 2005, p. 21). Kary Mullis, who received a Nobel Prize for inventing the polymerase chain reaction (PCR), a revolutionary technique for multiplying tiny amounts of DNA for use in genetic research, similarly attributed his innovation to his LSD use. In an interview for a BBC documentary, he explained how psychedelic experiences helped him imagine how DNA works:

> I wasn't stoned on LSD at the time, but my mind had learnt how to get there. I could sit on the DNA molecules and watch the polymers go by. And I didn't feel dumb about it. I felt like that's just the way I think, I put myself in all different kinds of spots. And I learnt it partially, I would think, this is again my opinion, through psychedelic drugs. (Eagles 1997)

When Jobs and Mullis experimented with LSD, microdosing was not yet popular. In an online interview with Dutch microdosing enthusiasts, Fadiman explained "with a high dose, set and setting is as important as the drug" (Microdosing Netherlands 2019). In contrast, he says, "with micro-dosing, unless your outerworld is terrible, it does not seem to matter much … Because its effect are so subtle, set and setting are far less important." The idea that LSD could be safely used at very low dosages is the innovating force behind microdosing.

Fadiman (2011) proposed a schedule of one day of microdosing, followed by two days off, and repeating the cycle starting on the fourth day. In the interview, Fadiman recalls that he proposed this schedule not as a standard practice, but as a tool for users to observe what microdosing did for them: "we wanted people to, on the third day, to experience how they feel without the substance, and reflect on the difference between 'on and off.'" He said that after one month of trying out this schedule, microdosers should be able to determine what works best for them. In *The Psychedelic Explorer's Guide*, Fadiman (2011) quotes a man named Charles, who used this schedule:

> The protocol I followed had me take a micro-dose one day, then carefully observe any ongoing or lingering effects the second day, and the give myself the third day completely off. By going slow, you give yourself a chance to really know, to really observe what is different, why it is different, and how you can best take advantage of it. … I've found that I've had some brilliant outbursts (at least they seemed brilliant to me) with respect to both work and personal creative projects. (p. 200)

This guide also describes the experiences of a woman named Madeline, who attested to the creative potential of microdosing. A documentary maker from Manhattan, married with a four-year-old child, Madeline says she has to review 50 hours of film footage and "knit it together in a story arc," and that when microdosing she feels deeply connected to her work: "I barely come up for air for the next five hours because I am so sincerely enjoying what I'm doing" (Fadiman 2011, p. 202).

A similar narrative is reported in the popular women's magazine *Marie Claire*, which ran a story entitled "Why Power Women Are Micro-Dosing LSD at Work" (Malone 2016), in which a woman named Karen Smith, a 32-year-old who lives in Chicago, explains in detail how she made capsules and dosed psilocybin. Karen is enrolled in a data science graduate program after working for 10 years in a tech startup. Confronted with cold Midwest winters, and having quit cigarettes and marijuana, she was looking for something else to improve her mental well-being. Her husband had read about the beneficial effects of psilocybin on the forum-based website Reddit (which at the time had a forum on microdosing with over 9000 subscribers). The couple was offered some "magic" mushrooms—psilocybin containing-mushrooms—from a friend, which they ground up in a spice grinder. They bought empty capsules on Amazon, and packed them with the powder: 10 micrograms for Karen's husband and half that amount for Karen. They took a capsule every few days for four months. Karen started feeling better and became very efficient. In Karen's words, "It gives you fresh eyes ... for programming or figuring out algorithmic stuff. It made me really productive in a motivated way." An added benefit was that Karen got a lot of household chores done.

Microdosing Narratives

In the earlier use of LSD, preparation mattered—users were given "flight instructions" and trip sitters guided the experience. The stories that we reviewed suggest that microdosing has little to do with managing preparation or setting as a runway for an unpredictable flight. Instead, it involves material work, as presented in the story of Karen—preparing capsules, cutting blots, and weighing—as well as attending to schedules that ensure the productive insertion of microdosing into a day's schedule. Figure 8.1 provides an example of such a schedule from Mishra's fieldwork. Note how it includes timeslots for meditation, sleeping healthy eating, and a reflecting on the success of the day's work.

Trip sitters are not seen as necessary for microdosing. Instead users keep records of their own experiences themselves, many of them inspired

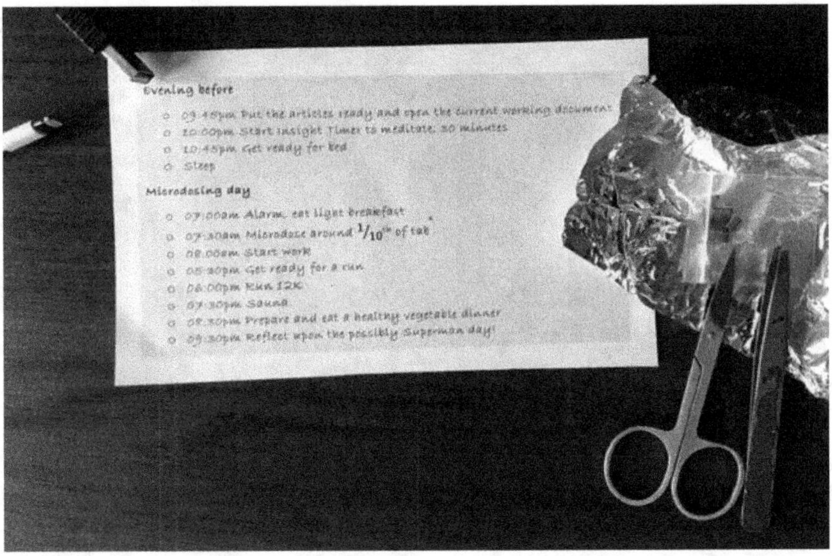

Fig. 8.1 Inserting microdosing into a "Superman" day (*Source* Photo Swasti Mishra, November 2017, Amsterdam)

by Albert Hoffman's laboratory notes. The narratives we examined suggest that microdosing had positive experience on users' moods and creativity, but that adverse events that interfere with the capacity to work could also occur. They also show that users compared the pros and cons of a range of substances (LSD, mushrooms, mescaline) for different tasks at hand. Finally, users commented on other medical benefits on microdosing, including their potential in the treatment of ADHD.

JingShu, one of Mishra's informants developed a scale to record the effects of microdosing over the course of 30 days, see Fig. 8.2. She divided effects into three categories: sexual, positive, and negative (each with their own summative indicator). She judiciously tracked various emotions and her work productivity, rating them on a scale of one to ten, and noting possible side effects.

Her positive mood indicators included being present, peace, joy, love, passion, confidence, acceptance, courage, celebration, and gratitude. Over the course of the 30 days, her scores on positive affects became

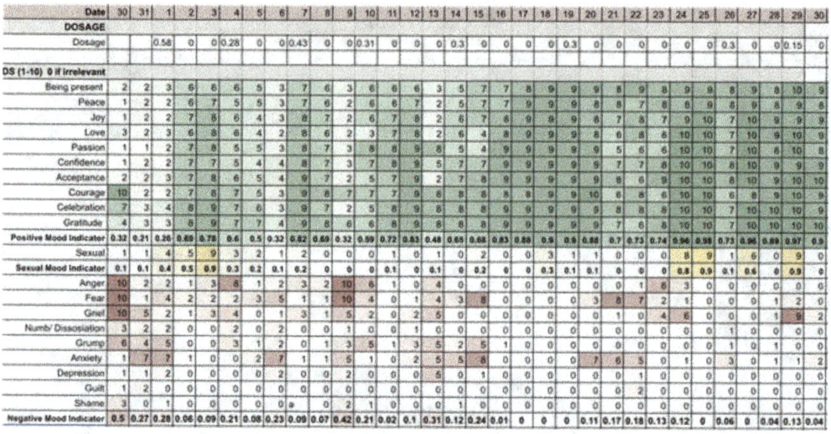

Date	30	31	1	2	3	4	5	6	7	8	9	10	11	12	13	14
DOSAGE																
Dosage			0.58	0	0	0.28	0	0	0.43	0	0	0.31	0	0	0	0.3
DS (1-10) 0 if irrelevant																
Being present	2	2	3	6	6	6	5	3	7	6	3	6	6	6	3	5
Peace	1	2	2	6	7	5	5	3	7	6	2	6	6	7	2	5
Joy	1	2	2	7	8	6	4	3	8	7	2	6	7	8	2	6
Love	3	2	3	6	8	6	4	2	8	6	2	3	7	8	2	6
Passion	1	1	2	7	8	5	5	3	8	7	3	8	8	9	8	5
Confidence	1	2	2	7	7	5	4	4	8	7	3	7	8	9	5	7
Acceptance	2	2	3	7	8	6	5	4	9	7	2	5	7	9	2	7
Courage	10	2	2	7	8	7	5	3	9	8	7	7	7	9	8	8
Celebration	7	3	4	8	9	7	6	3	9	7	2	5	8	9	8	8
Gratitude	4	3	3	8	9	7	7	4	9	8	6	6	8	9	8	8
Positive Mood Indicator	0.32	0.21	0.26	0.69	0.78	0.6	0.5	0.32	0.82	0.69	0.32	0.59	0.72	0.83	0.48	0.65
Sexual	1	1	4	5	9	3	2	1	2	0	0	0	1	0	1	0
Sexual Mood Indicator	0.1	0.1	0.4	0.5	0.9	0.3	0.2	0.1	0.2	0	0	0	0.1	0	0.1	0
Anger	10	2	2	1	3	8	1	2	3	2	10	6	1	0	4	0
Fear	10	1	4	2	2	2	3	5	1	1	10	4	0	1	4	3
Grief	10	5	2	1	3	4	0	1	3	1	5	2	0	2	5	0
Numb/ Dissosiation	3	2	2	0	0	2	0	2	0	0	1	0	0	1	0	0
Grump	6	4	5	0	0	3	1	2	0	1	3	5	1	3	5	2
Anxiety	1	7	7	1	0	0	2	7	1	1	5	1	0	2	5	5
Depression	1	1	2	0	0	0	0	2	0	0	2	0	0	0	5	0
Guilt	1	2	0	0	0	0	0	0	0	0	0	0	0	0	0	0
Shame	3	0	1	0	0	0	0	0		0	2	1	0	0	0	1
Negative Mood Indicator	0.5	0.27	0.28	0.06	0.09	0.21	0.08	0.23	0.09	0.07	0.42	0.21	0.02	0.1	0.31	0.12

Date	15	16	17	18	19	20	21	22	23	24	25	26	27	28	29	30
DOSAGE																
Dosage	0	0	0	0	0.3	0	0	0	0	0	0	0.3	0	0	0.15	0
DS (1-10) 0 if irrelevant																
Being present	7	7	8	9	9	9	8	9	8	9	9	8	9	8	10	9
Peace	7	7	9	9	9	8	8	7	8	8	9	8	9	8	9	8
Joy	7	8	9	9	9	6	7	8	7	9	10	7	10	9	9	9
Love	4	8	9	9	9	8	6	8	8	10	10	7	10	9	10	9
Passion	4	9	9	9	9	9	5	6	6	10	10	7	10	8	10	8
Confidence	7	9	9	9	9	9	7	7	8	10	10	8	10	9	9	9
Acceptance	8	9	9	9	9	9	8	6	9	10	10	8	10	9	10	10
Courage	8	8	8	9	9	10	6	8	6	10	10	6	8	9	10	9
Celebration	8	9	9	9	9	9	8	8	8	10	10	7	10	10	10	9
Gratitude	8	9	9	9	9	9	7	6	8	10	10	7	10	10	10	10
Positive Mood Indicator	0.68	0.83	0.88	0.9	0.9	0.88	0.7	0.73	0.74	0.96	0.98	0.73	0.96	0.89	0.97	0.9
Sexual	2	0	0	3	1	1	0	0	0	8	9	1	6	0	9	0
Sexual Mood Indicator	0.2	0	0	0.3	0.1	0.1	0	0	0	0.8	0.9	0.1	0.6	0	0.9	0
Anger	0	0	0	0	0	0	0	1	8	3	0	0	0	0	0	0
Fear	8	0	0	0	0	3	8	7	2	1	0	0	0	1	2	0
Grief	0	0	0	0	0	0	1	0	4	6	0	0	0	1	9	2
Numb/ Dissosiation	0	0	0	0	0	0	0	0	0	0	0	1	0	0	0	0
Grump	5	1	0	0	0	0	0	0	0	0	0	1	0	1	0	0
Anxiety	8	0	0	0	0	7	6	5	0	1	0	3	0	1	1	2
Depression	1	0	0	0	0	0	0	1	0	0	0	0	0	0	0	0
Guilt	0	0	0	0	0	0	0	2	0	0	0	0	0	0	0	0
Shame	0	0	0	0	0	0	0	0	0	0	0	0	0	0	0	0
Negative Mood Indicator	0.24	0.01	0	0	0	0.11	0.17	0.18	0.13	0.12	0	0.06	0	0.04	0.13	0.04

Fig. 8.2 The 30-day observations of JingShu (*Note* Retrieved on May 24 2020 from https://microdosing.nl/i-microdosed-on-psilocybin-for-30-days-and-tracked-its-lasting-effects/. *Source* Photo from Mishra [2020, p. 37])

higher. She tells Mishra that she was impressed by the "non-stickiness" to both positive and negative events that occurred in her life (Mishra 2020, p. 37).

There are many such individual reports of experiences with microdosing on online forum-based sites such as Reddit (used by Karen) and drug-using focused sites like Erowid (2020). Erowid is an "experience vault," which is filled through decentralized user engagement (Liu 2012, p. 25) via voluntary submissions, and which is managed centrally by two experienced drug users (named "Earth" and "Fire") who screen and edit reports before they are published on the website. Our analysis of user reports on Erowid shows that most of the participants in the experience vault are young (average age 23) and male (86% of reports are from men; 14% from women).[1] While Erowid accepts reports on a wide range of drugs, the most commonly mentioned substances are mushrooms ($N =$ 1715) and LSD ($N = 1168$). "Microdosing" was the most mentioned term in the LSD reports, which attests to the popularity of this practice.

An example of such a report is entitled "Psychedelic Microdosing: A Surprising ADHD Fix" (Erowid 2020). This report concerns 1P-LSD, a synthetic modification of LSD. "Designer drugs" such as 1P-LSD have emerged in this underground drug-use culture as a way of avoiding drug regulations that have defined LSD itself as illegal. The user who wrote up the experiences with 1P-LSD does not self-declare his/her age or sex, but does give his/her weight (60 kg) and the dose used (6 ug), while proposing a dosage scheme that consist of 1/16 rather than 1/10 of the regular dosage, and reports that he/she did not experience any side effects:

> I had been trying out magic mushrooms (or rather magic truffles) with… "interesting" results. But they are of tremendously repellent taste, and the reliable occurrence of nausea makes them unfit for daily utilisation. It was only then that I found out about 1P-LSD, a novel lysergamide that had entered the market only this very year and, being not yet statutory regulated, was being sold legally across Europe (and in some countries, still is). After reading up on it, I came to the conclusion that, judging by the majority of reports out on the interwebs, its biochemical response was indiscernible from that of its famous twin, LSD-25 [The drug that Sandoz branded as Delysid, which was taken off the market in 1966]. Excitedly, I ordered a sample from a research alchemist.
>
> A period of experimentation followed, and I had some profound experiences with this substance … the real revelation was the unexpected attenuation of my ADHD symptoms. Not only was I able to focus much better, both at work and university. Mood swings and impulsive behaviour basically vanished. During conversations, it has become easy for me to subdue my urge to interrupt, instead patiently listening to the other person and replying in a concise and considerate manner.
>
> Addendum: I have shared my find in my local ADHD support group. Several others have reported back with comments such as "helpful effects" "better concentration and general condition," "less thought racing," "less irritable" etc. One group member, who happens to be an alcoholic, happily recounted that each day he is microdosing, the urge to open yet another beer vanishes, and he will not even finish his first one.
>
> Addendum 2: To better assess the effects of 1P-LSD, I reverted back to Ritalin for a day while working on a very concentration-demanding job. In direct comparison, inattentivity is decreased to a similar extent with 20mg Ritalin as is with 6mcg 1P-LSD. In my opinion though, Ritalin does not feel quite natural, while the LSD does. It is just a more pleasing remedy.

This user turned to a new chemical (1P-LSD) that was similar to LSD, reporting not only on its effects but also on their research process; this suggests that, like many reporters on Erowid, this user is an experienced "psychonaut" (a user who tries out new designer drugs on a regular basis to examine the altered states of consciousness that the substances generate, see Berning and Hardon [2016] and Langlitz [2012]). This user was interested in trying out microdosing to be more creative and productive, as well as in doing research and connecting to others to share their experiences, especially with fellow ADHD sufferers.

Video reports of experiences with microdosing are also posted on YouTube, a platform that makes it easier to share the material aspects of "doing" microdosing and "real time" effects. Aleksi Hupli and Moritz Berning, who both participated in the ChemicalYouth project as ethnographers, used the YouTube Data Tool developed by the Digital Methods Initiative of the University of Amsterdam to explore these visual demonstrations of users' techniques (Hupli et al. 2019). The search, conducted in June 2016, resulted in 115 videos—six of which accounted for 92% of approximately 1 million total views. Subsequent extractions in November 2017 ($N = 351$) and October 2018 ($N = 447$) revealed a surge in video postings.

One of the two most popular videos, *Your Mate Tom*, presents Tom who consumes mushrooms in front of his camera, which the video declares are "props" (perhaps to avoid legal repercussions). Fifteen minutes after consumption Tom reports not feeling high but instead calm, despite his heart rate being slightly elevated. He says he feels "a bit chill, a bit calm, like I had one little tiny drag of a joint" (as quoted in Hupli et al. 2019, p. 133). He also tells his audience about an adverse event that happened when he took "three little mushrooms" on his way to the university to study for an exam and he "started to feel a bit funny," anxious and having mild visual distortions. Attesting to a need for cautious dosing, he says "that's what I get for not actually getting scales and measuring it. That's what I get for just estimating" (quoted in Hupli et al. 2019, p. 133).

Another highly viewed video, posted by PsychedSubstance, also calls for cautious dosing, suggesting that a person should first take half of the threshold amount; then, if they don't feel anything, slowly increase the amount by 25–50% until they "hit 1.5 of the threshold" (Hupli et al. 2019, p. 133). The video further recommends using a test kit, with a link to purchase it in the video description, to verify the purity of LSD. PsychedSubstance recommends that dosing every other day would be ideal,[2] since the body builds a tolerance to classical psychedelics immediately.

PsychedSubstance also compares the effects of different psychedelic substances, saying: "I can speak from personal experience being on mescaline microdose right now that it feels extremely similar to being on LSD microdose" (quoted in Hupli et al. 2019, p. 134). He tells the audience that his thoughts run a lot smoother on mescaline than on LSD, and that he experiences more auditory enhancement when using mescaline; when using LSD, in contrast, he experiences more visual enhancement.

Aggregating Experiences

The online platforms where users exchange experiences are convenient virtual spaces for academic researchers to engage with users and learn from their experiences. Efforts to aggregate user experiences confirm the observations of individual users: microdosing enhances creativity and elevates moods. But, the studies also point to adverse effects, and contra-indications for use.

Johnstad (2018), from the University of Bergen, engaged online users in a qualitative microdosing study. He posted an online thread that, after describing the purpose of the study, asked for input. He then approached users who reported on their microdosing practices via the private message function. Through open-ended, qualitative interviews he accumulated a great deal of data. Twenty-one respondents (all male, average age 30) agreed to be interviewed. Johnstad (2018) reports that his respondents reported positive health benefits, including feeling less depressed and anxious, though a few respondents experienced no effects at all and therefore stopped doing in. The participants in Johnstad's study, like many of the users referred to above, were interested in comparative efficacy. Some reflected on differences between LSD and mushrooms, as expressed by one informant: "LSD is just more practical for work and play, bounding energy and target mentality. Mushroom microdoses are more of a personal and 'fresh' interaction with the universe" (Johnstad 2018, p. 46). Despite general agreement on the lack of intoxication produced by microdoses, some respondents did report adverse events. They attributed these to taking a slightly higher dose, referred to as a "mini-dose," or to timing the use incorrectly, which resulted in tripping and having difficulty performing the tasks at hand. As one of Johnstad's (2018) respondents reported:

> I was feeling very tired and had a martial arts class to attend for the first time, so I didn't want to make a bad impression. This was my second time microdosing [mu]shrooms, and I dosed around 0.25–0.35 gram a few hours before in an attempt to peak well before the class and still just be stimulated and in a good positive mood for it. This backfired massively as I had a large meal around the time of dosing and it really kicked in once I got to the class. I found it very hard to follow instructions. (pp. 46–47)

Others reported insomnia after microdosing late in the day, and some also said that, after microdosing for a while, benefits faded and mental health conditions were exacerbated.

Fadiman and Korb (2019a, b) encouraged people who contacted them for advice to send reports of their experiences, using a Google form and a dedicated website (microdosingpsychedelics.com). They describe this work as "citizen science, a social agreement where researchers enlist those members of the public with an interest in a particular topic or issue to upload their own observations or local experiments into an unrestricted database" (Fadiman and Korb 2019a, p. 321). In citizen science, participants are not study subjects, but collaborators. The collaboration involved the researchers providing information on what they knew about the practice, and participants filling in Google forms, which, in addition to daily mood check-ins, included a modified version of the Positive and Negative Affect Scale (PANAS; see also Watson and Clark 1988). Over 18 months, 4000 people wrote in asking for information, and 843 responded to the request to fill in a Google form.[3]

Thus, the majority of people who were asked to join the study did not do so. This may have happened for many reasons: perhaps they decided not to microdose. Or perhaps they did try it, but stopped because it didn't work for them. Or they liked the effects, but didn't want to spend time participating. Fadiman and Korb (2019a) note that they had discouraged volunteers who appeared disorganized, were experiencing a bad period in life, as well as those with a history of psychosis, acknowledging that their findings were, therefore, not necessarily representative of the population of users:

> It is entirely possible that a sizeable percentage of the general population, were they to microdose, would experience no discernable effects. Another significant percentage might have a sufficiently negative experience such that they would not be inclined to continue or contribute a research report. (Fadiman and Korb 2019a, p. 322)

Those who did participate were asked to evaluate the following 23 affects (along with quality of sleep and pain):

- Attentive: paying close attention
- Focused: able to direct specific attention
- Depressed: generally unhappy or despondent
- Clear: free of unpleasantness or confusion
- Guilty: feeling regret for doing something wrong
- Proud: having a sense of achievement
- Irritable: feeling easily annoyed
- Strong: feeling able to cope with difficulties
- Ashamed: feeling shame for doing something wrong or foolish
- Interested: wanting to be involved in something
- Jittery: feeling agitated and edgy

Note that the list includes positive and negative affects in random order. Using this scale, Fadiman and Korb (2019b) found that 52.5% of the people who participated in the study experienced a relative improvement in the positive affects, and 31% experienced a decrease in negative affects. Overall, they reported elevated moods, and they found that microdosing was helpful for their productivity. A number of respondents said that they had been more creative, which they underscored by sending some of the art and music that they had crafted (Fadiman and Korb 2019b, p. 121). Interestingly in this large-scale survey, a substantial number of participants preferred microdosing to the use of ADHD drugs such as Ritalin for improving their productivity and focus, echoing the reports on Erowid (see above).[4]

Fadiman and Korb's "citizen science" approach aims not only at demonstrating benefits but also making microdosing safer. They write: "we tried to give the best and safest current information as we went along in these aggregated self-reports" (Fadiman and Korb 2019a, p. 327). Based on the data collected in their study, they advised lowering the suggested dose from 1/10 to 1/20 of a regular dose, warned that people with a red-green colorblindness could experience visual distortions for a number of days after discontinuing use, and warned of interactions with medications, such as lithium. They also called for more research: "The next steps are for research institutions to turn our search into research, establish safe methods and protocols, and scientifically verify or invalidate the claims we see in our inboxes and hypotheses we and others generate" (Fadiman and Korb 2019a, p. 322).

Academic researchers have been taking on this challenge in different ways. Here we present the findings from two such studies, one using an online questionnaire—an approach similar to that of Fadiman and Korb—and another extracting data from a real life microdosing event.

In 2018, the University of Maastricht's Department of Neuropsychology and Psychopharmacology conducted an online survey focusing on the benefits of microdosing on creativity, cognitive flexibility, and well-being (Hutten et al. 2019). Their online questionnaire was advertised to microdosers through online fora. The researchers received responses from 1116 respondents, largely young and male (18 years and older; 84% men; 14% women), of whom 80% were currently microdosing. The researchers report that performance enhancement was the most important stated purpose for microdosing. Enhanced creativity and enhanced mood were the most commonly reported positive effects. Psilocybin and LSD were the most used substance; dosing schedules varied. Around one-fifth of the respondents said that they had stopped microdosing completely, and one-third said they had stopped using at least one kind of psychedelic substance. Reasons given for stopping included doubt about efficacy and negative physical and psychological experiences (these are not specified in the study).

Researchers from the Brain and Cognition Institute of Leiden University, the Netherlands, in collaboration with the Psychedelic Society of the Netherlands, did a natural experiment at a microdosing event to assess the extent to which creativity is enhanced through microdosing (Prochazkova et al. 2018). Participants were asked to complete tasks to assess their creativity-related problem-solving skills, once before taking a microdose and once around 1.5 hours after taking a microdose. This timeframe was chosen because self-reports in the Erowid archive of user experiences suggest that effects of mushrooms peak between 30 and 90 minutes of use.

Out of 80 attendees at the event, 38 volunteered to participate in the experiment (23 men and 15 women, average age 31). In this experiment the amount of mushrooms was adjusted to their weight. Attendees with low body weight were given 0.22 grams, those with average weight 0.33 grams, and those with high body weight 0.44 grams, but participants were also free to adjust. The dosage was calculated based on the definition of microdosing as 1/10 of a recreational dose. The researchers also analyzed the presence of psychedelic alkaloids in the mushrooms, such as psilocybin.

The researchers report an increase in divergent idea generation, flexibility, and originality scores. The tests used included the Picture Concept Task, which measures visual creativity; it involves finding an association between several images. It also included the Alternative Uses Task, which is used to measure the possible uses of an object. The researchers write that the benefit of this study design is that it is done in a natural setting, but the disadvantage is that use is less controlled than in a laboratory, and that there is no control group. As a result, they do not know if the improved scores on creativity after using mushrooms are due to other factors, such as the learning that took place in the pre-mushroom-use tests, or the expectation that mushrooms increase creativity. Moreover, a positive mood and thrill of being part of the collective experiment could have influenced the test results. These researchers from the Brain and Cognition Institute of Leiden University were concerned with the "confounding" influence of users' expectations, a concern that set them apart from the first wave of psychedelic researchers, who explicitly aimed to create a positive expectation in order to enhance the effects of the psychedelic substances. In their scientific report on the experiment, the researchers emphasize that "future studies should seek to validate our findings using a lab-based randomized double-blind placebo-controlled experimental design" (Prochazkova et al. 2018, pp. 3409–3410).

Collaborative Trials

In the hybrid communities of users and academic researchers that participate in such online studies, there is an emerging call to study if the effects of microdosing are "real" through placebo-controlled controlled trials. A research group at the University of Maastricht has conducted a critical review of existing "evidence," finding that future studies need to examine whether there is an "expectation" effect (Kuypers et al. 2019). While microdosing is associated with positive effects in existing observational studies, these studies are of users who take the substances for the express purpose of increasing performance and creativity, and thus may expect positive effects. The researchers recommend "rigorous placebo controlled clinical studies with different low doses of the drug to determine whether there is any evidence for the claims being made by microdosers" (Kuypers et al. 2019, p. 1046). They also stress that, at the time their review was published, only one study had followed a double-blind, placebo-controlled protocol to look at the effects of microdosing LSD (see Yanakieva et al. 2019). This relatively small study (only 48 subjects were enrolled) reported a limited effect: a delay in time perception after the administration of single microdoses of LSD.

The UK-based Beckley Foundation, the founder of which openly admits to having benefited from experiences with LSD in the 1960s, is committed to supporting researchers who seek to generate more reliable evidence. On its website the foundation states:

> Although many underground adherents attribute a variety of psychological and physical benefits to microdosing, including enhanced mood,

> focus, and cognition, or even reduced pain, there is a dearth of reliable evidence of the benefits—or indeed any potential health effects—of the practice. (Beckley Foundation 2017)

Together with researchers from Imperial College in London, the Beckley Foundation is engaging users in the production of such reliable evidence. At the time of writing this book, the study was recruiting participants who already engaged in microdosing, or who were about to participate in a naturalistic *self-blinding* study, which would allow for the collection of more reliable evidence (see Fig. 8.3, the recruitment advertisement).

The website for the study contains a guide on how to carefully prepare microdoses and make capsules, which are either a placebo or a microdose, and how to pair the capsules up with QR codes in envelopes that are then randomly allocated over testing days, see Fig. 8.4.

Szigeti, one of the Imperial College researchers explains why "blinding" is necessary in an informational YouTube video entitled "Is Microdosing Placebo? The Self-Blinding Study" (b1987307 2019), which the

BECKLEY
FOUNDATION

We Are Recruiting For A New Psychedelic Microdosing Study!

Are you currently, or are planning to, microdose with a blotter-based psychedelic? We are now recruiting for our new observational psychedelic microdosing study!

The Beckley/Imperial Psychedelic Research Programme is excited to announce its new collaborative study on psychedelic microdosing. The Naturalistic Self-Blinding Microdose Study is designed and led by Dr. Balázs Szigeti and Dr. David Erritzoe MRCPsych of Imperial College London, in partnership with Amanda Feilding of the Beckley Foundation.

Fig. 8.3 Recruitment advertisement on the Beckley Foundation website (Beckley Foundation 2017)

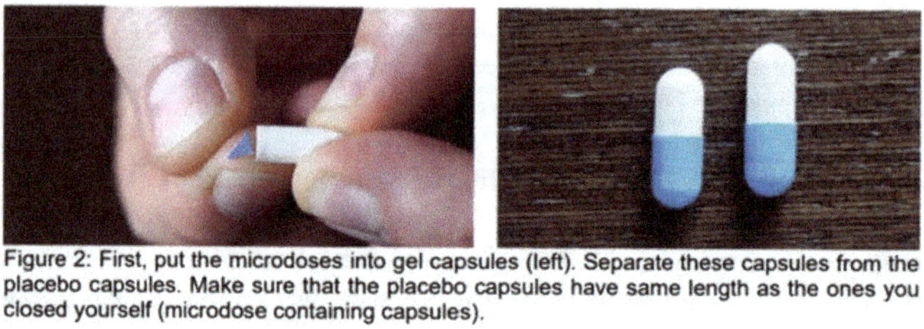

Fig. 8.4 The placebo and microdose capsules that users are expected to prepare themselves (*Source* Screenshot from the self-blinding manual [Imperial College London 2020])

Beckley Foundation links to on its website. He cites a pyramid of evidence, pointing to randomized controlled trials at the top of the pyramid and individual case reports at the bottom (Fig. 8.5).

Szigeti argues that, at present, "There is no evidence for microdosing, but also no evidence against it." Why don't the many user stories and results of observational studies count as evidence? He argues that the observational studies that have been done so far don't provide evidence because they do not account for the expectation effect. A self-blinding placebo-controlled study can provide more rigorous evidence, he suggests.

As we mentioned above, in the past, psychedelic researchers sought to cultivate a positive effect by setting expectations. The "flight instructions" developed by these early researchers were designed to produce specific kinds of positive effects, including capacities to problem solve as well as therapeutic efficacies. Preparing for such desired effects was considered as important as the consumption of the substance. Today, those engaged in microdosing, in contrast, appear intent on measuring the materials effects of LSD and mushrooms, purified from the influences of set and setting. Why is this so? To some extent, we can attribute self-blinding trials to the prohibition of psychedelics. Microdosing would be much easier if the substances used were studied, regulated, and allowed on the market. "Reliable" evidence from randomized controlled trials could

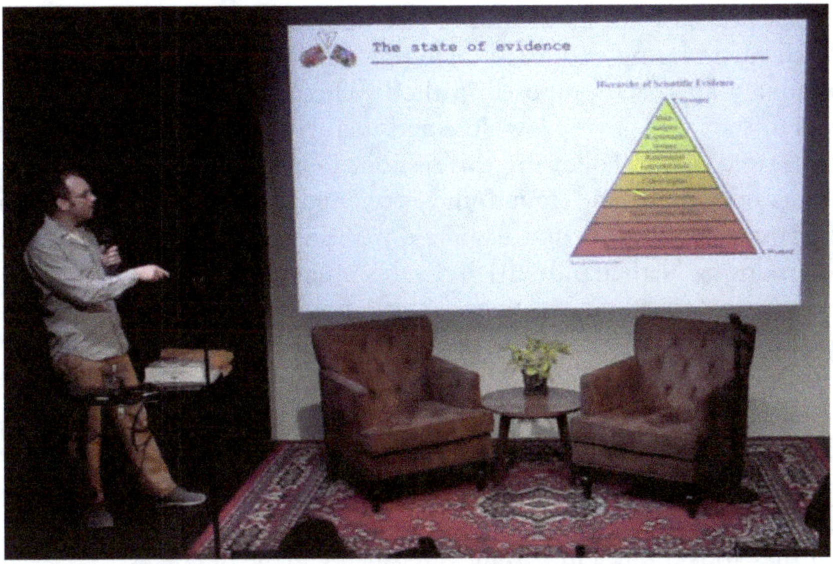

Fig. 8.5 Szigeti arguing for the need for more reliable evidence (b1987307 2019) (Note the comfortable, home-like surroundings in which Szigeti presents the state of the evidence. *Source* Screenshot by Anita Hardon, January 2020, the Netherlands)

help producers file for regulatory approval of microdoses of LSD and psilocybin for specific indications, such as ADHD.

Hubs of Concern and Collaboration

Toward the end of the ChemicalYouth project, I attended a talk on microdosing at the Trimbos Institute, a Dutch institute for mental health. Trimbos runs the Dutch Drugs Information and Monitoring Services (DIMS), which has observed an increase in microdosing of psychedelics because users increasingly come to DIMS to have their LSD tested. In the Netherlands, microdosers are in the luxurious position of living in a country where the use and sale of magic mushrooms is legal, and the quality of LSD can be tested through one of the 31 drug testing sites in the country (see also Chapter 2).

The speaker was a moderator of microdosing.nl, an online forum for Dutch microdosing enthusiasts. He presented a protocol similar to the cautionary approach proposed in the PsychedSubstance video, advising users to start with a very low dose and then gradually increase it to find one's "sweet spot." Following this session, I explored the Dutch website of microdosing.nl and found the very interesting interview between two young moderators and Fadiman, mentioned earlier in this chapter (Microdosing Netherlands 2019). In this interview, Fadiman emphasizes that online surveys of experiences are important, because they provide insights into what the substances can do. He also notes that scientists want to have clear biological endpoints; scientists like stuff that they can measure. But, he asks, can clinical trials be designed to measure the effects of microdosing? How do you measure having a good day or a productive one? What constitutes a good day will differ from person to person. People report working well, eating healthily, and even forgetting that they took a pill. How to measure such a range of effects?

The Dutch moderators asked Fadiman to reflect on users' embrace of microdosing to enhance their moods, creativity, and productivity. They ask: "Wouldn't it be better to have a good day without a supplement?" Fadiman responds: "The answer is: do you really need an apple? Or is there any point in having wine with your meal?" He points out that as far as is known today microdosing is safe. So why not take it? The Dutch moderator ends the discussion by comparing microdosing to cycling: "We all do it and don't want to live without it. We know there can be a danger, you assess the risk, you watch the traffic."

How popular microdosing had become was clear at the 2017 NextWeb conference for Tech innovators and start-ups, which was held in Amsterdam with 15,000 attendees from all over the world. The program included Paul Austin one of the leaders of the Third Wave—an online hub for responsible psychedelic use. Austin told the audience that microdosing can help business leaders excel, because it allows them to be creative, adaptable, patient and present: "It's about this sense of being in the zone. In the zone, present, in the moment. Microdosing psychedelics can do this, sex does this, extreme sports do this, being really engaged and focused and dedicated on a project that you really love does this" (Aronov 2019, p. 711).

In contrast, there is the more cautious conclusion of JingShu, interviewed by Mishra. More doubtful on the need for microdosing after trying it out for 30 days, Jingshu says, "I was quite skeptical of the mentality of optimization in this fast-paced, competitive world: what are we optimizing ourselves for?" (quoted in Mishra 2020, p. 37).

In Conclusion

This chapter describes how users and researchers have been exploring the effects of microdosing in three different ways, each of which generates different ways of "knowing" the substances. First, user narratives focus on a plurality of creativity, focus, and productivity-enhancing effects of these chemicals. They describe how users incorporate microdosing in daily schedules, attend to diets, and adjust dosages. Moreover, we observed users comparing the effects of different psychedelic substances, aiming to tailor the choice of substance to the task at hand. The online peer-to-peer sharing of experiences, support and co-creation of knowledge "constitutes an emergent and constantly evolving form of practical wisdom" (Boothroyd and Lewis 2016, p. 293). This chapter shows how, in a second way of exploring effects, researchers build on this practical wisdom in designing studies that seek to aggregate user experiences. These observational studies seek user collaboration through online fora and real life events to augment understanding of how the effects of microdosing are moderated by underlying conditions (such as anxiety and colorblindness), and interactions with other medicines. These researchers do not see this as conclusive evidence, but rather point to issues that need to be explored further: To what extent do the positive experiences just reflect placebo responses? Most users stop after a while—so what do we know about long-term effects? Does tolerance build after microdosing for a long time? The third way to study the effects of microdosing are randomized controlled trials. These aim to test if the effects of microdosing are "real," that is caused by the psychoactive substance used in the microdosing practice. The evidence generated by such studies depends on the "endpoints" chosen and the biological markers used.

While the first two ways of exploring microdosing are aimed at "improving" effects by trying different microdosing schedules, dosages and diets, and aggregating experiences through observations, the third way of doing research is aimed at "proving" effects through trials (Mol 2006). Improving through tinkering allows users to adjust dosages, experiment with diets as adjuncts to the treatment, and determine how best to embed microdosing in daily routines (Mol and Hardon 2020). It also allows users to adjust the microdosing regime to the work at hand: to perform during a job interview a different kind of microdosing is called for, than when aiming to solve a technical puzzle in the privacy of one's study.

Such tinkering is not possible in clinical trials which are designed to "prove" the effects of standardized treatments using pre-defined endpoints, while filtering out any "expectation" effects. Proving through clinical trials, however, has as advantage that if sufficient experiments have been done, the evidence can be submitted for review to the food and drug authority.

Though it is too early to tell, randomized controlled trials could prove that microdosing does indeed have specific beneficial material effects. But this does not mean that microdoses of LSD or psilocybin could immediately enter the market. Food and drug authorities will demand results from large-scale "phase 3" trials, which are expensive, and may be reluctant to review new indications for psychedelics, because these drugs were used recreationally in large doses in the past, resulting in its scheduling in the 1960s.

However, it can be done. The Multidisciplinary Association for Psychedelic Studies, a nonprofit organization based in Santa Cruz, California, received the green light from the US FDA to do phase 3 placebo-controlled trials of MDMA (a drugs which has also been used for recreational purposes) for the treatment of post-traumatic stress disorder, and in 2019 the association published positive results from these trials, which led to FDA approval to expand access to this treatment (Mithoefer et al. 2019).

Could researchers win such approval for the use of microdoses of LSD and/or psilocybin for creativity and productivity? It seems unlikely, because here the indications are not medical. But let's assume that large-scale trials were done, and that, as was the case for MDMA, the results were positive. Hypothetically, this could convince authorities that microdosing is effective, and that microdoses of LSD and/or psilocybin can be used safely. If this happens, the substances will be re-"informed," changing from illegal recreational substances to medicines for cognitive enhancement. We expect that, if this happens, microdoses would be incorporated into the vibrant online market for drugs used to enhance cognition, referred to as "nootropics." Web-based shops sell supplements such as "Rise," a daily nootropic for memory, and Sprint, a nootropic for energy and focus. HVMN (pronounced 'human'), the company that makes Rise and Sprint, "believes that the human system can be quantified, optimized and upgraded" (Angel 2018, p. 67). Given the wide range of positive user experiences, companies like this one are likely to be interested in adding microdoses to their product lines. If this happened, Karen and other users would not have to go through the material work of making capsules, weighing chemicals, and testing for purity. They could simply buy their preferred substance online.

That the products would be available in standardized forms, with precise advice on how to take it, does not mean that tinkering would end. Whether LSD and psilocybin are approved or not, users will continue to tinker with diets, dosages and schedules relying on shared practical wisdom online, which has been augmented with insights from surveys and trials. The chapter shows how throughout the different kinds of collaborative experimentation and every day tinkering the properties of LSD and psilocybin evolve—new benefits emerge, dosages are adjusted, and cautionary tales shared. The practice is fluid, and ways of knowing are always emergent (Hardon and Sanabria 2017; Mol and Hardon 2020). The peer-to-peer sharing, and collaborations with researchers make up a dynamic form of regulation from below, which acknowledges the experiences of users, and helps refine the practice so as to maximize a wide range of benefits, and prevent harm.

ChemicalYouth Ethnographers

Swasti Mishra is an anthropologist with interest in the intersections of health, drugs, biomedicine, and society. She completed her PhD under the ChemicalYouth project, at the University of Amsterdam. Her doctoral research focused on the generation and circulation of knowledge about psychedelic drugs, including from clinical trials, psychiatric practices, and public health centers, as well as their non-medical use in office spaces or festival venues, primarily situated in the United States and the Netherlands. She is currently part of a research project on the assessment of public health emergency preparedness across the European Union Framework contract with European Centre for Disease Prevention and Control (Fig. 8.6).

Fig. 8.6 Swasti Mishra

Lisa Krieg studied cultural anthropology at the University of Heidelberg, and defended her PhD on social memory in Germany in 2016 at Utrecht University. She joined the ChemicalYouth team as a virtual ethnographer, and conducted research collaboratively with other team members on digital archives of drug experience reports, working on platforms such as Erowid and Wikipedia. Currently, she works at the University of Bonn on human-nature-technology relations (Fig. 8.7).

Fig. 8.7 Lisa Krieg

Moritz Berning focused on mixing classical and virtual ethnographic research, trying to balance the limitations that come with each approach. For the ChemicalYouth project, he explored how risk is approached and managed with regard to old and new psychoactive substances. These included situational practices at festivals or clubs, as well as refined social mechanisms of testing substances in virtual spaces (Fig. 8.8).

Fig. 8.8 Moritz Berning

Aleksi Hupli has been trained as a medical anthropologist by the University of Amsterdam (2013) and as a sociologist by the University of Helsinki (2014). He is currently finishing his PhD in sociology at the University of Tampere focusing on cognitive enhancement drug use among student populations. He has also coordinated the Global Drug Survey in Finland since 2017, is a board member of the Finnish Association for Humane Drug Policy and Legalize NL, serves as the president of the Amsterdam Society of Medical Social Scientists, and is a member of the Finnish Bioethics Institute (Fig. 8.9).

Fig. 8.9 Aleksi Hupli

Notes

1. We developed an interactive website (https://chemicalyouth.org/visualising-erowid/) that provides insights into more than 9480 users' reports.
2. This dosing rationale differs from that proposed by Fadiman, who suggested that the second day be microdose-free, in order to experience what it is like to not be affected by the substance. Fadiman's advice was aimed at supporting research into the effects of microdosing, by contrasting substance-free days with those affected by the microdose.
3. Three hundred and sixty-six people sent in one day of data; 137 sent in data for more than one day and less than a week; 340 sent in data for longer than one week.
4. The advantage of microdosing LSD over ADHD drugs was also discussed by Mishra's (2020) interlocutors, who said that on LSD they didn't experience "the comedown of other stuff"; they also pointed to cost advantages, arguing that in the Netherlands microdosing was "even cheaper in the long run, though it depends on how you source it of course. An LSD tab cut into eight pieces is just five euros divided by eight, while Ritalin off-label you get for five euros per pill" (p. 42).

References

Angel, B. (2018). *Unstoppable: A 90-day plan to biohack your mind and body for success.* Irvine: Enterpreneur Press.

Aronov, M. (2019). (Micro-)"psychedelic" experiences: From the 1960s creativity at the workplace to the twenty-first century neuro-newspeak. *Ethnologie Francaise, 176,* 701–718.

b1987307. (2019). *Is microdosing placebo? The self blinding microdose study.* YouTube. https://www.youtube.com/watch?time_continue=14andv=QS8m0SZLxFMandfeature=emb_logo. Accessed on April 15, 2020.

BBC London News. (2018). *LSD microdosing.* BBC London News. https://www.youtube.com/watch?v=GPYzS9vxymQ. Accessed on April 15, 2020.

Beckley Foundation. (2017). *Recruitment flyer.* Beckley Foundation. https://beckleyfoundation.org/2018/09/03/we-are-recruiting-for-a-new-psychedelic-microdosing-study/. Accessed on April 20, 2020.

Berning, M., & Hardon, A. (2016). Educated guesses and other ways to address the pharmacological uncertainty of designer drugs: An exploratory study of experimentation through an online drug forum. *Contemporary Drug Problems, 43*(3), 277–292. https://doi.org/10.1177/0091450916662164.

Boothroyd, D., & Lewis, S. (2016). Online drug scenes and harm reduction from below as phronesis. *Contemporary Drug Problems, 43*(3), 293–307. https://doi.org/10.1177/0091450916654266.

Dean, J. (2017). *Micro-dosing: The drug habit your boss is gonna love.* GQ. https://www.gq.com/story/micro-dosing-lsd. Accessed on December 13, 2019.

Eagles, B. (1997). *Psychedelic science.* London: British Broadcasting Corporation.

Erowid. (2020). *Erowid*. Erowid. https://www.erowid.org. Accessed on March 20, 2020.

Fadiman, J. (2011). *The psychedelic explorer's guide: Safe, therapeutic, and sacred journeys.* Rochester, NY: Park Street Press.

Fadiman, J., & Korb, S. (2019a). Microdosing psychedelics. In M. Winkelman & B. Sessa (Eds.), *Advances in psychedelic medicine: State of the art therapeutic applications* (pp. 318–335). Santa Barbara, CA: Greenwood.

Fadiman, J., & Korb, S. (2019b). Might microdosing psychedelics be safe and beneficial? An initial exploration. *Journal of Psychoactive Drugs, 51*(2), 118–122. https://doi.org/10.1080/02791072.2019.1593561.

Fisher, S. (2016). *Interview with a corporate banker who microdosed his way to the top.* Vice. https://www.vice.com/en_au/article/5g9a4q/we-interviewed-a-corporate-banker-who-won-the-national-sales-award-while-microdosing-mushrooms. Accessed on March 1, 2020.

Gomart, E. (2002). Methadone: Six effects in search of a substance. *Social Studies Sciences, 32*(2), 93–135.

Hardon, A., & Sanabria, E. (2017). Fluid drugs: Revisiting the anthropology of pharmaceuticals. *Annual Review of Anthropology, 46*(1), 117–132. https://doi.org/10.1146/annurev-anthro-102116-041539.

Hofmann, A. (1979). *LSD: My problem child*. New York: McGraw-Hill Book Company.

Hupli, A., Berning, M., Zhuparris, A., & Fadiman, J. (2019). Descriptive assemblage of psychedelic microdosing: Netnographic study of YouTube videos and on-going research projects. *Performance Enhancement and Health, 6,* 129–138. https://doi.org/10.1016/j.peh.2019.01.001.

Hutten, N. R. P. W., Mason, N. L., Dolder, P. C., & Kuypers, K. P. C. (2019). Motives and side-effects of microdosing with psychedelics among users.

International Journal of Neuropsychopharmacology, 22(7), 426–434. https://doi.org/10.1093/ijnp/pyz029.

Imperial College London. (2020). *Self-blinding microdose study set up manual for blotter psychedelics.* London: Creative Commons.

Johnstad, P. G. (2018). Powerful substances in tiny amounts: An interview study of psychedelic microdosing. *Nordic Studies on Alcohol and Drugs, 35*(1), 39–51. https://doi.org/10.1177/1455072517753339.

Krieg, L. J., Berning, M., & Hardon, A. (2017). Anthropology with algorithms? An exploration of online drug knowledge using digital methods. *Medicine Anthropology Theory, 4*(3). https://doi.org/10.17157/mat.4.3.458.

Kuypers, K. P., Ng, L., Erritzoe, D., Knudsen, G. M., Nichols, C. D., Nichols, D. E., et al. (2019). Microdosing psychedelics: More questions than answers? An overview and suggestions for future research. *Journal of Psychopharmacology, 33*(9), 1039–1057. https://doi.org/10.1177/0269881119857204.

Langlitz, N. (2012). *Neuropsychedelia: The revival of hallucinogen research since the decade of the brain.* Berkeley: University of California Press.

Liu, A. (2012). The state of the digital humanities: A report and a critique. *Arts and Humanities in Higher Education, 11*(1–2), 8–41. https://doi.org/10.1177/1474022211427364.

Malone, N. (2016). *Women are micro-dosing on LSD: Psychedelics and the working woman.* Marie Claire. https://www.marieclaire.com/culture/news/a23669/power-women-microdosing-lsd/. Accessed on April 20, 2020.

Markoff, J. (2005). *What the dormouse said: How the 60s counterculture shaped the personal computer industry*. London: Penguin Books.

Microdosing Netherlands. (2019). *James Fadiman about microdosing.* Microdosing.nl podcast. https://www.youtube.com/watch?time_continue=6andv=k7dQj92WPugandfeature=emb_title. Accessed on April 16, 2020.

Mishra, S. (2018). *Microdosing at work: Reworking bodies and chemicals.* Cultural Anthropology. https://culanth.org/fieldsights/microdosing-at-work-reworking-bodies-and-chemicals. Accessed on May 24, 2020.

Mishra, S. (2020). *Drug craft: On the configurations of psychedelic efficacies.* Doctoral dissertation. Anthropology department. Amsterdam: University of Amsterdam. https://pure.uva.nl/ws/files/47924549/Front_matter.pdf.

Mithoefer, M. C., Feduccia, A., Mithoefer, A. T., Feduccia, A. A., Jerome, L., Wagner, M., et al. (2019). 3,4-methylenedioxymethamphetamine (MDMA)-assisted psychotherapy for post-traumatic stress disorder in military veterans, firefighters, and police officers: A randomised, double-blind, dose-response, phase 2 clinical trial. *The Lancet Psychiatry, 5*(6), 486–497. https://doi.org/10.1016/S2215-0366(18)30135-4.

Mol, A. (2006). Proving or improving: On health care research as a form of self-reflection. *Qualitative Health Research, 16*(3), 405–414. https://doi.org/10.1177/1049732305285856.

Mol, A., & Hardon, A. (2020). Caring: A fluid concept for adaptable engagements. In J. Bowen, N. Dodier, J. W. Duyvendak, & A. Hardon (Eds.), *Pragmatic inquiry: Critical concepts for social sciences*. London: Routledge.

Oram, M. (2014). Efficacy and enlightenment: LSD psychotherapy and the drug amendments of 1962. *Journal of the History of Medicine and Allied Sciences, 69*(2), 221–250.

Pollan, M. (2019). *How to change your mind: The new science of psychedelics*. London: Penguin Books.

Prochazkova, L., Lippelt, D. P., Colzato, L. S., Kuchar, M., Sjoerds, Z., & Hommel, B. (2018). Exploring the effect of microdosing psychedelics on creativity in an open-label natural setting. *Psychopharmacology (Berl), 235*(12), 3401–3413. https://doi.org/10.1007/s00213-018-5049-7.

Watson, D., & Clark, L. A. (1988). Development and validation of brief measures of positive and negative affect: The PANAS Scales. *Journal of Personality and Social Psychology, 54*(6), 1063–1070.

Woods, B. (2016). *Can very small doses of LSD make you a better worker? I decided to try it.* Vox. https://www.vox.com/2016/3/2/11115974/lsd-internet-addiction. Accessed on April 20, 2020.

Yanakieva, S., Polychroni, N., Family, N., Williams, L. T. J., Luke, D. P., & Terhune, D. B. (2019). The effects of microdose LSD on time perception: A randomised, double-blind, placebo-controlled trial. *Psychopharmacology (Berl), 236*(4), 1159–1170. https://doi.org/10.1007/s00213-018-5119-x.

9

Youth and the Future of Chemical Use

Think of what you did today. You woke up in the morning and got out of bed. First you put your left foot onto the carpet, the skin of the sole in direct contact with the molecules of the flame retardant that coats the fibers of your carpet, just like in every industrially manufactured carpet around the world. And then the right foot followed. You yawned and inhaled deeply the fine particles of plastic that combustion and friction had leached into the air. Perhaps they came from the scented candle you lit the night before, and the one before that? Or the countless plastic objects that had passed through your room in the past few days? Or maybe the minute compounds simply came in through the window with the warm breeze of the dense, bustling city where you live.

I am guessing, and this is a pretty good guess, that you brushed your teeth. You did so conscientiously, moving the brush in thorough tooth-wide strokes, making sure that the butylparaben, propylparaben, and triclosan—all preservatives put into toothpaste to make it last longer on supermarket shelves and in bathroom cabinets, and also well-known endocrine disruptors—penetrate well into your gums. Then you took a shower, washing with a gel, shampoo, and perhaps facial scrub if you were not in a rush. If you are a woman, you may have also used an intimate douche. Your rinsed most of the cocktail of parabens, phthalates, artificial scents, and colorants off your body, although some of these molecules,

> even if you could not feel or see it, had already penetrated your skin. You stepped out of the shower and dried your body with a towel that still contained some of the pesticides used to grow the cotton it is made of. After all, 16 percent of the worlds' insecticides are sprayed on cotton crops. You then got dressed and applied some kind of deodorant, and for a second you might have worried, like a growing number of people around the world does, about the suggested links between cancer and the aluminum salts contained in most antiperspirants. Finally, you rubbed on some lotion that contains a highly polluting polyethylene glycol as emulsifier (no wonder it is so silky), and if on that particular day you wanted to make a good impression, you may have splashed a few drops of perfume or cologne on your neck. And then you got dressed. (Rios Sandoval 2019, pp. 21–22)

This is the introduction to Mariana Rios Sandoval's PhD thesis "There Is Politics in Your Shampoo," in which she describes young people who belong to the activist organization Générations Cobayes (Guinea pig generations). The Cobayes launched an "Éco-Orgasme" campaign to call on youth to avoid using sex-related products that contain potentially toxic chemicals, such as lubricants, and sex toys, as well as other products young people might encounter in dating, such as bed linens, processed foods, cosmetics, and lotions (Fig. 9.1).

The Cobayes' main concern is the potential of such chemicals to cause endocrine disruption, infertility, and cancer. Manufacturers have denied this toxicity, but regulators have been slowly and partially recognizing the risk (Bellanger et al. 2015; Colborn et al. 1997; Tessaro 2020). The Cobayes call on their peers to avoid endocrine disruption by making their own soaps with safe ingredients, using reusable menstrual cups rather than sanitary pads, and buying locally sourced foods. By calling for consumer action, the Cobayes are making micro-level toxicities—not immediately apparent when consuming chemicals—into a tangible and graspable problem, one that can and should be addressed (Rios Sandoval 2019).

In this chapter we turn to the strategies that young people use to prevent chemical harms, not just those related to single chemicals but also, more broadly, those that comprise "chemical regimes of living" (Murphy 2008). Most of the ethnographies presented in this book

Fig. 9.1 The Éco-Orgasme tour, a youth-led campaign in France (*Source* Photo taken by Mariana Rios Sandoval, March 2017, France)

concern deliberative acts of inhaling, swallowing, and injecting chemicals, as well as applying them to hair, faces, and bodies. We show that young people engage in such practices to achieve their aspirations for wellness and productivity at work, and that many of our interlocutors were not aware of how these practices simultaneously involve multiple, entangled toxicities. Two questions thread their way through this book: why do these youth trust that chemicals will not bring them harm, and what contributes to the relative invisibility of toxic risks?

Throughout this book we have pointed to the agency of youth in making chemicals do things for them through their situated practices, highlighting the creativity of their do-it-yourself chemical regimes, and the dense webs of human relations and things in which chemical efficacies and ways of knowing take shape. In these constellations of doing and knowing, chemicals should be understood as fluid (Hardon and Sanabria 2017). We have described how, across the field sites, young people viewed their skin tone, body shape, gendered identity, and mental and creative potential as modifiable through situated chemical practices.

They tinkered with dosages, shared experiences, and substituted products in order to achieve desired states of being, while also moderating their use in order to prevent adverse effects.[1] Having referred throughout to their risk-mitigating practices as "harm reduction from below," in this chapter we propose that youth should be supported with "harm reduction from above."

In Search of a Good Life

In the seven empirical chapters, we discussed three general reasons for using chemical products. The first pertains to wellness: the young people we spoke with used chemicals to be attractive, healthy, connected, happy, and muscular; the second concerns desires to achieve diverse gendered ways of being in the world; and the third entails enhancing work capacity, productivity, and creativity. We noted how the positive potential of chemicals for these projects is amplified through advertising, tailored face-to-face sales, and online sharing, and is enabled by the easy accessibility of products in malls, pharmacies, and corner stores.

Youth's engagement with wellness and beauty products suggests a pervasive trust in and reliance on their beneficial effects (see also Rodrigues 2016). Chemicals gave our interlocutors a sense of control as they faced multiple insecurities in their everyday lives, especially the work-related precariousness that was present across our fieldwork sites although in different ways. The daily engagements of young people with multiple chemicals is fueled by a neoliberal global economy, in which working conditions are characterized by flexibility and the lack of worker protections, causing job insecurity (Beck 2000; Harvey 2005; Kallenberg 2009; Vallas and Prener 2012). In addition to seeking a good education, youth invest in their bodies and minds (Anagnost et al. 2013), and acquire skills to be able to compete in an increasingly precarious labor market (Gershon 2017). Advertising campaigns feed on young people's insecurities about their ability to accomplish all this, depicting cosmetics, cigarettes, energy drinks, and supplements as the means through which they can gain confidence and succeed in life (Chua 2000).

Growing up in a post-industrial era, their lives have overflowed with chemicals promoted by a multi-billion dollar beauty, wellness, and supplements industry. The industrial practices involved are under-regulated in neoliberal political constellations that favor economic progress and protect corporate interests. All sorts of claims are permitted in advertisements, as long as they do not make medical promises. In the absence of information on the potential toxic effects of the chemicals contained in these products, young people observed their own bodies to see what chemicals did, and they shared their experiences with others. If products didn't work or had unwanted effects, they tried out new products and other brands.

Social theorists argue that in times of "uncertain global conditions" (Misztal 1996, p. 6), people increasingly rely on trust, which Misztal defines as "believ[ing] that the results of somebody's intended action will be appropriate from our point of view" (p. 24). The mediation of experiential knowledge by peers, sales people, and multilevel marketeers, we observed, plays a key role in building such trust. Indeed, the "concreteness" of face-to-face communication fosters it (Brown and Calnan 2012). Thus, we argue that the amplification of benefits of products through advertising, along with the interpersonal relations through which young people try out chemicals and share information on them, together shaped our interlocutors' overall trust in the chemicals that pervaded their lives.

Trust is typically described in social science literature as a benign dynamic, involving productive reciprocity. Here, we find it has a darker side. While providing our interlocutors with tools to confront the uncertainty in their lives, mechanisms of trust also rendered toxic risks of chemical invisible. Our analysis suggests that our interlocutors' trust in the products that they used was unwarranted and even harmful. Interpersonal relations can be manipulated (Skinner et al. 2014); in our field sites, this occurred when companies paid youth to market chemicals to their friends, peers, and family. Our youth ethnographers observed these dynamics in multiple contexts, for example, where youth are paid to use their social media accounts to promote e-cigarettes to their peers (Chapter 3), or are lured to sign up to sell supplements with exaggerated health claims in multilevel marketing schemes, capitalizing on their networks of friends and family to make a living (Chapter 7).

In many cases, our interlocutors ended up worse off than when they started using chemicals, which they believed would help them achieve their aims in life. Whitening exfoliants harmed some of the young women working in karaoke bars, and their disfigured skin made it harder for them to attract clients. Potent painkillers used by sex workers to feel confident ended up causing dependency on the drugs, forcing them to keep working to maintain their drug habit. E-cigarettes used by youth as safe alternatives to cigarettes cause severe pulmonary conditions and can even be lethal. The overconsumption of energy drinks left low-income workers exhausted, while using high dosages of hormones to modify their bodies put transgender people at risk of getting cancer later in life. Buying supplements for resale through multilevel marketing companies left hopeful entrepreneurs in debt. Though government authorities may warn about the addictive potencies and toxicities of cigarettes and narcotic substances, our interlocutors were kept in the dark on the risks of cosmetics, pharmaceuticals, supplements, and e-cigarettes, all of which—in part because they are accessed easily in groceries and online stores—were widely considered safe. While our ethnographies reveal that young people across our sites sought to mitigate immediate chemical harms, the effects of the multiplicity of toxic exposures on their future health tended to escape their attention, precisely the problem the Cobayes sought to address.

Regimes of Invisibility

Social scientists are increasingly examining and theorizing how chemical toxicities make up our everyday lives (Murphy 2008; Fortun 2012; Davis and Abraham 2013; Fortun et al. 2014; Povinelli 2017; Roberts 2017) and how they are governed by what Fortun and colleagues (2014) call "regimes of invisibility." Immense resources are invested in keeping the toxicity of chemicals secret, to avoid state regulation and scientific scrutiny. Corporations prioritize their sales, while neoliberal governments protect commercial interests. Chemical manufacturers oppose precautionary measures, they question the methodologies used to measure toxicities, and exaggerate scientific uncertainties with the aim of sabotaging decision making (Markowitz and Rosner 2002; Homberg & Vaupel 2019). Fortun and colleagues (2014) note that, even in a world of big data and widespread surveillance, some things seem to systematically "fall off the radar," such as the monitoring of air and water quality, and the health impact of toxicants. Such invisibility obscures the "synthetic toxic relations" that surround us (Murphy 2008).

Proctor (2011) coined the term "agnotology" to refer to the deliberate strategies of making things invisible. The term foregrounds how uncertainty is not simply the absence of knowledge; rather it may be actively produced by social practices (Sanabria 2016). Proctor (2011) illustrates how agnotology works in an incisive historical study that shows how Big Tobacco diffused evidence that smoking was associated with lung cancer. Tobacco companies funded researchers to produce divergent interpretations of that evidence, in order to create uncertainty and prevent regulatory action, while simultaneously engaging in public campaigns that represented smoking as freedom and an adult choice, which created a political smokescreen in which regulatory action became hard to justify. Chapter 3 shows how, facing a global treaty on tobacco control, companies shifted their communication strategy to the promotion of "safer nicotine products," a term that renders e-cigarette toxicities invisible.

Similar regimes of invisibility have been documented in public debates on the safety of cosmetics, such as Johnson's Baby Powder as we discussed in Chapter 5. Lawyers, representing US women who suffered from cancers associated with the product, reviewed company communications and found that Johnson and Johnson hand known for more than 40 years that its talc may be contaminated by asbestos, a potent carcinogenic (Rabin and Hsu 2018). In hundreds of pages of internal company documents, executives worried about the consequences of admitting to regulatory authorities that their product was unsafe. The company defended its commercial interests by discrediting research on the presence of asbestos, while also proposing new ways to measure the purity of the product; evidence of these efforts was unearthed by the *New York Times*, after obtaining company documents through the US Freedom of Information Act.

In Chapter 7 we discussed how the supplements industry also produces regimes of invisibility, by successfully preventing more stringent oversight on safety and efficacy by the US FDA. Highly orchestrated lobbying efforts to prevent stronger regulation involved doctors, who argued patients had rights to use supplements and vitamins in complementary medical treatments, and consumers, who fought for their freedom to use these "natural" products (Offit 2013; Scrinis 2013; Cohen 2016). As such products are now able to acquire a status of "generally recognized as safe," the market for them is growing rapidly worldwide, driven by aggressive promotion of their benefits through social media and multilevel marketing. The products are promoted as protective shields for metabolic conditions, such as diabetes and cardio-vascular conditions, the occurrence of which is exacerbated by fast food diets containing high levels of salt and sugar (Scrinis 2013). Marketing their products as prevention, the supplements industry helps render invisible the negative role that food corporations play in current epidemics of metabolic diseases, while reinforcing industry rhetoric that individual choices determine health (Moodie et al. 2013; Sanabria 2016).

The agnotological mechanisms that take place in Big Pharma-sponsored trails of psychiatric pharmaceuticals produce ignorance that makes it possible for psychiatric medications to be approved by regulatory committees despite their potential for severe adverse effects (Healy 2012; Medawar and Hardon 2004). For example, when clinical trials funded by Eli Lilly and Company showed an increased risk for suicide among children taking Prozac, the manufacturer decided to not report this risk to authorities. Healy (2012) states, "When a company is faced with defending of a brand that is essential to its survival, commercial logic dictates that it will take any steps necessary to preempt the emergence of a hazard, including doctoring the evidence" (p. 53). Similar suppression of evidence has occurred in other pharmaceutical domains. For example in the field of pain medication, Purdue Pharma has been charged of suppressing information on the addiction potential of slow-release oxycontin, thereby fueling the current opioid crises in the United States (Lexchin and Kohler 2011; Kanouse and Compton 2015). We saw in Chapter 2 how similar epidemics of addiction occurred in Indonesia, where our interlocutors bought potent pain killers over the counter to enable them to work without realizing that the pills can cause dependence.

These industry-sponsored regimes of invisibility make it near impossible for youth to fully understand the risks of using chemicals to achieve their aspirations for wellness, sexuality, productivity, and creativity. The Cobayes address this by drawing attention to the potential toxicities involved in everyday chemical regimes. They encourage youth to exchange their daily chemical products for safer alternatives, efforts that, along with other practices of youth to mitigate harm, we label "harm reduction from below."

Harm Reduction from Below

Strategies and efforts to reduce harm from below can involve a multiplicity of collaborative strategies that recognize young people's chemical regimes of living and mobilize embodied resistance to the conditions of precarity which perpetuate chemical harm (cf. Medina 2013; Sabsay 2016). Harm reduction from below, as we propose it, builds on young people's existing interest in mitigating the risks of chemicals, the hybrid nature of the networks in which they experiment with chemicals, and the protective nature of the social networks in which young people experiment with drugs. It amplifies the cautionary tales shared by young people online, supports their modes of self-regulation, and counters the exaggeration of benefits by industry. It also seeks to prevent adverse effects by drawing attention to less tangible, slowly accumulating toxicities; we can understand the campaigns of the Cobayes in this light, playfully working against the "merchants of doubt" (Markowitz and Rosner 2002), to make such toxicities visible.

Harm reduction programs emerged in the 1980s to prevent the transmission of HIV in communities of injecting heroin users, and since have targeted a wide range of substances, including speed, cannabis, nicotine, and alcohol. Harm reduction programs offer safer means to administer substances, such as clean needles to inject heroin or patches to deliver nicotine, and they promote safer chemicals, such as using buprenorphine or methadone to replace heroin. But they are not usually designed from "below." Harm reduction efforts have tended to locate chemical risk in the actions of individuals, calling on heroin users, (cannabis) smokers, and binge drinkers to take responsibility for their own health (Hardon and Hymans 2016). Our research leads us to conclude that such efforts threaten to misfire, or be misunderstood by youth, because they fail to build on the ways that young people already exchange experiences and self-regulate drug use in face-to-face and online social collectives.

For example, in New South Wales (Australia), a 2015 government-led harm reduction campaign had as its slogan: "You're Worse on Weed." The creative design firm Saatchi and Saatchi was hired, and they developed three YouTube videos featuring a human-size sloth named Jason (compilation uploaded by YouTube user "Aa4398743873" [2015]). The videos depict Jason's siblings and peers responding to him when he is stoned in diverse circumstances (a dinner table, classroom, a party). In one, Jason sits at the dinner table; his mother asks him to pass the salt, and he reacts confusedly and passes the salad instead. His sister, apparently disgusted, calls him "Stoner Sloth." The videos appear to be intended to make cannabis users fear being similarly shamed (Fig. 9.2).

The campaign failed (Nudd 2015), though, because youth thought the videos were hilarious and started sharing them through social media for laughs. In comments posted on the YouTube channel, where the videos are shared, a commenter named Milos asks, "is this video a joke or what?" and Richard answers, "I have absolutely no idea. I just find it unreasonably funny" (Aa4398743873 2015). The campaign seems strangely out

Fig. 9.2 Screenshots form StonerSloth Campaign Videos (Aa4398743873 2015) (*Source* Photos taken by Anita Hardon, the Netherlands, April 2020)

of touch, not only with global moves toward legalizing cannabis as a relatively safe drug but also with young people's capacity to moderate their use. Their capacity to do so is increased if they are adequately informed of risks, for example, regarding the high THC content of many varieties of cannabis, or of potential lung toxicity when vaping the substance (Chapter 3).

With their focus on individual behavior and on the risks of addiction and overdose, many such educational campaigns against alcohol, drugs, and smoking downplay the normalized status of the substances. They also fail to acknowledge the way such substances are embedded in and foster social relations, and that they can generate positive feelings such as relaxation, excitement, and pleasure (Malins 2004; Hunt et al. 2007; Duff 2008; Martinic and Measham 2008). Failing to recognize what many young people consider to be the benefits of substance use, and failing to build on young people's collective self-regulation strategies, the effectiveness of harm reduction programs is reduced (Hardon and Hymans 2016).

In developing our own harm reduction from below efforts, we built on successful strategies undertaken in Amsterdam, where experimenting youth advised each other on harm reduction techniques, such as using micro-gram scales and "allergy-dosing" new kinds of drugs (Chapter 2). Through online forums, this community was able to adapt to challenges, for instance through substance warnings and providing advice for members experiencing problems (van Schipstal et al. 2016). We were impressed by the pragmatic way that municipal authorities supported young people in their efforts to reduce harm, including providing access to testing facilities where young people could have their ecstasy pills and LSD blots tested for purity, and training peer supporters to keep an eye on drug users during festivals. These pragmatic harm reduction efforts had been developed as an alternative to individual-oriented, nudging approaches to harm reduction, and to drug policies that stigmatize, criminalize, and marginalize drug users.

Concerned about the precariousness of drug users in Indonesia, where there is no effort to reduce harm from above or below, we organized deliberative dialogs between drug experts and youth. In one of these sessions, a pharmacy professor from the University Hasanuddin in

Makassar met with a group of heavy drug users. He walked them through his understandings of the pharmaco-kinetics of the drugs that they used, pointing to the hard work that their livers needed to do to metabolize the large dosages of psychoactive prescription drugs that they used on a daily basis. He asked them whether they had friends who had died, and what the cause was. When he was told by the drug users that a friend had died of hepatitis, he asked follow up questions, eventually explaining that “becoming yellow,” could be caused by liver failure and discussed the stresses of heavy drug use on the kidneys of users. Our respondents had been evaluating the safety of drugs, and mitigating harm, by observing acute effects. They considered their drug-use practices safe enough if they woke up the next morning feeling reasonably well. But the slower, and much less visible effects on their livers and kidneys had not been part of their experiential knowledge. By taking their experiences seriously and creating space to discuss different perspectives on risk, we were able to create a reflective space that allowed many of our respondents reconsider their drug-use habits.

To reach a larger audience, we developed a harm reduction from below campaign with two youth communication collectives in Jakarta, Pamflet and Kok Bisa. They proposed to spread “tales of caution” on social media, a strategy that had proven successful in other campaigns. This collaboration resulted in a short YouTube video on the growing use of psychopharmaceutical drugs and their adverse effects, conveying that (1) all pharmaceuticals can have side effects and should be used with caution, and (2) product packaging contains important information about pharmaceutical content, indications for use, dosage, and side effects. As of April 2020, this experimental 3-minute educational video had been viewed 360,000 times and attracted nearly 8000 likes (Fig. 9.3).

Confronting Toxic Uncertainties

The harm reduction from below approach that we propose intends to address less visible chemical exposures and slow toxicities, as in the Cobayes’ campaigns. Murphy’s (2008) conceptualization of chemical

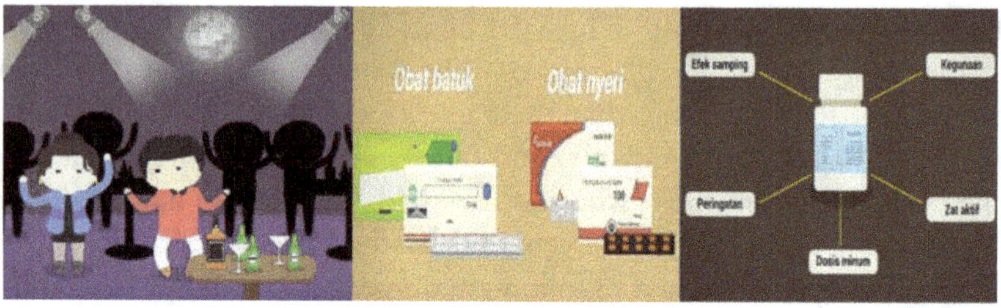

Fig. 9.3 Three images from the Kok Bisa/Pamflet YouTube video *Apakah Minum Obat Bisa Membahayakan Kesehatan Kita?* (Can taking medicines cause harm?)

regimes of living provides a useful framework for analyzing slow toxicities, related to the multiplicity of synthetic chemicals used by young people every day. The concept invites us to examine the totality of soaps, creams, supplements, e-cigarettes, hormones, and psychoactive substances that young people inhale, ingest, inject, and rub on their skin on a daily basis. It asks us as well to attend to the complex feedback loops through which chemicals pass through our bodies, combining with environmental pollutants—pesticides, factory emissions, sewage, and transportation exhaust—that then re-enter our bodies entangled with food, water, and air (Roberts 2017; Hardon and Sanabria 2017).

Attending to toxic entanglements is not easy, especially given the regimes of invisibility described above. Over the past two hundred years of industrialization, societies and scientists have struggled to keep track of the safety profiles of chemicals, both the long-used ones and the constant stream of new chemicals, used in agriculture and homes, and in cosmetics, supplements, and pharmaceuticals. More often than not, when chemicals appear on the market, their risk profiles are poorly understood and are used for many years before evidence on harm emerges (MacKendrick 2018; Homberg and Vaupel 2019).

Moreover, knowledge of toxicities is generated by researchers working in a range of disciplines, each of which producing field-specific knowledge with their own measurement techniques, resulting in their own "agential cut" (Barad 2007, p. 176) on the problem of the toxic entanglements. These disciplines include environmental sciences, ecology, epidemiology, reproductive medicine, dermatology, forensic and military medicine, pulmonology, and occupational health. Evidence of toxicities does not necessarily travel across disciplinary domains, as we see in the case of e-cigarettes. Chemicals used to flavor e-cigarettes had been identified as toxic by occupational health scientists who conducted studies of workers' health in the food industry, but this toxicity was not associated with e-cigarettes until pulmonologists noted that vaping could cause severe lung pathology.

Measurements of chemical toxicities furthermore change over time. For example, in the early twentieth century, animal studies were used to define threshold levels below which substances were deemed safe. When I studied biology in the early 1980s, we were taught that such thresholds could be defined by measuring the LD_{50}, the lethal dose at which half the population of test animals would die due to exposure to the substance. Research on the teratogenic and mutagenic effects of chemicals in the latter decades of the twentieth century, however, demonstrated that some chemicals could disrupt endocrine systems and cause cancers even at very low levels of exposure.

How can we make poorly understood slow toxicities visible? We are inspired by the Éco-Orgasme campaign of the Cobayes, designed to raise awareness of the multitude of chemicals in youth's everyday lives that can cause endocrine disruption, the effects of which are not immediate and are hard to perceive. The campaign attracted youth by playfully registering their chemical sexualities. This is what Camille, a 24-year-old Cobayes activist, told an audience of French students about what they could expect:

> Is there anyone here that already knows the eco-orgasm? You came here because you saw the word orgasm in the title of this morning's workshop? Is that it? [Audience giggles.] Ah, yes, very good choice, very good choice indeed. Well, I will begin by introducing us briefly; here we have Thibault who is an eco-orgasm giver, Alice too, she gives eco-orgasms also. … What we will present this morning is how to go from a nice, simple orgasm, to an *orgasm de ouf* [crazy, cool], an *orgasm écolo,* inventive, creative and sustainable, and voilà, that's the program for this morning until 12:30. Is that OK with you?". (Rios Sandoval 2019, pp. 83–84)

Rios Sandoval describes how this highly interactive event, which traveled to many French university towns, warned youths about toxic chemicals hidden along the "*parcours de la drague*" (cruising route). The event was highly structured, with 15 minutes of sharing facts about the mechanisms and consequences of exposure to endocrine-disrupting chemicals, followed by theatrical sketches to engage the audience. The sketches played out practical solutions, such as a dazzling date with a meal free of pesticides, and condoms and self-made lubricants free of endocrine-disrupting chemicals. Rios Sandoval (2019) writes that her interlocutors "apprehend toxicity through the re-appropriation of production chains, a mutually triggered and reinforced process. Do-it-yourself practices are tools for young people to intervene in the toxic relations making up everyday toxicity" (p. 251) (Fig. 9.4).

Fig. 9.4 Do-it-yourself preparation of make-up remover.

We found video and photo projects to be extremely useful in making visible young people's chemical regimes of living. The ChemicalYouth project, committed to the implementation of multimodal anthropology (Collins et al. 2017) has provided an experimental space for several visual arts projects. In Cagayan de Oro, for example, we asked students participating in the field school of the Anthropology Program of the University of the Philippines to take pictures using their mobile phones of chemical information, and access points in town. As the photos contained GPS coordinates, participants were able to make an interactive ChemicalYouth map of the city.[2]

In Manado, the youth ethnographers took stock of all the chemicals consumed by students in one day using a GoPro camera, a video of which can be found on our website, www.chemicalyouth.org (Fig. 9.5).

Fig. 9.5 Screenshot from a GoPro exploration of the chemical lives of students.

We also worked with young filmmakers from to produce the documentary *Sweet Medicine* on the dark-side of multilevel marketing of supplements (see Chapter 7),[3] and two mini-documentaries that examined skin-whitening practices in Manila, contrasted these with the embrace of brown skin in a surfing community in the south of the Philippines (see Chapter 5).[4]

We were also inspired by the potential to make visible chemical regimes of living that were presented in the evocative documentary *Toxic Beauty* (Ellis 2019). This documentary addresses the lack of regulation of cosmetics, and presents the litigation by a group of women claiming that Johnson's Baby Powder caused the cancer they have suffered. The documentary maker presents Nguyen, a young Vietnamese woman pursuing a master's degree in medical sciences at Boston University, who has become worried about the toxic effects of the multiplicity of cosmetic products, including whitening creams that make up her chemical regime of living. In her classes she learns about the endocrine-disrupting effects of parabens and phthalates found in the cosmetics that she uses. She also writes a term paper, inspired by Stein and Lourie's (2019) *Slow Death by Rubber Duck*, about experiments to lower the level of toxins in one's everyday life. Nguyen self-experiments to lower the amount of parabens and phthalates in her body, listing all the contents of the 27 different products that she usually uses, and measuring chemicals in her urine with a "chemical body burden kit" distributed by the Silent Spring Institute. The test involves collecting a urine sample on three consecutive days: on the first day, she applies her regular skin care and beauty products; the second day she uses no products; and the third day she uses "clean" products, which are allegedly free from phthalates and parabens.

When she receives her results, Nguyen is shocked by the high levels of phthalates in her urine on a "normal" day, when she uses all her regular products. She worries about her future fertility, given that has been using these products for a long time. The graph shows how the levels of toxins are much lower on the second day, and that level is maintained on the third day, when she uses clean cosmetics. Using such testing and self-experimentation to raise awareness of chemical toxicities is a good harm-reduction-from-below approach, not only because it fits with the way young people already tinker with chemicals and monitor effects in their bodies but also because it helps them overcome the limits of what they can directly feel and see.

Helping people "see" slow chemical toxicities may be informed by the bio-ethnographic approach being developed by Roberts and Sanz (2017). Their approach combines "two methodological bundles – ethnographic observation and biochemical sampling – in a synthetic analysis that understands environment interactions as always relational, contingent and constructed phenomena" (Roberts and Sanz 2017, p. 749). They point out that combining divergent methodologies and epistemologies is a slow process, but one that can bring together disparate practitioners and practices.

If we were to do a follow-up project to the ChemicalYouth project, we would seek to involve young people not only in the ethnography of their chemical consumption but also in generating understanding of the slow, less visible toxicities that make up their chemical regimes of living. Facing the daunting array of chemicals that make up our everyday lives, we would suggest that such studies are best done locally, as a way to put some spatial boundaries around the objects of inquiry.

Having provided ethnographic descriptions of young peoples' situated chemical practices, and outlining the toxicities at stake, we now propose to expand our inquiry to include also less visible, unintentional environmental exposures. This might include examining the chemical safety of water, air, housing materials, working spaces, food, and soils that make up young people's everyday lives. But we feel firmly that deciding what to examine should be co-determined by the young people who face the toxic risks, if only because this will also encourage them to act on the chemical regimes of their lives.

Toxicities involve complex feedback loops and emergent effects. Bio-ethnographic strategies can help us unravel some of the complexities, so as to prioritize societal actions that may reduce chemical harm. Focused bio-ethnographic studies can invite young people to measure the existence of toxins in the environments in which they live, observe seepage into and out of their bodies (as in the urine tests described above), while analyzing also the routes through which pollution takes place.

The ChemicalYouth project has developed collaborative ways of engaging young people in such research, to not only collect data but also write-up reports and publish scientific articles, and the distributed nature of this project has allowed for contrasting analyses across sites and collaborative analysis and action. A ChemicalYouth 2.0 could involve a wider range of researchers, advisors, and laboratories, in order to make more visible and tangible the multiple toxicities that make up young people's everyday lives—taking our cue from the multiple intersecting strategies employed by activists and researchers in the field of endocrine disruption (Wylie 2018). ChemicalYouth 2.0 could thus take stock of the multitude of chemicals present in the commodities they consume, as well as the presence of toxins in their blood and urine, while surveying also the prevalence of benefits as well as adverse effects such as endocrine disruption, skin conditions, and respiratory problems.

We saw in Chapter 8 that similar collaborative research emerged around the testing of safety and efficacy of microdosing, which involved experimentation with a single category of chemicals. The challenge at stake is to broaden this collaboration to involve a wide range of chemicals, and to develop other ways of measuring both efficacy and potential toxicities. Roberts and Sanz (2017) point out that in practice bio-ethnography involves bridging diverse ways of knowing chemicals, while attending to "logistical minutiae and methodological challenges" (p. 751). We have experience in doing this and are ready to take on the next challenge. Collective advocacy, along with collaborative research to produce situated evidence of harm, can support efforts to implement the precautionary principles in policies to regulate chemicals, and to confront the regimes of invisibility that constrain effective regulatory action.

Reducing Harm from Above

These harm-reduction-from-below efforts would gain much traction if they were reinforced by concerted efforts "from above" to unmask the invisibility forged by a range of societal actors. In pointing to the need for such a multi-pronged approach, we are inspired by the historical analysis conducted Gaudillière and Hess (2013), who describe the regulatory potentials of multiple stakeholders who co-produce regulatory regimes. We have highlighted the pragmatic approach, chosen by Amsterdam's city government, to provide youth access to pill-testing facilities, and the work of the Trimbos Institute in developing youth-friendly educational materials. Such institutional efforts can help. A similar role is played by organizations like the Silent Spring Institute in testing urine, thereby giving people a valuable impetus for changing their everyday chemical regimes.

EU regulators too are taking action. In the introduction we pointed to the European Union's Registration, Evaluation and Authorization of Chemicals (REACH) Policy, which has led to the banning of 1328 chemicals that are known or suspected to cause cancer, genetic mutations, reproductive harm, and/or birth defects from cosmetics. Finally, global treaties, such as the Framework Convention on Tobacco Control, can help hold nation states accountable for the implementation of policies and laws to prevent harm. Through this concerted action, misinformation on tobacco safety has been neutralized and tobacco consumption dramatically reduced across the globe.

Harm reduction from above strategies would also counter the harmful effects of white privileging that are reinforced by the making and marketing of skin-whitening products. These could include a ban on advertising skin creams and soaps, as such ads reinforce discriminatory policies that discipline young women into whitening their faces, as observed in the malls in Cagayan de Oro. Harm reduction from above would recognize the sexual health needs of youth, as well as the pragmatic ways they use emergency contraception to prevent unwanted pregnancies, achieve sexual hygiene through vaginal washes and penile tissues, and shape their (trans)gendered ways of being in the world. Harm reduction from above efforts could offer young people avenues for developing safer sexual health chemicals that meet their needs (Hardon et al. 2019).

Acute and slow toxicities can be reduced, and we have many tools: collective action by youth, harm reduction from below programs that build on young people's self-regulation, collaborative research and development, responsible entrepreneurship, better science communication, multi-modal arts projects, transparent governance by food and drug authorities and consumer protection agencies with an aim of upholding the precautionary principle, and public scrutiny. These efforts begin by acknowledging the benefits that youth seek in their situated chemical practices.

Accounting for Emergence

All harm reduction efforts, from below and above, need to also acknowledge the fluidity of chemical toxicity, which means examining the chains of events through which chemicals enter youths' lives and accounting for always-emergent toxicities. In the case of Johnson's Baby Powder, for example, it means accounting for the asbestos present in the mines where talc is extracted, and in the case of supplements it means attending to the regulatory space that allows manufacturers to make claims about a product's metabolic benefits without being required to present evidence of its safety. In the case of e-cigarettes, it means attending to the reactions between lung cells and chemical vapors, examining nicotine content and the added flavors and thinners that may cause severe pathologies in the lungs of some users, which puts them at further risk for disease when a novel coronavirus emerges.

Attending to fluid toxicities also requires attention to corporate responses to societal trends and regulatory practices. We have seen across the chapters that when regulations are adopted by governments, societal actors respond (Black 2008). Users seek substitutes for their needs, while corporations can pay expensive lawyers and public relations firms to create smokescreens around the measurement of toxicity, in order to sow doubt about scientific evidence, and they frequently reinvent their products to circumvent regulation, just as Johnson and Johnson replaced talc with corn starch. When 180 states worldwide committed to stringent regulations on cigarettes sales and marketing, companies introduced e-cigarettes, referring to them as "safer nicotine products," as we saw in Chapter 3. They market e-cigarettes online through social influencers, making it harder for regulators to sanction.

Further attending to the fluidity of toxicity entails the monitoring of global market dynamics and global disparities in the "under-regulation of chemical hazards, and corporate impunity" (Lee 2020, p. 8). When people in France or the United States stop buying products associated with toxic risks, corporations seek new markets in the global South, as we saw in Chapter 3, where we described how the manufacturers of JUUL, faced with US sales restrictions, are now expanding the distribution of e-cigarettes in Indonesia, a densely populated country that has not endorsed the global treaty on tobacco control. Faced with diminishing sales due to toxicity concerns, Johnson and Johnson decided to discontinue sales of its Baby Powder in the United States. What will happen with the product in Indonesia and the Philippines, where the product is (still) very popular?

Attending to fluidity, finally, entails studying ways of knowing that generate new ways of understanding toxicities (Liboiron et al. 2018). Environmental researchers are calling for new ways of sensing chemicals, including long-term studies to measure the cumulative effects of toxins, which may lead to the reassessment of the safety and efficacy of chemicals in everyday life (Gabrys et al. 2016; Fortun et al. 2014; Shapiro 2015; Balayannis and Garnett 2020). The Center for the Health Assessment of Mothers and Children of Salinas (CHAMACOS) study, conducted by scholars at the University of California Berkeley, for example, measured the effects of organophosphates in children born to 600 pregnant Latino women in farming communities in Salinas Valley. The study determined that children's cognitive development, as tested at age seven, decreased with higher amounts of pesticides used during their mothers' pregnancies (Sanchez Barba 2020; Gunier et al. 2017). They found: "reduced IQ, attention deficit disorders, developmental delays, autism, and other pervasive developmental disorders correlated with exposures to organophosphates" (Sanchez Barba 2020, p. 4). Based on these studies, the U.S. Environmental Protection Agency concluded that there is no safe level of chlorpyrifos, one of the more commonly used organophosphates (Sanchez Barba 2020).

New ways of knowing chemicals may also lead to the re-evaluation of regulatory actions. In Chapter 8, we saw how LSD (a psychedelic drug that was banned in the 1960) is increasingly used by young people in very low dosages to enhance creativity at work. We described how this new microdosing practice was accompanied by collaborative studies to take stock of benefits and adverse effects, which involved users working together with academic researchers in online communities. These collaborations inspired new ways of doing placebo-controlled trials, in which users themselves were responsible for randomizing (Chapter 8). The evidence that is emerging from studies may result in new assessments of the risks of LSD, and new psychoactive products, which can then be appropriated by youth in their search for wellness, creativity, and productivity at work.

Harm reduction efforts need to be pragmatic and flexible in order to respond to the emergence of new knowledge, to innovations in ways of measuring toxicities and efficacies, to new products and revamped marketing strategies, and to revised regulatory assessments. And with the same dedication of purpose, they must simultaneously be alert to the creative ways that young people "do" chemicals in their ongoing quests for a good life.

ChemicalYouth Ethnographers

Mariana Rios Sandoval's PhD focused on the toxicity of everyday life and things in late industrial society, and on how young environmental activists in France made it visible, through political action and everyday practice, in order to fight it. This kind of toxicity was often articulated as the presence of endocrine-disrupting chemicals, but referred more generally to the myriad toxicants mediating the most ordinary, yet life-sustaining activities, such eating, keeping bodies and homes clean, having sex, and breathing. Mariana is now a Marie Curie post-doctoral fellow at CERMES3 with a project that explores how young French feminists integrate environmental considerations into their contraceptive practices (Fig. 9.6).

Fig. 9.6 Mariana Rios Sandoval

Notes

1. Neuroscientists have recently argued that youths' brains are wired to take risks (Bessant 2008), and social scientists have found that youth experience thrills when engaging in edgework (Lyng 1990). Our focused ethnographies suggest that young people's chemical practices involve balancing benefits and harms. Our interlocutors had no appetite for living on the edge, and if they did so, it was usually caused by conditions of precarity beyond their control.
2. https://chemicalyouth.org/#/projects/mapping-chemicals-in-cagayan-de-oro.
3. https://vimeo.com/234326045.
4. https://vimeo.com/156004560 (password: fairandflawless) and https://vimeo.com/110724981 (password: brownisbeautiful).

References

Aa4398743873. (2015). *Stoner sloth compliation.* YouTube. https://www.youtube.com/watch?v=7rHm8GbTHyE. Accessed on March 1, 2020.

Anagnost, A., Arai, A., & Ren, H. (2013). *Global futures in east Asia: Youth, nation, and the new economy in uncertain times.* Palo Alto, CA: Stanford University Press.

Balayannis, A., & Garnett, E. (2020) Chemical kinships: Interdisciplinary experiments with pollution. *Catalyst Special Section on Chemical Entanglements: Gender and Exposure, 6*(1), 1–10. https://doi.org/10.28968/cftt.v6i1.33524.

Barad, K. (2007). *Meeting the universe halfway: Quantum physics and the entanglement of matter and meaning.* Durham, NC: Duke University Press.

Beck, U. (2000). The cosmopolitan perspective: Sociology of the second age of modernity. *The British Journal of Sociology, 51*(1), 79–105. https://doi.org/10.1111/j.1468-4446.2000.00079.x.

Bellanger, M., Demeneix, B., Grandjean, P., Zoeller, R. T., & Trasande, L. (2015). Neurobehavioral deficits, diseases, and associated costs of exposure to endocrine-disrupting chemicals in the European Union. *Journal of Clinical Endocrinology and Metabolism, 100*(4), 1256–1266. https://doi.org/10.1210/jc.2014-4323.

Bessant, J. (2008). Hard wired for risk: Neurological science, "the adolescent brain" and developmental theory. *Journal of Youth Studies, 11*(3), 347–360. https://doi.org/10.1080/13676260801948387.

Black, J. (2008). Constructing and contesting legitimacy and accountability in polycentric regulatory regimes. *Regulation and Governance, 2,* 137–164.

Brown, P., & Calnan, M. (2012). *Trusting on the edge: Managing uncertainty and vulnerability in the midst of serious mental health problems.* Bristol: Policy Press.

ChemicalYouth. (2020). *ChemicalYouth.* ChemicalYouth. www.chemicalyouth.org. Accessed on April 4, 2020.

Chua, B.-H. (2000). Where got Japanese influence in Singapore! In J. Ben-Ari & E. Clammer (Eds.), *Japan in Singapore: Cultural occurrences and cultural flows* (pp. 133–149). Surrey: Curzon Press.

Cohen, P. A. (2016). The supplement paradox: Negligible benefits, robust consumption. *Journal of the American Medical Association, 316*(14), 1453–1454. https://doi.org/10.1001/jama.2016.14252.

Colborn, T., Dumanoski, D., & Peterson Myers, J. (1997). *Our stolen future: Are we threatening our fertility, intelligence, and survival? A scientific detective story*. New York: Penguin Books.

Collins, S. G., Durington, M., & Gill, H. (2017). Multimodality: An invitation. *American Anthropologist, 119*(1), 142–146. https://doi.org/10.1111/aman.12826.

Davis, C., & Abraham, J. (2013). *Unhealthy pharmaceutical regulation: Innovation, politics and promissory science*. New York: Palgrave Macmillian.

Duff, C. (2008). The pleasure in context. *International Journal of Drug Policy, 19*(5), 384–392. https://doi.org/10.1016/j.drugpo.2007.07.003.

Ellis, P. (dir). (2019). *Toxic Beauty*. Canada: Kew Media.

Fortun, K. (2012). Ethnography in late industrialism. *Cultural Anthropology, 27*(3), 446–464. https://doi.org/10.1111/j.1548-1360.2012.01153.x.

Fortun, K., Fortun, M., Bigras, E., Saheb, T., Costelloe-Kuehn, B., Crowder, J., et al. (2014). Experimental ethnography online: The asthma files. *Cultural Studies, 28*, 632–642. https://doi.org/10.1080/09502386.2014.888923.

Gabrys, J., Pritchard, H., & Barratt, B. (2016). Just good enough data: Figuring data citizenships through air pollution sensing and data stories. *Big Data & Society, 3*(2), 1–14.

Gaudillière, J.-P., & Hess, V. (2013). *Ways of regulating drugs in the nineteenth and twentieth centuries*. London, UK: Palgrave Macmillan.

Gershon, I. (2017). *Down and out in the new economy: How people find (or don't find) work today*. Chicago: University of Chicago Press.

Gunier, R. B., Bradman, A., Harley, K. G., Kogut, K., & Eskenazi, B. (2017). Prenatal residential proximity to agricultural pesticide use and IQ in 7-year-old children. *Environmental Health Perspectives, 125*(5), 057001–057002-8.

Hardon, A., & Hymans, T. D. (2016). Guest editors' introduction: Harm reduction from below. *Contemporary Drug Problems, 43*(3), 191–198. https://doi.org/10.1177/0091450916663247.

Hardon, A., & Sanabria, E. (2017). Fluid drugs: Revisiting the anthropology of pharmaceuticals. *Annual Review of Anthropology, 46*(1), 117–132. https://doi.org/10.1146/annurev-anthro-102116-041539.

Hardon, A., Taqueban, E., Pell, C., & Narasimhan, M. (2019). Implementing do-it-yourself sexual and reproductive health care for women and girls: Insights from ethnographic studies. *British Medical Journal*. https://doi.org/10.1136/bmj.l1333.

Harvey, D. (2005). *A brief history of neoliberalism*. Oxford: Oxford University Press.

Healy, D. (2012). *Pharmageddon*. Berkeley: University of California Press.

Homberg, E., & Vaupel, E. (2019). *Hazardous chemicals: Agents of risk and change, 1800–2000*. New York: Berghahn Books.

Hunt, G. P., Evans, K., & Kares, F. (2007). Drug use and meanings of risk and pleasure. *Journal of Youth Studies, 10*(1), 73–96. https://doi.org/10.1080/13676260600983668.

Kallenberg, A. L. (2009). Precarious work, insecure workers: Employment relations in transition. *American Sociology Review, 74*(1), 1–22.

Kanouse, A. B., & Compton, P. (2015). The epidemic of prescription opioid abuse, the subsequent rising prevalence of heroin use, and the federal response. *Journal of Pain and Palliative Care Pharmacotherapy, 29*(2), 102–114. https://doi.org/10.3109/15360288.2015.1037521.

Lee, R. (2020) A lattice of chemicalized kinship: Toxicant reckoning in a depressive-reparative mode. *Catalyst Special Section on Chemical Entanglements: Gender and Exposure, 6*(1), 1–27. https://doi.org/10.28968/cftt.v6i1.33904.

Lexchin, J., & Kohler, J. C. (2011). The danger of imperfect regulation: Oxycontin use in the United States and Canada. *International Journal of Risk and Safety in Medicine, 23*(4), 233–240. https://doi.org/10.3233/JRS-2011-0539.

Liboiron, M., Tironi, M., & Calvillo, N. (2018). Toxic politics: Acting in a permanently polluted world. *Social Studies of Science, 48*(3), 331–349.

Lyng, S. (1990). Edgework: A social psychological analysis of voluntary risk taking. *American Journal of Sociology, 95*(4), 851–886. https://doi.org/10.1086/229379.

MacKendrick, N. (2018). *Better safe than sorry: How consumers naviage exposure to everyday toxics*. Berkeley: University of California Press.

Malins, P. (2004). Machinic assemblages: Deleuze, Guattari and an ethico-aesthetics of drug use. *Janus Head, 7*(1), 84–104.

Markowitz, G., & Rosner, D. (2002). *Deceit and denial: The deadly politics of industrial pollution*. Berkeley: University of California Press.

Martinic, M., & Measham, F. (2008). *Swimming with crocodiles: The culture of extreme drinking*. New York: Routledge.

Medawar, C., & Hardon, A. (2004). *Medicines out of control: Antidepressants and the conspiracy of goodwill*. Amsterdam: Aksant.

Medina, J. (2013). *The epistemology of resistance: Gender and racial oppression, epistemic injustice, and resistant imaginations*. Oxford: Oxford University Press.

Misztal, B. (1996). *Trust in modern societies: The search for the bases of social order*. Cambridge, MA: Polity Press.
Moodie, R., Stuckler, D., Monteiro, C., Sheron, N., Neal, B., Thamarangsi, T., et al. (2013). Profits and pandemics: Prevention of harmful effects of tobacco, alcohol, and ultra-processed food and drink industries. *The Lancet, 381*(9867), 670–679. https://doi.org/10.1016/S0140-6736(12)62089-3.
Murphy, M. (2008). Chemical regimes of living. *Environmenal History, 13*(4), 695–703.
Nudd, T. (2015). *Australia's "Stoner sloth" anti-marijuana campaign is an instant and classic fail*. YouTube. http://www.adweek.com/creativity/australias-stoner-sloth-anti-marijuana-campaign-instant-and-classic-fail-168702/. Accessed on April 2, 2020.
Offit, P. (2013). *Do you believe in magic? Vitamins, supplements and all things natural—A look behind the curtains*. London: HarperCollins.
Povinelli, E. A. (2017). Fires, fogs, winds. *Cultural Anthropology, 32*(4), 504–513. https://doi.org/10.14506/ca32.4.03.
Proctor, R. (2011). *Golden holocaust: Origins of the cigarette catastrophe and the case for abolition*. Berkeley: University of California Press.
Rabin, R., & Hsu, T. (2018). Johnson & Johnson feared baby powder's possible asbestos link for years. *The New York Times*. https://www.nytimes.com/2018/12/14/business/baby-powder-asbestos-johnson-johnson.html. Accessed on April 15, 2020.
Rios Sandoval, M. (2019). *There's politics in your shampoo: On youth activism, endocrine disruption, and making everyday toxicity visible in France*. Doctoral dissertation. Anthropology Department, University of Amsterdam, Amsterdam. https://pure.uva.nl/ws/files/32459798/Thesis.pdf.
Roberts, E. F. S. (2017). What gets inside: Violent entanglements and toxic boundaries in Mexico City. *Cultural Anthropology, 32*(4), 592–619. https://doi.org/10.14506/ca32.4.07.
Roberts, E. F. S., & Sanz, C. (2017). Bioethnography: A how to guide for the twenty-first century. In M. Meloni, J. Cromby, D. Fitzgerald, & S. Lloyd (Eds.), *The Palgrave handbook of biology and society* (pp. 759–776). New York: Palgrave Macmillan.
Rodrigues, C. F. (2016). Medicines and therapeutic pluralism in Maputo: Exploring modalities of trust and the (un)certainties of everyday users. *Health, Risk and Society, 18*(7–8), 385–406. https://doi.org/10.1080/13698575.2016.1271403.

Sabsay, L. (2016). Permeable bodies: Vulnerability, affective powers, hegemony. In J. Butler, Z. Gambetti, & L. Sabsay (Eds.), *Vulnerability in resistance* (pp. 278–303). Durham, NC: Duke University Press.

Sanabria, E. (2016). Circulating ignorance: Complexity and agnogenesis in the obesity "epidemic." *Cultural Anthropology, 31*(1), 131–158. https://doi.org/10.14506/ca31.1.07.

Sanchez Barba, M. G. (2020). 'Keeping them down': Neurotoxic pesticides, race, and disabling biopolitics. *Catalyst Special Section on Chemical Entanglements: Gender and Exposure, 6*(1), 1–31. https://doi.org/10.28968/cftt.v6i1.32253.

Scrinis, G. (2013). *Nutritionism: The science and politics of dietary advice*. New York: Columbia University Press.

Shapiro, N. (2015). Attuning to the chemosphere: Domestic formaldehyde, bodily reasoning, and the chemical sublime. *Cultural Anthropology, 30*(3), 368–393.

Skinner, D., Dietz, G., & Weibel, A. (2014). The dark side of trust: When trust becomes a 'poisoned chalice.' *Organization, 21*(2), 206–224. https://doi.org/10.1177/1350508412473866.

Tessaro, L. (2020). Potency and power: Estrogen, cosmetics and labeling in Canadian regulatory practices, 1939–1953. *Catalyst Special Section on Chemical Entanglements: Gender and Exposure, 6*(1), 1–13. https://doi.org/10.28968/cftt.v5i2.32339.

Vallas, S., & Prener, C. (2012). Dualism, job polarization, and the social construction of precarious work. *Work and Occupations, 39*(4), 331–353. https://doi.org/10.1177/0730888412456027.

Van Schipstal, I., Mishra, S., Berning, M., & Murray, H. (2016). Harm reduction from below: On sharing and caring in drug use. *Contemporary Drug Problems, 43*(3), 199–215. https://doi.org/10.1177/0091450916663248.

Wylie, S. A. (2018). *Fractivism: Corporate bodies and chemical bonds*. Durham, NC: Duke University Press.

Permissions

All chapters in this book were first published in CYNUSGL, by Springer by Anita Hardon; hereby published with permission under the Creative Commons Attribution License or equivalent. Every chapter published in this book has been scrutinized by our experts. Their significance has been extensively debated. The topics covered herein carry significant information for a comprehensive understanding. They may even be implemented as practical applications or may be referred to as a beginning point for further studies.

We would like to thank the editorial team for lending their expertise to make the book truly unique. They have played a crucial role in the development of this book. Without their invaluable contributions this book wouldn't have been possible. They have made vital efforts to compile up to date information on the varied aspects of this subject to make this book a valuable addition to the collection of many professionals and students.

This book was conceptualized with the vision of imparting up-to-date and integrated information in this field. To ensure the same, a matchless editorial board was set up. Every individual on the board went through rigorous rounds of assessment to prove their worth. After which they invested a large part of their time researching and compiling the most relevant data for our readers.

The editorial board has been involved in producing this book since its inception. They have spent rigorous hours researching and exploring the diverse topics which have resulted in the successful publishing of this book. They have passed on their knowledge of decades through this book. To expedite this challenging task, the publisher supported the team at every step. A small team of assistant editors was also appointed to further simplify the editing procedure and attain best results for the readers.

Apart from the editorial board, the designing team has also invested a significant amount of their time in understanding the subject and creating the most relevant covers. They scrutinized every image to scout for the most suitable representation of the subject and create an appropriate cover for the book.

The publishing team has been an ardent support to the editorial, designing and production team. Their endless efforts to recruit the best for this project, has resulted in the accomplishment of this book. They are a veteran in the field of academics and their pool of knowledge is as vast as their experience in printing. Their expertise and guidance has proved useful at every step. Their uncompromising quality standards have made this book an exceptional effort. Their encouragement from time to time has been an inspiration for everyone.

The publisher and the editorial board hope that this book will prove to be a valuable piece of knowledge for students, practitioners and scholars across the globe.

Index

H

I

M

N

O

P

R

S

www.ingramcontent.com/pod-product-compliance
Lightning Source LLC
LaVergne TN
LVHW051049220926
848485LV00001BA/49
* 9 7 8 1 6 4 7 2 6 6 2 7 1 *